Dear John:

With my personal best regards,

Jeffrey.

2/11/94

Prof. John Mylopoulos

Knowledge-Based Software Development for Real-Time Distributed Systems

SERIES ON SOFTWARE ENGINEERING AND KNOWLEDGE ENGINEERING

Series Editor-in-Chief
S K CHANG (*University of Pittsburgh, USA*)

Vol. 1 Knowledge-Based Software Development for Real-Time Distributed Systems
Jeffrey J-P Tsai and Thomas J Weigert (Univ. Illinois)

Forthcoming titles:

The Impact of CASE Technology on Software Processes
edited by Daniel E Cooke (Univ. Texas)

Advances in Software Engineering and Knowledge Engineering
edited by Vincenzo Ambriola (Univ. Pisa) *and Genoveffa Tortora* (Univ. Salerno)

Series on Software Engineering and Knowledge Engineering

Vol. 1

Knowledge-Based Software Development for Real-Time Distributed Systems

Series Editor

S K Chang

Jeffrey J-P Tsai
Thomas J Weigert
University of Illinois

World Scientific
Singapore • New Jersey • London • Hong Kong

Published by

World Scientific Publishing Co. Pte. Ltd.
P O Box 128, Farrer Road, Singapore 9128
USA office: Suite 1B, 1060 Main Street, River Edge, NJ 07661
UK office: 73 Lynton Mead, Totteridge, London N20 8DH

**KNOWLEDGE-BASED SOFTWARE DEVELOPMENT
FOR REAL-TIME DISTRIBUTED SYSTEMS**

ISBN 981-02-1128-7

Printed in Singapore by Utopia Press.

Contents

1

The Science of Software Development

Software engineering is a discipline concerned with developing correct software products. We begin by introducing paradigms relied upon in the software engineering community to model the software development process. These paradigms describe the path from an abstract description of the problem to be solved by a software system (the specification) to its implementation (the program). In this book, we subscribe to a view of the software development process maintaining that the specification is a formal theory and that the program is obtained from this theory by applying correctness-preserving transformations.

1.1 Software Engineering as Theory Construction

We want to liken the activity of the software engineer to the job of a scientist. Part of the task of the scientist is to describe phenomena. Scientists do so by formulating theories, i.e., sets of sentences of an appropriate language, intended to capture that part of the world under consideration.[1] What makes a description of a phenomenon a good scientific theory?

Consider the following description of the motion of a (large) pendulum (with only a small angle of deviation from the resting position). It is well known that the motion of such a pendulum can be approximated by a one-dimensional linear harmonic oscillator. A one-dimensional linear harmonic oscillator is a system consisting of a single mass constrained to move in one dimension only. Taking its rest position as origin, the total energy of the system is

$$H = T + V = \frac{p^2}{2m} + \frac{1}{2}kx^2, \text{ where } p = m\frac{dx}{dt}.$$

[1]Obviously scientists do not only describe the world, but their theories should also explain the phenomena. Various accounts have been given of what makes a certain description of a phenomenon an explanation of that phenomenon. Suggestions range from the claim that an explanation of a phenomenon has to license a prediction of the phenomenon, to the claim that to explain a phenomenon is to derive the sentence describing it from the theory and sentences stating initial conditions. This issue will not concern us here. The claim that any scientific theory will be a description of the phenomenon is uncontroversial.

The development of the system over time is given by solutions to the following equations of motion:

$$\frac{dx}{dt} = \frac{\partial H}{\partial p'} \text{ and } \frac{dp}{dt} = -\frac{\partial H}{\partial x}.$$

Let these equations define a theory Θ. Surely, a theory will not be good (under any reasonable interpretation of "good") unless its theorems are true. The theorems are true if there is a model that makes them true. Assume standard interpretations of theoretical terms like mass, position, etc., then let the model that makes Θ true be the linear harmonic oscillator.[2] The linear harmonic oscillator exhibits all the characteristics specified in the theory Θ. For example, the mass of the linear harmonic oscillator exhibits perfectly sinusoidal motion.

A real-life pendulum is *not* a linear harmonic oscillator since it does not exhibit the exact behavior specified by Θ (for instance, its motion exhibits dampening). Thus, such a pendulum is not a model for the theory Θ. However, we think the pendulum can be described by Θ. What makes Θ a good theory of the pendulum is the existence of a model (namely the linear harmonic oscillator) approximately isomorphic to it. By approximate isomorphism, we mean that the two models are isomorphic in specified respects to a specified degree. For example, we might claim that all quantities in the pendulum system remain within ten percent of the quantities in the linear harmonic oscillator for the first minute of operation. When a theory adequately describes a phenomenon we call the theory "*valid.*"

Definition 1.1 *A theory Θ of a phenomenon is valid if and only if there exists a model for Θ which is isomorphic to the subset of the domain containing the phenomenon in respects and to degrees specified by Θ.*

We want to claim that the software engineer is involved in a similar process. The software engineer also wants to describe a domain through a theory (the software system). The scientist's descriptions generally constitute discoveries whereas the software engineer's descriptions do not make any claim to novelty. This difference is one of purpose, but not a difference in the semantics of descriptions. For the software engineer, the theory (software system) is not formulated in natural language or set theory but in a programming language. Just as for the theories a scientist constructs, the notion of praise for a software system is that of validity.

Example 1.1 Consider a software system managing all the student records of Chicago State University. If the software system states, there exists a student A.N. Other with social security number 123-45-6789, then the system will not be correct unless there is indeed a student attending Chicago State University which can be mapped onto the object that is the interpretation of A.N. Other, having a social security number

[2]More precisely, the linear harmonic oscillator is a class of models, obtained by specifying unique values for all parameters of the system.

that can be mapped onto 123-45-6789. Conversely, for any student the model of the software system should contain an object that can be mapped onto the student.

Software engineering studies the development process of software systems. It mainly studies methodologies to produce theories describing a domain in a programming language.

Construction of a theory (a software system) begins by identifying the subset of domain which is to be described. This isolated subset of the domain will be the model that bears an approximate isomorphism to a model of the software system. We will call this model the domain model for the software system.

Definition 1.2 *The domain model for a software system is a subset of the domain that the software system is intended to describe.*

The domain model is that subset of the domain which the model of the software system bears an approximate isomorphism to if the software system is a valid description of the domain. The model of the software system which is approximately isomorphic to the domain model will be termed the conceptual model of the software system.[3]

The conceptual model is described by the requirements specification (requirements theory) of the software system. It forms the starting point for the software system building process. Software engineering studies and provides methodologies for the efficient and reliable transformation of the requirements into the implemented system. It is the study of the process that advances from a theory merely describing the conceptual model to a theory which, besides describing the conceptual model, is efficiently executable (the program/software system). The view that the software building process is but a process of theory transformation has been advanced by other researchers as well [138].

1.2 Software Engineering Paradigms

In the late sixties, software engineers and system designers were faced with what was then termed the "software crisis." This crisis was the direct result of the introduction of a new generation of computer hardware. The new computers were substantially more powerful than hardware available until then, making large applications and software systems feasible. However, the strategies and skills employed in designing software for the new systems did not match the new hardware capabilities. The result

[3]This terminology deviates from standard usage. At the stage in the development of a software system at which one (the prospective users, the system designers) acquires a vague idea of what the software system should be able to do and how it should perform, one is often described as having a "conceptual model" of the software system. In this sense, "conceptual model" bears no relation to semantics; a conceptual model resembles a scale model of the software system. According to our usage, however, the conceptual model is the semantic entity which models the software system.

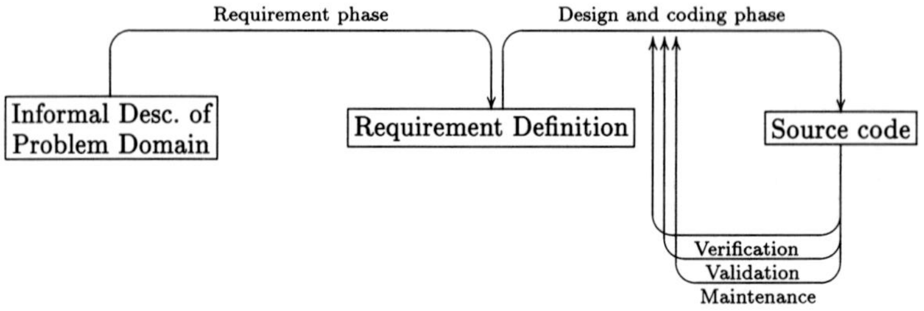

Figure 1.1. Software development life-cycle paradigm.

was delayed projects (often for years), considerable cost overruns, as well as unreliable and poorly performing applications. The need arose for new techniques and methodologies to design large software systems.

The methodology proposed as an answer to the software crisis was the Software Development Life-Cycle Paradigm (also known as the "Waterfall" Paradigm). This methodology was first proposed by Royce [273] and later modified by [33, 108, 160, 222] and others (see Fig.1.1). The life-cycle paradigm has seen many variations, amendments, and deletions, but all these share the basic assumption that software is developed in a sequence of distinct stages.[4]

- *Requirements phase* — The requirements phase (analysis phase) is concerned with understanding what the system is designed to accomplish. Starting from an informal description of the problem and the system's requirements, the designer formulates a system to solve the problem and defines it in terms of "what" it does. The definition of the requirements treats the system as a black box describing all required characteristics of the external behavior as well as the constraints on the system ("what"), but no characteristics of its internal structure that will generate that behavior ("how").

- *Design and coding phase* — The internal structure of the software system is determined in the design specification. The designer decomposes the system into abstract software components which shall produce the behavior demanded by the requirements. The interfaces between software components are frozen. Although the relationships between these abstract software components are defined, the components themselves are again treated as black boxes. In top-down fashion, a detailed design is formulated for each abstract software component in terms of simpler abstractions, until the problem is divided into many small,

[4]The U.S. Department of Defense currently requires contractors to follow the "Waterfall" model of software development (DOD Standard 2167A).

easily understood and implemented pieces. The design phase determines the optimal structure of the software components and how they interface. Ideally, the design specification should be complete enough to reduce the implementation effort to little more than a translation to a target programming language.

The design is implemented in a programming language. This involves the realization of the internal mechanism of the abstract software components as a (set of) program(s) in some programming language. Knowledge of both the design and target environment is incorporated to produce the final system software. All the physical aspects of the system are addressed during implementation.

- *Verification phase* — Information from the previous three phases is used in verifying the software system. Test plans can be derived from requirements and design specifications. Verification confirms that the software conforms to requirements and design specifications and that the code is correct.

- *Maintenance and validation phase* — Bug fixes and adaptations which result from experience with the software are activities of the maintenance phase. The software is now being used. Users will come across errors and discover where the system does not meet their expectations. Maintenance involves the correction of errors which were not discovered in early stages, improving the implementation, and enhancing the services the system renders.

During the software engineering process the system builder is confronted with the following two questions:

- Are we building the *correct system*?

- Are we *building* the system *correctly*?

Correspondingly, validation determines whether the services and functions rendered by the system (as specified in the requirements definition) comply with the customer's informal requirements. Verification determines whether the system under construction meets the requirements definition. In the terminology introduced in the previous section, validation attempts to determine whether the conceptual model is isomorphic to the domain model. Verification determines whether the conceptual model is a model of the implemented software system.

Obviously, a software engineer must be able to answer both questions affirmatively. At what stage can this be determined to be the case? One of the major criticisms of the software life-cycle paradigm applies here. Although most explications of the paradigm provide for some feedback loops between stages, validation and verification cannot be performed conclusively until after the coding stage. At this point, most of the effort has been applied. Detection of errors can send the system back into the requirements stage. The system may have to be redesigned (or even re-specified) should severe misunderstandings of the users' requirements have occurred. As indicated in Fig.1.1, however, this is typically not the case. Often, the system is merely adjusted to meet the users' requirements by changing its source code. This results in a system with obsolete requirements specification.

Software development usually begins with an attempt to recognize and understand the users' requirements and then proceeds to implement a software system which satisfies those requirements. The users' requirements specification is formulated in a dialogue between users and system analysts. Typically, the requirements definition reflects the developers' interpretation of the users' needs. Where the communication of these needs has been distorted, either by preconceptions or by general unfamiliarity on either side, it is unlikely that misunderstandings become apparent until the users test (examine) the near-ready product. Thus, maintenance is performed at the implementation level (at the source code). At this point, the programmer has applied considerable skill and knowledge to optimize the code. But optimization spreads information: it takes advantage of what is known elsewhere in the system and substitutes complex but efficient realizations for the simple abstractions of the specification. The result being a system more difficult to understand due to increased dependencies among its components and scattering of information [15]. Correcting errors deriving from the requirements phase during software maintenance becomes exceedingly expensive [34].

The main assumption of the life-cycle paradigm is that it begins with well-understood requirements and that those requirements, and thus the design specification, are fixed. Tools supporting this paradigm usually enforce this rigidity by static type-checking and interface descriptions. In practice, though, standard techniques do not allow one to arrive at exact specifications. Often, the users do not know, and cannot anticipate their exact requirements. (The users' informal requirements description is more aspiration than specification.) Since the users have no experience on which to ground those aspirations, it is only by exploring the properties of some putative solutions that the users can find out what is really needed.

These problems are serious, and many critics have called for a replacement of the software life-cycle methodologies by new paradigms for software engineering—e.g., [4, 15, 119]. Three new methodologies emerged:

- Rapid Prototyping [5, 54, 133, 278, 302, 328].
- Executable Specification [4, 17, 53, 298, 379, 380].
- Transformational Implementation [14, 26, 58, 166, 247, 369].

Rapid prototyping is the process of building a working model of a software system (or part of a system). Using this model one can validate the requirements or perform feasibility studies. An operational specification is a system model that can be evaluated or executed to generate the behavior of a software system at an early software development stage. Transformational implementation is an approach to software

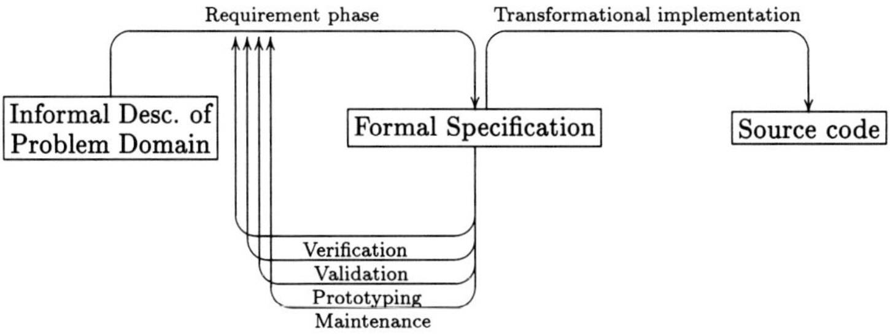

Figure 1.2. Modified software life-cycle paradigm.

development that uses automated support to apply a series of transformations that change a specification into a concrete software system. These new software engineering paradigms all strive to avoid errors in the requirements phase by demonstrating to the users the system behavior during an early stage of the software development process.

Although each of these methodologies addresses a slightly different problem with the conventional life-cycle methodology, they all share (or can share) an underlying paradigm, as depicted in Fig.1.2.

The requirements specification is a theory of the domain model (the subset of the domain under consideration), and is interpreted by the conceptual model. It states the problem to be solved by the software system including the constraints it must meet. The new paradigm insists that maintenance, verification, and validation be performed as close to the conceptual model as possible.

- *Requirements analysis* — The requirements definition of the life-cycle paradigm generally is a description of the system's behavior in natural language. It may be constrained by structure or supplemented by pictures, diagrams, etc. This type of description is psychologically distant from the conceptual model and from the final system itself. The same is true for requirements definitions in terms of automata. According to the new paradigm the end product of requirements analysis is a formal specification which is executable (prototype, operational specification). It is so possible for the users to be exposed to a "working model" of the system at a very early stage in its development. Misinterpretations can be revealed before the coding phase. The users may also gain a better understanding of their informal requirements and the conceptual model in turn resulting in a better specification.

- *Validation and verification* — The requirements specification is then subject to careful evaluation. The users can validate the system's requirements by interacting with the rapid prototype/operational specification. These representations are much closer to the users' view of the final system than the diagrams and natural language descriptions of traditional requirements specifications. Misunderstandings of the users' needs, or misunderstandings that the users may have of their own needs, quickly become apparent. In addition, if the requirements specification language provides a mechanism to infer consequences of the specification these can also be compared to the domain model. Furthermore, the requirements specification may be subject to formal checks attempting to show the absence of typical sources of incorrectness.

- *Coding* — When the system designers obtain the final formal specification, they then possesses a formal description of the system which is modeled by the conceptual model. It expresses all the requirements and constraints on the system (if the conceptual model is indeed approximately isomorphic to the domain model). By adhering to the life-cycle paradigm possession of such a specification does not guarantee correctness of the final system, since errors could still be introduced in the coding phase. Implementing the specification must not change the functionality of the system. The new paradigm wants to eliminate such a possibility. The assumption of the new paradigm is that progress from specification to program is made by applying only transformations known to preserve the correctness of the involved constructs. These transformations may choose data structures, replace algorithms with equivalent algorithms, change control structures, etc., but they do not change the behavior of the system itself. The final product is then guaranteed to behave as the specification did.

- *Maintenance* — Most maintenance costs result not from system errors but from changing system requirements after the system has been put into operation. Whereas the users generally have little difficulties incorporating such changes into their conceptual model of the system, these changes usually have a massive effect at the implementation level due to the scattering of information after optimization. If it is the specification that is maintained, such changes are kept at a level before information is spread throughout the system. Similarly, the discovery of errors is far easier before implementation has taken place.

According to these paradigms, the software building process begins with the construction of a theory (requirements specification) that has a model (the conceptual model) which is isomorphic to the domain model. One then proceeds to transform this theory into another theory formulated in a programming language (source code, implemented system). Coding is then, in a sense, merely a linguistic exercise: the replacement of expressions of one theory with semantically equivalent expressions of another theory. This transformation must not affect the semantics of the theory, i.e., the transformation must be model-preserving. The testing phase of the life-cycle methodology should establish that the conceptual model does indeed model the implemented system. Whereas the life-cycle methodology has no means of ensuring that the conceptual model is also a model of the implemented system, according to the new paradigm the transformations applied are correctness-preserving and thus also preserve the model. Note also that the verification and validation phases have moved to a much earlier stage in the lifetime of the software system.

Any software development process based on the new paradigms builds on formal languages for representing system requirements. As will be pointed out below, such a language must meet several desiderata to be effective in supporting the new software engineering paradigms.

1.3 The Path from Problem to Program

The new paradigm for software engineering presented in the previous section splits the path from problems to programs into two essentially different steps. Given the objects of the problem domain and the relations they bear to each other, plus constraints pertinent to the domain model (the subset of problem domain under consideration), we want to obtain a valid linguistic description. It is generally referred to as "specification;" we would prefer the terminology "requirements theory" but shall not depart from common usage. The minimum requirement is that this linguistic description have a model (the conceptual model) isomorphic to the domain model. In a second step, the linguistic description is transformed into the executable program. The linguistic description of the conceptual model should be (if very inefficiently) executable (operational specification, rapid prototyping) or at least formal and capable of validation.

At either of these steps, knowledge enters massively into the software engineering process. Representing the conceptual model through the requirements specification involves knowledge of the problem domain itself. The second step, from requirements specification to program, requires knowledge of programming. Due to the involvement of knowledge, the software engineering process lends itself to artificial intelligence techniques, which can be applied at either of these steps.

Current research most often considers the second step. Extensive work has been done on gradually refining a requirements specification into a program, on obtaining the explicit knowledge to facilitate these transformations, and on representing knowledge allowing these transformations to be performed automatically.[5]

Until recently, little thought has been given to the first step mentioned. Currently requirements specifications are mostly functional specifications of the program's behavior and are normally not in a form allowing them to be automatically transformed into a program.[6] Requirements specifications often do not capture the problem domain adequately, in the sense that their conceptual model is not isomorphic to the

[5] For an overview consult [130], the relevant section in the collections [266] and [301].

[6] For current work in this area, refer to [41]. Recently, a trend developed to specify nonfunctional requirements [106].

domain model. Others have shared this sentiment: *We do not primarily need a specification of what the program should do, but a theory that is valid for the problem domain*–see [17, 40, 50, 271, 370, 377].

Specifying system requirements, as currently practiced, unnecessarily mixes programming and domain knowledge: To produce the requirements specification programming knowledge is needed; to transform it into a program requires domain-knowledge beyond that conveyed by the requirements specification. We feel that these sets of knowledge are, and should be, separate:

- A valid requirements specification is a theory describing the problem domain that should be reflected in the program completely (since it has a model isomorphic to the domain model), and therefore, no further domain knowledge should be necessary to transform it into the program. The requirements specification captures all knowledge of the domain needed by the programmer and system designer.

- The requirements specification describes only the problem, not its solution, thus no knowledge of programming should be required to formulate a problem into a requirements specification. Information about algorithms or the specification of any nonabstract data types is particularly foreign to the spirit of a requirements specification.

Both claims are standard desiderata; yet two remarks are in order here.

We are not arguing that to describe the problem domain in a requirements specification no knowledge about how to solve the problem is necessary. There is a strong connection between describing and solving a problem. A formal description of a problem is already one way in which to solve that problem. Consider a formal description of the property "list y is a sorted version of list x":

$$\forall x \cdot \forall y \cdot \mathsf{sort}(x, y) \equiv \mathsf{permutation\_of}(x, y) \wedge \mathsf{ordered}(y)$$

The predicate $\mathsf{sort}(x, y)$ expresses the above property and describes it in the following way: $\mathsf{sort}(x, y)$ is true if and only if y is a permutation of x, and y is ordered.[7] This obviously captures the meaning of $\mathsf{sort}(x, y)$. This description also presents us with a method of computing a sorted version of a list: look for permutations of the original list until you hit upon a permutation which is ordered. This method is, of course, hopelessly inefficient (taking time 2^n to sort a list of length n), but even this innocent looking specification is a method of solving the given problem. The following explication of $\mathsf{sort}(x, y)$ is extensionally equivalent to the one above, but presents a far better method.[8]

[7] We will ignore how to express permutation_of and ordered.

[8] Let a list be represented in familiar list-notation [65].

$$\begin{aligned}\forall x \cdot \forall x \cdot \mathsf{sort}(x, y) \equiv \\ &x = [\,] \wedge y = [\,] \\ &\vee (\exists z \cdot \exists zs \cdot x = [z \mid zs] \wedge \\ &\quad \exists u \cdot \exists u' \cdot \exists v \cdot \exists v' \cdot \\ &\qquad \mathsf{partition}(z, zs, u, v) \wedge \mathsf{sort}(u, u') \\ &\qquad \wedge\, \mathsf{sort}(v, v') \wedge \mathsf{append}(u', [x \mid v'], z))\end{aligned}$$

Provided that $\mathsf{partition}(z, zs, u, v)$ is true if and only if u is the list of all members of list zs less than or equal to z, and v is the list of all members of zs greater than z, the latter description also gives the meaning of $\mathsf{sort}(x, y)$. The method of solving the problem given is the "quicksort"-algorithm. These two descriptions are equivalent to each other in the sense that both predicates will be true for the same pairs of terms. The point is that for the sake of a requirements specification it should not matter which of these descriptions is chosen. The requirements specification does not commit us to a particular method of solving the problem, although it, necessarily, presents us with some such method. "No information about how to solve the problem" should read "no information about how to do it efficiently" instead.

Furthermore, in the transformation phase domain knowledge can be used to reduce the complexity of the search space for a program implementing the requirements specification. For example, consider the problem of determining the amount of hydrocarbons in a ground formation [23]: since hydrocarbons are not uniform (the density of gas varies depending on temperature, depth, etc., to a considerable degree), the effect of hydrocarbons on measurements is difficult to capture precisely. Human experts interpreting oil well logs have developed a simple heuristic: "Since light hydrocarbons are uncommon all calculations should be performed assuming there are no light hydrocarbons. If the results are implausible, consider the possibility that light hydrocarbons are present." [23] In Barstow's system, this heuristic is reflected in two subproblems: porosity analysis and hydrocarbon correction. During program synthesis domain specific knowledge enables one to reduce a complex problem into two simpler subproblems.

Another area where domain knowledge enters the program transformation process is the selection of alternative possible implementations. For example, various techniques exist to represent real numbers. The knowledge that a sensor reads temperatures to within an accuracy of, say, +0.03 centigrade would have a direct bearing on how we choose to represent temperature to the software system. Or consider the problem of solving a complex system of nonlinear polynomial equations: From a mathematical point of view this may not be tractable due to the multiple solutions for the same unknown. However, only one solution with a physically plausible range of values may exist [23]. If an approximating numeric technique is necessary, domain knowledge might allow us to predict the number of iterations required to achieve the desired accuracy. Using the temperature sensor above, if two iterations result in 4-digit accuracy, nothing more is required.

The programming knowledge that is applied at the second step enables us to transform the requirements specification into a working program. It is during this step that efficiency considerations and implementation issues are addressed: How should the representations of the requirements specification be implemented in the programming language, i.e., how are the abstract data types of the requirements specification to be reduced to data types of the programming language? Which algorithms should be employed to solve the problem?[9]

How should requirements specifications be formulated? Any software engineering methodology requires that there be some correspondence between the domain model, the requirements specification, and the program. According to the new paradigm it is insisted that

- The domain model is isomorphic to a model of the requirements specification (the conceptual model).
- The program is a theory obtained from the requirements specification by application of model-preserving transformations only.

Therefore,

- The conceptual model is a model of the program.
- The domain model is isomorphic to a model of the program.

It is the insistence on the isomorphism between conceptual model and domain model that makes the application of the new paradigm possible. It ensures the correctness of the program as well as the possibility of the transformation.

First, the transformation from requirements specification to program is carried out through model-preserving transformation steps only. Thus, the conceptual model is also a model of the program. Since validity of a theory was defined in terms of an isomorphism between a model of the theory and the domain, the validity of a program consists in this isomorphism between the model of the program and the domain model.

Second, the transformations are based on knowledge of the domain. This knowledge must, therefore, be specified in the requirements specification. If the model of the requirements specification is isomorphic to the domain, then for every relevant fact of the domain (these are just the facts in the domain model), there exists a sentence that is entailed by the requirements specification, such that the fact under consideration can be mapped onto the interpretation of this sentence. Consequently, the description of every relevant fact of the domain can be derived from the requirements specification.

[9]Although the requirements specification gave us some algorithm, the system is not committed to this algorithm, but can replace it by any algorithm which is functionally equivalent.

1.4 Knowledge-Based Software Development

Various knowledge-based systems geared to assisting the users in producing software have been developed. These systems tackle different phases of the software life-cycle. Knowledge-based techniques can help in elicitation and formalization of requirements, they can aid in software design and implementation as well as assist during testing and debugging phases.

1.4.1 Requirements Elicitation and Formalization

KBRA [74] (Knowledge-Based Requirements Assistant) is a component of the KBSA (Knowledge-Based Software Assistant) developed by Sanders Associates, Inc. KBSA is intended to support software development spanning a system's life-cycle from requirements to code.

KBRA provides computer assistance from the project's beginning, presenting multiple views of the system being specified. These views support capturing and enforcing ramifications of design decisions, handling reusability at the requirements level, and critiquing and automatically completing certain aspects of requirements specifications (e.g., acquisition, analysis, and communication).

Czuchry [74] identified knowledge representation issues associated with requirements acquisition and analysis. He also employed artificial intelligence techniques to provide consistent reasoning for the intelligent assistant: inheritance of properties from generic object types, automatic classification based on discriminators, and constraint propagation for processing ramifications of requirements decisions.

KB/RMS (Robert Binder Systems Consulting, Inc.) [31] is a knowledge-based requirements definition assistant. It uses rule-based inference and natural language processing to create a high-level system model from a collection of natural language statements. KB/RMS also assists the software developers in refining the requirements specification.

KB/RMS is independent of any particular application domain, software development method or implementation platform. It identifies the objects in the problem and solution spaces. The so obtained model also serves as the logical schema for the KB/RMS database.

Requirements Apprentice (RA) [265] is designed to assist the analyst in the creation and modification of software requirements which focus on the boundary between informal and formal specifications. RA has been developed in the context of the Programmer's Apprentice project, whose goal is to automate the analysis, synthesis, modification, specification, verification, and documentation of software systems. RA consists of three modules.

- CAKE, a hybrid knowledge representation and reasoning system. CAKE supports dependency-directed reasoning aiding in disambiguation of informal specifications and in contradiction detection.

- EXECUTIVE, an aid for interacting with the analyst and providing high-level control of the reasoning performed by CAKE.

- A repository for storing domain-independent and domain-dependent information.

RA attempts to resolve the ambiguities and incompleteness inherent in informal specifications, as well as over-generalizations and inconsistencies, by resorting to a library of prior domain knowledge or "clichés." A cliché is a representation of commonly occurring structures of the domain. Mechanisms are provided to instantiate a cliché in a particular situation. RA also contains a requirements knowledge base and a knowledge-based editor (KBEmacs) which automatically implements a program from algorithmic fragments.

WATSON (AT&T Bell Labs.) [168] is an artificial intelligence-based software development environment for reducing the complexity of formal specifications elicited for new features in telephone switching software.

WATSON uses a variety of design knowledge to bridge the gap between informal English "scenarios" and an executable finite-state skeleton:

- Domain specific knowledge of telephone hardware, telephone network protocols, expected end-user etiquette, and principles of finite-state automata design.

- WATSON relies on novel heterogeneous knowledge representation techniques incorporating goal-directed plans (generalized from the English scenarios), temporal logic, and relational approximations to finite-state automata. These representation techniques are interrelated through theories to allow for internal consistency checking.

- Background knowledge is embedded in prefabricated plan templates, axioms of temporal logic, and constraints on finite-state automata.

Designers of new telephone features present a natural-language scenario. Internally scenarios are represented in the form of finite-state automata with temporal logic constraints on transitions. WATSON expands these scenarios to resolve inconsistencies and incomplete information.

1.4.2 Software Design and Implementation

ASPIS (Application Software Prototype Implementation System) [258] encourages a more flexible and effective software-development life cycle by smoothing the transition between users' needs, analysis, and design.

ASPIS consists of several assistants:

- The analysis assistant and design assistant are used directly by the developers of a particular application. They embody knowledge about both the particular software development methodology employed and the application domain.

- Once defined, the specifications can be executed by the prototype assistant, which verifies the system's properties.
- The reuse assistant aids developers in reusing specifications and designs.

The design schemas in *IDeA* (Microelectronics and Computer Technology Corp.) provide a refinement paradigm of software development and support a uniform view of software specification, design, and prototyping. Reusable design information is abstracted in the form of domain-oriented design schemas applicable to various design families. Constraint information, such as design dependencies and consistency requirements of a users' specifications are also included in the design schema. In addition, rules for design specialization and refinement are included to support a top-down refinement-based methodology. Some support is also provided in the form of bottom-up design through planning, rapid prototyping, and goal management.

IDeA (Intelligent Design Aid) [203, 204] is a prototype design environment integrating knowledge-based support for software reuse, analysis, and testing. The design schema representation in IDeA is based on data-flow modeling. This representation supports the techniques of structured analysis and data-flow design and facilitates the use of process graph structures for simulation.

KIDS (Kestrel Interactive Development System) [295] formalizes and automates various sources of programming knowledge and integrates them into a highly automated environment for developing formal specifications into correct and efficient programs.

KIDS provides an open architecture for experimenting with the automated development of formal specifications into correct and efficient programs. The system has components for performing algorithm design, deductive inference, program simplification, partial evaluation, finite differencing optimizations, data type refinement and other development operations. Although their application is interactive, all of KIDS operations are automatic except the selection of an algorithm design tactic. Design tactics provided by KIDS are divide-and-conquer, global search, and local search.

Users of KIDS develop a formal specification into a program by interactively applying a sequence of high-level transformations. During development, the users view a partially implemented specification annotated with input assumptions, invariants, and output conditions.

All KIDS transformations are correctness-preserving and perform significant, meaningful steps from the users' point of view. Their intent is to provide a collection of program transformations that can be composed through tactics or a meta-programming language to yield higher-level and domain-specific transformations.

Marvel [18, 164] is a programming environment that provides early error-checking and answers questions about a program under development. Marvel has a certain understanding of the systems being developed and how tools are used to produce software.

Marvel supports two aspects of an intelligent assistant: it provides insight into the system and it actively participates in development through opportunistic processing.

Marvel consists of two key components:

- An object data base stores data represented as objects. This data base defines object classes and the relationships among objects.
- A process model imposes structure on programming activities. The model is an extensible collection of rules specifying conditions that must exist so that particular tools may be applied to an object. Rules are relevant only when users invoke a tool or when the environment initiates processing.

MicroScope (Hewlett-Packard) [9] is a knowledge-based programming environment designed to improve quality and productivity of software development. The MicroScope program analysis system helps programmers in comprehending and modifying programs.

MicroScope provides a framework for navigation through different views of programs to help programmers focus on the parts they want to understand. MicroScope contains rules for reasoning about program properties which enable it to advise the programmer during code evolution (debugging and modification).

Programmers can extend or change the rule base and request explanations of MicroScope's reasoning. MicroScope stores program information in a central knowledge base, so different services have access to the same information, saving programmers from using separate tools having different levels of programming knowledge. MicroScope provides a common user interface among its services and allows programmers access to each service at any time.

1.4.3 Software Testing and Debugging

To support fault-driven bug localization, Falosy [285] incorporates a knowledge base of heuristic associations between output discrepancies and possible causes. Each fault model in the knowledge base relates fault symptoms to hypotheses regarding possible faults. Function-driven fault localization relies on relations between less specific fault hypotheses and functions. In addition, Falosy's knowledge base contains functional prototypes that describe implementation alternatives.

Given the program to be debugged and a list of output discrepancies, Falosy checks whether any expected faults listed in the fault model are present (fault-driven localization), and identifies the discrepancies between the functional prototype and the closest matching section of the code as bugs (function-driven localization).

Falosy uses a straightforward fault-localization strategy. On the basis of output discrepancies, it decides which fault-localization tactic (fault-driven or function-driven) it will initially pursue. The output discrepancies are then matched against the symptoms of which the system is aware.

Tsai proposed a noninterference architecture [338, 339] to collect the program execution history of a target system without interfering with its execution. It guarantees the preservation of timing requirements as well as the reproduction of errors. His system detects synchronization errors and timing related errors. To eliminate redundant information in the collected execution history, a post-processing mechanism to organize the information necessary for testing and debugging is introduced. A knowledge-based debugging aid [337] automates the examination of collected data and assists the users in localizing errors.

MTA [141] it is intended to help debug process-structured programs with message-based interprocess communication. MTA examines the message trace and outputs a list of suspect processes and anomalies discovered in the communicated messages. MTA identifies illegal message sequences in the trace and determines the processes at fault.

Proust [161, 162] uses a less-formal problem description in the form of a list of goals to be satisfied and a description of objects the program manipulates. Proust utilizes programming plans to understand programs. Programming plans contain statements and subgoals, and show how particular programming goals can be realized.

A problem in the matching process arises when no known plans for the currently considered goal exactly match the code. Proust then decides whether it is faced with an unknown implementation or with buggy code. Plan-difference rules are triggered by discrepancies between the plan being matched and the code, and may either transform the program code into a correct form or explain the differences as a bug.

Program-analysis based debugging compares the program to specifications, e.g., Laura [3] or output assertions, e.g., PUDSY [208]. Comparison typically proceeds through several stages: standardization transformations, graph matching (to bind the corresponding variables, nodes, and arcs), and error detection. The program to be debugged must implement the same algorithm as the specification, or derive the same output assertions, respectively.

1.4.4 Roadmap to This Book

We have developed a software development environment encompassing the whole life-cycle from requirements specification to testing and debugging [336, 337, 340–342, 346–348, 350–352]. This environment adheres to the new software engineering paradigm as presented above. It is based on a requirements specification language based on the representational constructs of frames and rules, appropriately termed FRORL (this acronym stands for "Frame- and Rule-oriented Requirements specification Language").

Software system development starts from the formation of informal requirements by the client according to the problem domain. The requirements may include functional operations requirements, reliability requirements, performance requirements, communication protocols, interface/environment accommodations, or timing constraints. Starting with the client's informal requirements the developers build up a conceptual model of the proposed software system.

The developers form the FRORL specification from the conceptual model by following the six steps of the frame-and rule-oriented development methodology as described in Section 2.5. This methodology guides the users to construct specifications systematically that appropriately model the problem domain. Now the developers must check the correctness of the specification. The FRORL analyzer performs various consistency checks on the specification and attempts to detect desirable and undesirable properties of the specification. These include static and dynamic functional properties (i.e., properties concerned with the functional aspects of the systems), temporal properties, and timing constraints consistency (see Chapter 6). Inference mechanisms are provided to compare consequences of the requirements specification to the domain model, and to determine whether important facts of the domain model hold in the requirements specification.

The requirements specification is executable (i.e., the specification is a rapid prototype). During prototype evaluation clients and developers cooperate to validate the prototype by inspecting its behavior and by comparing consequences of the requirements specification with the domain model. The abstractions of the requirements specification are then implemented by a transformation system in a conventional programming language.

This is *not* a book about the aforementioned software development environment. Instead, it introduces applications of artificial intelligence and knowledge-based techniques applied to the software development process. During recent years this field has expanded considerably. Many different approaches of solving subproblems have been presented, often based on radically different theoretical and philosophical foundations. A book of this length could not completely cover the field of software engineering and still do justice to the approaches presented. We have opted not to attempt to cover the field of software engineering in its entirety. We have selected important aspects of the software development process and discuss in-depth particular approaches of applying knowledge-based techniques to those selected aspects. Survey sections at the beginning of relevant chapters relate the presented techniques to other approaches.

For the sake of continuity we decided to base the discussion of presented techniques on our FRORL requirements specification language [348, 350, 352]. However, we have excluded material that is unique to the development of software systems specified in FRORL, except where it proved necessary to maintain coherence of the text. We intend this book as a guide to developing software systems starting from formal specifications (provided that the specification language has a clean, well-understood semantic foundation).

The next chapter begins by presenting demands a requirements specification language should meet. We argue that any requirements specification language should provide freedom from implementation concerns, allow as natural a representation of the system's requirements as possible, and provide mechanisms for verification and validation of the requirements specification against the domain model. After giving a short survey of types of requirements specification languages, we present FRORL (a "Frame- and Rule-Oriented Requirements specification Language") which we rely

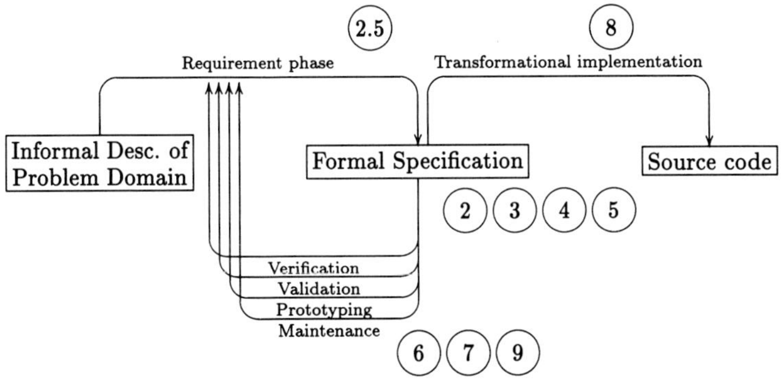

Figure 1.3. Relationship between chapters and phases of the software life-cycle.

on throughout this book. A discussion of a methodological approach to constructing requirements specifications concludes this chapter.

If the requirements specification language is expected to allow for thorough verification beyond mere syntactic checks and execution of the specification, then a sound formal basis is necessary. In Chapter 3, we present the formal foundations of FRORL together with schemes for translating constructs of FRORL into its underlying logic. To support features such as default inheritance and exceptions, we base the FRORL requirements specification language on a nonmonotonic variant of Horn-clause logic. In this chapter, we also prove this logic to be both sound and complete.

Real-time distributed systems require additional features to be represented completely: Multiple processes and inter-process communication must be supported. Mechanisms are necessary to express timing constraints and nondeterministic behavior. After discussing the special aspects of real-time distributed systems modeling, we present various real-time specification languages. Chapter 4 also introduces the features of FRORL peculiar to the specification of real-time distributed systems.

To permit the formal verification of specifications of real-time distributed systems the formal foundation of the requirements specification language must also include the concept of time. In Chapter 5, we present the temporal fix-point calculus which serves to verify the time-dependent aspects of the specification. Through model checking, we can determine whether a temporal sentence expressing some timing constraint on the system holds for a given specification. We show how the timing-related constructs of FRORL can be translated into the temporal fix-point calculus.

Chapter 6 is devoted to the verification of a requirements specification. Verification may apply to both functional and time-dependent aspects of a specification. The functional aspects of the specification are concerned with ensuring the functionality of the system. Dynamic analysis may determine liveness, reversibility, consistency, and similar properties. The time-dependent aspects of the specification are concerned with timing-constraints imposed by the system's environment. Timing consistency analysis determines whether it is possible to meet these constraints. Through model checking, various important temporal properties of a specification, such as safety properties (partial correctness, mutual exclusion, deadlock freedom), liveness properties (total correctness, guaranteed accessibility), precedence properties, and fairness are established.

In Chapter 7, we discuss the development of knowledge-based systems and show that it can be guided by the same principles that assist in developing conventional software. We develop verification techniques for the specification of knowledge-based systems and argue that the paradigms underlying this book are equally well applicable to the development of knowledge-based systems.

The implementation of a specification in conventional programming languages is discussed in Chapter 8. We focus on the technique of transformational implementation: the step-by-step transformation of constructs of the specification into constructs of the implementation language by correctness-preserving transformation rules. Two major aspects of implementing a logic-based specification are data dependency and flow analysis and the implementation of the backtracking control mechanism inherent in the specification. For one, constructs of a logic-based specification are assumed to be logical descriptions and can be used, procedurally speaking, to compute multi-directionally. On the other hand, all possible solutions of a given logic-based specification can be computed by way of backtracking. Neither of these features is present in conventional programming languages. We present techniques to determine the intended direction of the flow of computation and to eliminate unnecessary nondeterminism from a specification. The spirit of transformational programming is illustrated by the example of canonicalizing transformations which are a necessary first step for the data flow analysis techniques presented.

The debugging and testing process is indispensable to producing a good program. It becomes more difficult as the complexity of the program increases and yet more difficult when programs are written in concurrent languages where several tasks may be executing in parallel. Traditionally, debugging is performed in the implementation phase of the software life cycle. The executability of a specification makes it possible to apply debugging techniques earlier, during validation of the requirements specification which will exhibit errors in the specification. In Chapter 9 we discuss techniques that aid in locating such errors and correcting it.

The appendices contain two examples of system specifications using FRORL (the alternating bit protocol and the specification of part of the subscriber-line controller in a telephone exchange). We present the formal grammar of FRORL, as well as theoretical results governing fix-points relied upon throughout this book.

Fig.1.3 relates the phases of the software life-cycle to parts of this book. As pointed out earlier, because the techniques presented in this book are discussed in-depth it is not possible to cover all the presented issues in complete breadth. For example, although Chapter 8 discusses the implementation of FRORL specifications in conventional programming languages, no mention is made of how the inheritance hierarchy of a FRORL specification is converted into data structures of the implementation language. Neither do we discuss data flow analysis as it applies to the concurrent subparts of specified systems. This book should not be interpreted as a complete discussion the steps necessary for arriving at a correct implementation starting from a FRORL specification. Instead, this book attempts to present, for each of the phases of the software life-cycle, particular applications of knowledge-based techniques to aid software developers.

1.4.5 Acknowledgments

The research presented here would have been impossible without the assistance and contributions of our graduate students involved in the development of the FRORL software development environment. H. Jang contributed to the implementation of the verification mechanisms discussed in Chapter 6. T. Moritz implemented the development and verification environment for knowledge-based systems presented in Chapter 7 and developed the potential-conflict backtracking scheme relied upon in this environment. R. Sheu and B. Li have conceived and implemented the data dependency and data flow analysis techniques of Chapter 8. A. Liu and K. Nair have contributed to the discussion of specification debugging in Chapter 9.

We are grateful to Fujitsu America, Inc., National Science Foundation under Grants CCR-8809381 and CCR-9106540, IEEE and Engineering Foundation under a Grant RI-A-88-11, and the Science and Technology Agency (STA) of Japan, for supporting the research reported in this book.

2

Knowledge Representation as a Basis of Specifying Requirements

This chapter begins with presenting demands that have been placed on languages intended to formulate requirements specifications. After describing classes of requirements specification languages, we present a formal requirements specification language, FRORL (*Frame- and Rule-Oriented Requirements specification Language*) developed to facilitate specification, analysis and development of software systems. The surface syntax of FRORL is based on the concepts of frames and production rules. The frames and rules of a FRORL specification may bear hierarchical relationships to each other relying on multiple inheritance. However, to provide a thorough semantic foundation, FRORL is based on a nonmonotonic variant of Horn-clause logic. The underlying logic of FRORL is proven sound and complete in Chapter 3.

2.1 Demands on a Requirements Specification Language

In the literature, e.g., [16, 100, 348, 352], it has been argued extensively that a requirements specification language should meet the following desiderata.

2.1.1 Freedom from Implementation Concerns

A specification language should provide freedom from the need to prescribe specific methods of problem-solving to such a degree that a behavior may be nondeterministically specified. Implementation then must determine appropriate choices for each of the nondeterministic constructs of the requirements specification. Nondeterministic specification of behavior often includes computationally undesirable behavior. By adding constraints during the implementation phase, the range of possible interpretations is narrowed to eliminate undesirable choices.

Methods that achieve the prescribed behavior need data to operate on. A requirements specification language, particularly one used to specify functional requirements, should be unconcerned with providing necessary data and how that data is accessed.

Furthermore, there should be no distinction between explicitly declared and derived information: From given information we can often deduce new information not explicitly stated through implicit inference rules. The access of explicitly stated information should, in terms of the requirements specification language, be indistinguishable from accessing derived information.

2.1.2 Naturalness of Representation

Many formal specification languages are difficult to write and understand. Recently, knowledge representation techniques have been incorporated to amend the expressive power of requirements specification languages. The languages currently available often lend themselves easily only to the description of certain aspects of problem domains. Some are good in describing the objects of a domain and relations between those objects but lack the means to represent rules and constraints. These include languages based on the entity-relationship approach, frames, or object-oriented programming [44, 365]. Generally, these languages also make it difficult to present queries to the requirements model when validating the correctness of specifications. On the other end of the spectrum, we have languages which easily lend themselves to stating constraints and rules, but fail to capture essential aspects of the objects in the conceptual model.

Ideally, a language capable of expressing a requirements specification should also allow representation of the problem domain in every aspect with equal ease. Today the prevalent assumption is that real-world objects bear hierarchical relationships to each other; thus the specification language should allow representation of such objects in hierarchies. We must be able to represent the inheritance of features, as well as defaults and exceptions present in hierarchical domains. Inheritance allows upper-level entities in the hierarchy to share information with the lower-level entities. So far, few specification languages are known to support default or multiple inheritance. However, these properties always tend to appear in real world applications. In addition, one must be able to state constraints and rules.

2.1.3 Operational Interpretation

To allow for the rapid prototyping design methodology the specification should be executable, although efficiency considerations are not brought to bear.[1] If the requirements specification *is* the executable prototype, programming knowledge and domain knowledge become even further separated. The designer of the requirements specification can immediately determine the feasibility of the design approach and further refine it to satisfaction.

---

[1]The rapid prototyping and executable specification paradigm are, of course, not identical. For the purpose of this book we will, however, neglect this distinction and claim that prototyping is accomplished using an executable requirements specification language.

2.1.4 Validity Checking

It has already become commonplace in software engineering folklore that an error occurring in the requirements analysis phase is expensive to fix when discovered later (requirements errors have been cited to be ten to thousand times more expensive to correct if discovered in the maintenance phase than when discovered during the requirements phase [34]). Validating a requirements specification, i.e., checking whether the domain was indeed represented in the requirements specification, is therefore extremely important. If a requirements specification is valid relative to a problem domain, the domain model is isomorphic to a model (the conceptual model) of the requirements specification.

Along with examination of the behavior of a requirements specification through rapid prototypes or executable specifications, formal correctness checking is desirable. There are only a few requirements specification languages that currently provide support for rigorous checking of requirements specifications. This is particularly true for requirements specification schemes which surpass the expressiveness of standard first-order logic. To determine whether the conceptual model is isomorphic to the domain model involves testing to see whether facts in the domain model also hold true in the conceptual model, and whether the interpretations of all theorems of the requirements specification can be mapped onto facts in the domain model.[2] Comparing theorems of a requirements specification to the domain allows us to detect surprising consequences of the requirements specification. On the other hand, checking whether facts of the domain important to the users can be mapped onto theorems of the requirements specification will reveal where the specification fails to capture the problem domain adequately, before this surfaces in the programming and testing phases. Therefore, the specification language must provide an inference mechanism which allows deducing the logical consequences of the requirements specification. It is unlikely that validating the specification, in contrast to its verification, can be accomplished completely. However, checking the specification against the domain model will add credibility and correctness to the specification. The requirements specification language should lend at least some support to this process.

2.1.5 Verification

Given that we will not be able to formally validate the requirements specification in its entirety, it becomes even more important that we establish the absence of undesirable properties from the requirements specification (surely an *incorrect* specification will not adequately model the users' domain model).

The requirements specification language should facilitate verification of the specification. It should provide for mechanisms which thoroughly check for correctness of the specification. This becomes even more important when building real-time or

[2]Of course the "all" here is not meant literally. There are many unimportant theorems, such as those obtained by adding disjuncts onto existing theorems which we would not want to check.

distributed systems. The different components of such systems are often intricately connected as far as their timing requirements are concerned. For such systems, inspection is usually incapable of revealing problems lurking in an incorrect specification.

Typically, it is assumed that the absence of certain undesirable properties will amount to correctness of the specification. Among the properties that should be checked for are dynamic properties (reversibility, liveness, consistency, bounded fairness, etc.) and static properties (redundancy, subsumption, unnecessary conditions, etc.).

2.1.6 Soundness and Completeness

Validity checking requires a calculus for the specification language which allows the derivation of sentences entailed by the requirements specification. Validity checking will only be possible if the calculus associated with the language used in describing the domain is sound (so that we are not allowed to infer theorems not true in its model) and complete (which allows us to infer all the theorems true in the model). The completeness and soundness of the calculus used to specify the users' requirements should not be confused with the validity of the requirements specification relative to the problem domain.

2.1.7 Ease of Modification and Construction

When constructing a requirements specification one should be concerned with human comprehension and assimilation abilities. According to common tenets of problem representation, complexity is the main barrier to understanding. A specification language must, therefore, provide for improving the conceptual clarity of the problem domain and be supported by a development methodology. The methodology should support the hierarchical representation of a complex system. A hierarchical representation enables the users to start conceptualizing the system at the highest level of abstraction, and then continue downwards for further levels of detail. A top down approach frees the users from examining unnecessary details when concerned with the overall view of the system. On the other hand, parts of the system may be explored in detail while other parts are not yet defined.

One of the major pitfalls of software development is that software developers are always forced to make assumptions about the users' requirements. Often, the users have an incomplete understanding of their own needs, or are not fully aware of the consequences of all those needs. The users' needs may even be inconsistent. Therefore, as software development progresses and the users become more familiar with their own needs, such assumptions will often have to be withdrawn. The requirements specification language must provide for an easy mechanism to adapt to these types of changes.

Inheritance supports management of such changes by allowing that information is shared between objects in the hierarchy instead of being duplicated. Less abstract objects may override inherited information. Components of a system unrelated in the hierarchy should be specified in a self-contained manner. A certain level of object-orientedness helps to ensure that components are encapsulated and have clearly defined interfaces.

2.2 Languages to Formulate Requirements Specifications

Unlike a conventional software specification, a requirements specification with operational interpretation of its language constructs can exhibit the behavior of the proposed software system. To be able to interpret the requirements specification operationally, it is expressed in a language that allows it to be evaluated to show system behavior.

An operational requirements theory addresses a key shortcoming of the conventional life-cycle paradigm, in which users and developers must wait well into the design phase before they have linguistic constructs (in this case, procedures and modules) producing system behavior. At this point, design commitments have already been made. If the system behavior is not acceptable, unraveling those commitments is costly. If the requirements specification is executable, the users' feedback can be gathered early in the software development process.

Design errors exposed by a rapid prototyping design methodology typically resulted in the requirements specification defining behavior other than the intended behavior. A system designer who committed errors of this kind selected a different subset of the domain as the conceptual model than the users had in mind. In a sense, a software system with such design errors is correct in so far as the requirements specification is valid. But the system is the wrong system, due to the selection of a wrong conceptual model.

We pointed out above that any statement of a problem through a theory is also a method to solve that problem. Let us call the point of view that looks at a theory as the statement of a problem to be solved ("what to do") the declarative point of view, while referring to the "how to do it" aspect as the procedural point of view. There is a continuum of languages with logic at one end of the spectrum purely assuming the declarative point of view. At the other end of the spectrum are conventional programming languages which allow only the procedural point of view.

Several techniques to execute requirements specifications while keeping the language used to state the requirements purely declarative (or nearly so) have been proposed. In the following, we show the most prevalent approaches exemplified by particular systems using that approach.[3]

[3]Note that for each of the mentioned approaches, there would be several examples readily available, but we are not concentrating here on the comparison of requirements specification languages.

2.2.1 Abstract Data Types

SETL [85, 280, 282] and V/REFINE [2, 137, 166, 251, 296] are both examples of very-high level languages which offer a multitude of abstract data types. The users concentrate only on the description of the algorithm relying on the abstract data types offered. The system will then select a proper realization of the abstract data types in terms of more efficient constructs of an underlying programming language.

In such specifications, the data representation that eventually realizes an algorithm depends on the code. Algorithms are coded without specifying any nonabstract data structures. The expressions appearing in a specification are dynamically assigned appropriate abstract data types from the basic data types supported by the language. In the implementation phase, such abstract data types are viewed as place-holders for a collection of more specific data structures capable of representing that abstract data type. For example, the data type **set** abstracts hash tables, linked lists, bit strings, etc., since these can be used to implement the set construct. The code itself is independent of the data-structure selection and need not be modified when this selection is made [280].

These languages provide finite set-theoretic expressions, such as finite sets, maps, tuples, and support many operations over these structures. Functional programming, including partial functions, is supported. Incidentally, both examples mentioned also provide the standard control structures of Algol-like, block-structured languages, including if-then-else, case selectors, while-loops, iteration, etc. In addition, first-order logic constructs (particularly, bounded quantifiers) and iterations over sets are provided for specifying control. The quantifier **some** nondeterministically evaluates expressions.

2.2.2 Algebraic Term Rewriting

OBJ [126] is based on the principle of abstract data types being specified as (initial, many sorted) algebras [126, 129]. OBJ relies on the assumption that a software system can be considered a collection of abstract data types representing objects in the problem domain. The abstract data types are described algebraically.

OBJ considers every object of the system model an interpretation of an abstract data type (an OBJ object). The algebraic specification of an abstract data type consists of two parts, one for syntactic declarations and the other for axioms. The syntactic part is its signature and consists of a set of sort names, one for each sort of data involved (such as **nat** and **bool**, for natural numbers and truth values), and a set of declarations for operation symbols (such as declaring + a binary infix operation on **nat**, or ˆ a unary operation on **bool**). The axioms of the algebraic specification define the meaning of the operations by stating their relationships to one another. In OBJ, axioms are equations, i.e., pairs of terms which denote the same value in every valid interpretation. To make OBJ operational these equations are treated as left-to-right rewrite rules, and are assumed to exhibit the Church-Rosser property. Informally, a set of rewrite rules is Church-Rosser if, whenever one applies a rewrite rule to reduce a term, then a rule to reduce the resulting term, and so on until there are no more applicable rules, the result is independent of the order in which one chooses to apply the rules. For a method to prove that a set of rewrite rules is Church-Rosser, see [174]. Operators in OBJ do not denote procedures in the usual sense but implicitly define them by algebraic equations.

2.2.3 Symbolic Evaluation

In GIST [17], all possible behaviors of the system are characterized through symbolic evaluation techniques. Symbolic execution allows many different execution paths to be examined simultaneously [67].

A GIST specification defines a collection of behaviors, where each behavior is a sequence of situations. A GIST specification is composed of structural declarations, which define a space of potential states of the system; stimulus-response rules, which define both situations that initiate activities and the range of behaviors ensuing from these situations; and constraints, which prune the space of possible behaviors defined by the elements above [17].

The structural declarations describe the types of objects in the domain, any relevant instances of these types, and the relationships which exist between objects. The objects of the domain are described as standing in a hierarchy of types. An inference mechanism is provided which allows global declarations describing the relationships between objects. The logical structure of the domain is captured in a relational and associative data model (therefore no access scheme is imposed). GIST defines operations on those objects using familiar programming constructs: sequencing, iteration, loops, etc. In addition, GIST provides demons; asynchronous processes which respond to defined stimuli. When a demon's stimulus (an arbitrary predicate) becomes true, the demon's response (an arbitrary statement) will be executed. The various lines of control due to multiplicity of demons are interleaved and merged nondeterministically, which generates the space of possible behaviors ensuing from a given situation. From the possible behaviors, those situations and behaviors not considered to be acceptable system behaviors are pruned by constraints (specified as global declarations). Constraints also prune behaviors which do not agree with system history and ongoing activities. In addition, GIST provides historical reference, i.e., the ability to refer to past process states.

2.2.4 (Extensions to) First-Order Logic

Early formal requirements specification languages, just as early artificial intelligence systems, relied on a full first-order predicate logic as the language for representing domain knowledge. Although such schemes were fully general and semantically well understood, they have been inadequate for organizing large knowledge bases and encoding complex objects. In an attempt to extend the power of first-order logic, new requirements specification languages have been developed. Greenspan's RML language [139] is based on strict inheritance and typed first-order logic. Goguen's FOOPS language [128] tries to unify functional, object-oriented and relational programming with logical semantics. Dubois uses temporal logic in his ERAE language [87].

FDL [324, 325] and our own proposal FRORL [346, 348, 350, 352] are based on the Horn-clause subset of first-order predicate logic (rather than a full-fledged first-order calculus). Horn-clause logic allows two different semantic interpretations of its sentences: A declarative semantics based on the standard model-theoretic semantics of first-order logic and a procedural semantics. The latter is the set of ground clauses which are instances of queries solved by the theory. Execution of theories expressed in Horn-clause logic relies on the interpretation of expressions of the form "*A* if *B* and *C* and ..." as procedures "to do *A*, do *B* and *C* and ...," which can be executed using the mechanisms of an abstract interpreter.

In contrast to other specification languages, logic has well-understood semantics and is known to be both sound and complete. The inference mechanism provides not only the means for correctness checking, but also allows us to view all data present in the specification as if it were contained in a relational data base (imposing no access mechanisms). Objects are represented in terms of abstract data types. Relationships between objects express the activities and actions possible in the system specified. Control information need not be stated; instead, it is implicit in the inference mechanism.

2.3 The FRORL Requirements Specification Language

The FRORL requirements specification language is based on Horn-clause logic [179, 180, 190, 199]. As Kowalski has repeatedly pointed out [179, 182], Horn-clause logic allows two different semantic interpretations of its sentences:

- The declarative semantics of Horn-clause logic is based on the standard model-theoretic semantics of first-order logic. The intersection of all models of a theory is also a model for the theory and is known as the minimal model. The minimal model is the declarative meaning of a theory expressed in Horn-clause logic.

- The procedural semantics is a way of describing procedurally the meaning of a theory. The procedural meaning of a theory is the set of ground clauses that are instances of queries solved by the theory using an abstract interpreter.

Horn-clause logic in itself would not meet all the demands on requirements specification languages as stated in Section 2.1.

It does not completely grant freedom from finding a method for solving a problem. The abstract interpreter follows a prescribed evaluation order. Thus, control information is provided by the ordering of the clauses in the data base and the presence of the cut mechanism in most concrete realizations of Horn-clause logic (such as in the Prolog programming language). Furthermore, some care has to be taken to avoid enumeration of infinite data structures, lest the execution will not terminate.

Horn-clause logic does not meet the demand of naturalness of representation. A commonplace in software design is that the objects of the domain should be considered bearing hierarchical relationships to each other. Properties and constraints can be inherited down this hierarchy, and provide default information about objects. In exceptional cases, property inheritance can be overridden. Standard Horn-clause logic provides neither a hierarchical structure with property inheritance nor an exception mechanism to its rules and constraints.

FRORL builds on Horn-clause logic for its clear semantics and the ability of extensive verification of the specification it provides. However, we have augmented Horn-clause logic by various mechanisms (presented in this and the following chapters). FRORL does meet the desiderata stated above:

- *Freedom from implementation concerns* — Specifications need not be efficient to be executable, and complete nondeterminism is available to state a problem solution. If a solution exists, the abstract interpreter will find it through backtracking. All data in a FRORL specification is global. In addition, the FRORL fact base can be treated as a relational database model (data access freedom). Inferred and explicitly stated information are completely indistinguishable.

- *Naturalness of representation* — People have little difficulty in constructing object hierarchies using frames. Production rules can be easily understood by domain experts. FRORL uses a frame representation for object-oriented modeling and employs production rules for specifying actions and constraints of the domain to enhance the naturalness of representation. We have chosen a set of abstract mechanisms, such as instantiation, generalization, and aggregation for the expression of abstract relations in FRORL. These abstract relations establish hierarchical relationships (relying on default and multiple inheritance) between objects and activities in the representation.

- *Validity checking* — The procedural interpretation of the axioms of a requirements specification expressed in Horn-clause logic also provides the inference mechanism required for the validity checking of the requirements specification against the domain model. One can formulate goal-clauses expressing facts about the software system and determine whether those facts can be derived from the requirements specification. Here Horn-clause logic provides an additional advantage over standard first-order logic. Any theory with a large number of axioms, formulated in a standard first-order language, will have many theorems, most of them irrelevant for the validation of the requirements specification (think only of the many disjunctions one can derive using standard first-order inference). Horn-clause logic is not susceptible to this problem since the procedural interpretation of Horn clauses treats conditionals as having only one inferential direction (thus, escaping the complexity problem validation is victim to in a standard first-order framework).

- *Operational interpretation* — Provided through the procedural interpretation of Horn-clause logic.

- *Verification* — The cited language features are only elements of the surface syntax of FRORL. The semantics of FRORL is built upon an extension of Horn-clause logic (Horn-clause logic augmented with nonmonotonicity). We rely on the duality of declarative and procedural meaning of this augmented Horn-clause logic for determining the correctness of a specification. Chapter 6 discusses in detail the various schemes provided for the verification of a requirements specification.

- *Soundness and completeness* — In contrast to other specification languages, the semantics of Horn-clause logic is well-understood. FRORL is shown to be both sound and complete relative to the nonmonotonically augmented semantics.

- *Ease of modification and construction* — FRORL is based not on standard logic, but instead, on nonmonotonic logic. In standard logic, it is very difficult to deal with the types of change typical during the software development process or with exceptions to generalizations (also typical for usable requirements specifications). Standard logic is monotonic: Adding information cannot invalidate previously holding facts. However, software developers constantly struggle with invalidation of facts through newly acquired information. Nonmonotonic logic abandons the assumption of monotonicity and attempts to provide an inference mechanism dealing with this phenomenon.[4] In Section 2.5, we present a methodology to construct FRORL specifications.

The FRORL modeling primitives are *objects* and *activities*. Each object in the model represents some entity in the domain being modeled. Changes occurring in the domain and relations between entities of the domain are represented as activities in the requirements model. Each object and activity has certain properties, assumptions, and constraints associated with it. The information related to objects and activities is expressed using frame representation. The structure of the executable specification written in FRORL is modularized into different activities. Because of this modularization, frames are relatively easy to reuse.

Using FRORL for specifying a software system is similar to the object-oriented design strategy as described in [37].[5] As far as inheritance is concerned, the three reserved words **an_instance_of**, **a_kind_of**, and **a_part_of** represent the hierarchical

[4]This direction is also pointed out by other researchers [40]. For a more detailed motivation of the use of nonmonotonic logic in requirements specifications refer to [347, 367].

[5]The object-oriented approach has also been applied to deductive databases to offer structured objects plus deductive capabilities [170].

relationships of instantiation, generalization, and aggregation among frames, respectively. Generalization allows a class to capture common characteristics shared by a group of individuals. Instantiation allows us to obtain an individual from a prototype (class). Aggregation is an abstraction which allows an object to be constructed from its constituent components. We encourage the developers to apply the proposed three kinds of abstract relations to represent hierarchical inheritance among frames. Thus, the requirements specifications will be more concise. More inferential information can be obtained by way of abstract relations.

2.3.1 Object Frames

Objects represent "things" in the domain being modeled. An object can also be viewed as a data structure or a data type in a software system. Each object has its own attributes or properties. The syntax for an object frame is introduced here mainly by example (for the precise statement of the syntax of FRORL consult the Appendix).[6]

Object: ⟨object-name⟩
  ⟨abstract-relation-type⟩**:** ⟨parent-name⟩, ⟨parent-name⟩, ...
  ⟨attribute-name⟩**:** ⟨value⟩
  ⟨attribute-name⟩**:** ⟨value⟩
  ⋮

Details of an object are stated in slots of the object frame. The abstract-relation slot indicates the type of hierarchical relationship an object frame bears to its parent frame. The type of abstract-relation may be one of **a_kind_of**, **a_part_of**, or **an_instance_of**. The value of the abstract-relation slot permits multiple object names because FRORL allows a frame to bear an inheritance relationship to more than one parent (multiple inheritance). The attribute slots represent particular properties of an object. Each property may have a value defined in the frame (which may either be a single object or a list of objects represented in Prolog list notation [65]). The value of an object may also be empty, in which case it will either be defined by an object which descends from the given frame in the inheritance hierarchy, or it will be defined through later computation.

We introduce the following example of object frames and represent their inheritance properties. The object phone_call, which is a general class, has the two attributes caller_id and callee_id as its main characteristics. three_way_call is a subclass of phone_call (three_way_call is *a kind of* phone_call). A three_way_call allows three parties to talk on the same line simultaneously. The main addition of three_way_call compared to phone_call is 2nd_callee_id. That is, a three_way_call has the attributes of phone_call

[6] In the following, we will use the convention that FRORL reserved words are typeset in bold sans-serif font, variable expressions are formatted in *italics*, whereas all other code text is set in plain sans-serif font.

which it inherits plus this additional attribute. Lastly, call_1 is an instance of the class **three_way_call** (an individual which belongs to the class **three_way_call**, and in virtue of the inheritance relationship between **three_way_call** and **phone_call** also to the class **phone_call**). The class **three_way_call** and its instance call_1 will inherit all attributes defined in the class **phone_call**. They may possess different attributes from those of their parents if they choose to override them. The three objects described above are defined in FRORL as follows.

Object: phone_call
  caller_id:
  callee_id:

Object: three_way_call
  a_kind_of: phone_call
  2nd_callee_id:

Object: call_1
  an_instance_of: three_way_call
  caller_id: 226-7083
  callee_id: 996-7251
  2nd_callee_id: 413-5352

2.3.2 Activity Frames

FRORL refers to changes taking place in the domain as activities. Each activity is represented as a frame. The activity frame has four slots, namely parts (**Parts**), precondition (**Precond**), action (**Actions**), and alternative action (**Alt_actions**) slots. The structure of the activity frame is as given below.

Activity: ⟨activity-name⟩(⟨variable⟩, ⟨variable⟩, ...)
  Parts: ⟨variable⟩: ⟨object-name⟩, ⟨variable⟩: ⟨object-name⟩, ...
  Precond: ⟨activity-desc⟩, ⟨activity-desc⟩, ...
  Actions: ⟨activity-desc⟩, ⟨activity-desc⟩, ...
  Alt_Actions: ⟨activity-desc⟩, ⟨activity-desc⟩, ...

The parts slot states the objects partaking in an activity. Specifically, it describes the class to which the objects partaking in the activity belong. The action slot contains a sequence of references to activities or facts.[7] The precondition slot describes constraints associated with the activity. If the precondition is satisfied, then the actions stated in the action slot will be executed. If the precondition is not satisfied, the sequence of actions that may be stated in the alternative action slot will be executed.

[7] A fact is some assertion about the domain; as such it either postulates objects or activities that have no preconditions associated with them.

Actions and preconditions are stated as a list of predicates. Any of the slots (except the parts slot) may be empty.

Activities are passed values as arguments, or they may be passed uninstantiated variables which will receive values as a result of performing the activity. Variables may be instantiated to lists [65]. Variables refer to instances of objects. It is also possible to refer to the object that is the value of an attribute slot of an object. This is done by using dot-notation. For example, call_1.caller_id refers to the value at the caller_id slot of object call_1. We continue the example from above to illustrate the representation of activity frames. Suppose, in a telephone system, a caller wants to dial a sequence of digits. It is required that the time duration between dialing two consecutive digits, as well as the time lag between going off-hook and dialing the first digit should be within some specific time slot or the switching system will signal a timeout (send a reorder tone) and abort the dialing process. We construct the activity get_digit. get_digit will operate on *call* which is a kind of phone_call, as stated in the parts slot. If the timing constraint is not violated (**not** alarm()), the system will wait for further dialed digits (await_further_digits) and pass the dialed digit to that action. Otherwise, the reorder tone is applied to the caller's line (alternative action reorder_tone()) and the call is aborted.

> **Activity:** get_digit(*call*)
> **Parts:** *call*: phone_call
> **Precond:** **not** alarm()
> **Actions:** await_further_digit(*call*)
> **Alt_Actions:** reorder_tone(), abort_call()

Activities may also bear hierarchical relationships to each other. These relationships are mediated through the inheritance hierarchies that exist between the objects partaking in the activities. Lets assume a safe_call is a type of phone_call in which dialing is monitored for the presence of tones not ordinarily in phone numbers (i.e., the tones generated by the "#" and "*" buttons). A safe_call aborts dialing immediately, when such a tone is received:

> **Activity:** get_digit(*call*)
> **Parts:** *call*: safe_call
> **Precond:** **super**, numeric_tone()

The get_digit activity for a safe_call inherits its action and alternative action from the get_digit activity for an ordinary phone_call (of course this requires that the object safe_call is a kind of phone_call, which we assume). However, the behavior of the precondition is changed. In addition to the behavior inherited from its successors in the inheritance hierarchy (as indicated by the keyword **super**), a safe_call adds the constraint that numeric_tone() must hold. Note that if we had not specified the keyword **super** in this case, the precondition would have overridden preconditions defined in parent classes, rather than augmenting their behavior. The same is possible for actions and alternative actions.

There are various predefined basic operations which provide convenient facilities typically needed during software development and relieve the developers from having to define them. Common primitive functions can be defined as built-in operations and embedded into the system. Domain-independent operations provide widely used common functionalities. Domain specific operations provide special purpose utilities which have been predefined in the development environment. If enough domain-specific utilities are provided, the developers can produce the specification in a nearly domain-specific language.

2.4 LSSGR Protocol Example

We illustrate the use of FRORL in stating a specification through the example of a subsection of the Local Switching System General Requirements (LSSGR) protocol for automatic completion of reverting telephone calls. This part of the LSSGR protocol defines a reverting call to be a call in which a party-line customer dials another party on the same line. Reverting call service allows a two- and four-party line customer to complete a call to other parties sharing the same line without the assistance of an operator.

The customer perspective on reverting calls depends on whether the telephone company elects to provide automatic completion. It also depends on the class of service of the line, the number of parties on the line and the type of ringing. Depending on their particular type of party-line service, customers may or may not be required to dial a digit identifying the calling party.

The requirements document describing the LSSGR protocol is shown in Fig.2.1. We define the following object frames, based on the informal description of the requirements:

Object: reverting_call
    caller_id:
    callee_id:

Object: two_party_call
    a_kind_of: reverting_call
    party_line_type: two_party

Object: four_party_semisel_call
    a_kind_of: reverting_call
    party_line_type: four_party_semisel

Object: four_party_semisel_iddigit_call
    a_kind_of: four_party_semisel_call

1. *Do not complete:*

   This option imposes no requirement on the local switching system other than to return a busy tone if a customer dials a number on the same line. The customer has to dial the operator, who may complete the call after instructing the calling customer to hang up, delay long enough for the called party to answer, and then go off-hook. The operator then supervises the call.

2. *Complete automatically*

   With this option, reverting calls are completed by the local switching system. A calling party identifying digit may or may not be required, as follows:

   (a) *Identifying digit not required:*

   The identifying digit is not required for two-party lines and is the preferred method of implementation for four-party semi-selective ringing lines. After dialing a reverting call, the calling party hears a busy tone. The calling party then hangs up and both the calling and called customers receive ringing. The calling customer is rung first to indicate initiation of the ringing sequence. Cessation of ringing informs the calling customer that the call has been answered. The calling customer goes off-hook to complete the talking connection. If the called customer does not answer, the calling party may go off-hook momentarily to trip the ringing.

   (b) *Identifying digit required:*

   The identifying digit is required for four-party fully selective ringing lines. After dialing a reverting call, the calling party hears a second dial tone and dials an additional digit identifying the calling station. The customer is informed of the procedure and of the correct identifying digit by instructions provided separately by the telephone company. After dialing the identifying digit, the calling party hears a busy tone and the call progresses as explained above.

3. Types of lines available

   (a) *Two-party line.* The called party should receive normal ringing. It is desirable that the calling party receive normal ringing but it is acceptable to ring the calling party with a special reverting ringing code. This design option allows the same ringing procedure to be used for two-party fully selective and four-party semi-selective lines.

   (b) *Four-party semi-selective line.* Only one of the following is needed depending on the method of implementation selected. The preferred method is without an identifying digit.

      i. *Without identifying digit.* The called party should receive normal ringing. The other side of the line should receive the special reverting ringing code.

      ii. *With identifying digit.* Normal ringing should be applied to both the calling and called parties if they are on opposite sides of the line. If the parties are on the same side of the line, only that side of the line should be rung using the normal ringing code of the called party.

   (c) *Four-party fully selective line.* Both parties should be rung with their normal ringing codes.

Figure 2.1. LSSGR protocol. Partially modified from A module of TR-TSY-000064, FSD 20-10-0000, LSSGR. Tech.Rep. 2, TR-TSY-000530, AT&T, 1987.

Object: four_party_semisel_nodigit_call
  a_kind_of: four_party_semisel_call

Object: four_party_fully_sel_call
  a_kind_of: reverting_call
  party_line_type: four_party_fully_sel

Unless the telephone company has elected the option of denying reverting calls, the system should attempt to complete reverting calls automatically by taking the following steps: initiate application of a busy tone to the calling party's line and then ring the two parties.

Activity: complete(x)
  Parts: x: reverting_call
  Actions: initiate_busy_tone(x), ringing(x)

A busy tone should be applied to the line immediately after the call is recognized as a reverting call or once an identifying digit has been detected (in case of a four-party semi-selective line with identifying digit). The line should be monitored for disconnect and the tone should be removed on disconnect. An invalid identifying digit will lead to a failure response. We have the following two initiate_busy_tone activities.

Activity: initiate_busy_tone(x)
  Parts: x: reverting_call
  Actions: apply_busy_tone(x.caller_id), wait_for_disconnect(x)

Activity: initiate_busy_tone(x)
  Parts: x: four_party_semisel_iddigit_call
  Precond: correct_identifying_digit(x.Digit)
  Alt_Actions: failure_response(x.caller_id), **fail**

Note that the latter activity is defined for a four_party_semisel_iddigit_call only. It inherits from any initiate_busy_tone activity which is defined for objects higher up in the hierarchy, here from reverting_call. It does not have any actions defined (it inherits its actions) but adds a special precondition and an alternative action, should this precondition fail. Upon detection of disconnection the busy tone is removed from the calling party's line, as shown below. If disconnection is not detected, the line is monitored continuously. The alternative action calls wait_for_disconnect recursively and thus creates a continuously running process which monitors the calling party's line until the precondition succeeds and the action fires, in which case the busy signal is removed.

Activity: wait_for_disconnect(x)
  Parts: x: reverting_call

Precond: is_disconnected(x)
Actions: remove_busy_signal(x.caller_id)
Alt_Actions: wait_for_disconnect(x)

Ringing should be applied to both the calling and called parties. The following activities show how ringing is applied in the general case: Normal ringing is applied to the calling party's line first, and after a 0.5 second delay the called party's line is rung, followed by another delay to allow the ringing isolator circuitry to turn off. The ringing continues in this manner until either party goes off-hook (again the continuously running process is represented as a recursive call).

Activity: ringing(x)
Parts: x: reverting_call
Precond: is_off_hook(x.caller_id)
Actions: stop_ring(x)
Alt_Actions: ring(x)

Activity: ringing(x)
Parts: x: reverting_call
Precond: is_off_hook(x.callee_id)
Actions: stop_ring(x)
Alt_Actions: ring(x)

Activity: ring(x)
Parts: x: reverting_call
Actions: apply_normal_ring(x.caller_id), delay_for_0.5_seconds,
apply_normal_ring(x.callee_id), delay_for_0.5_seconds,
ringing(x)

The above frames describe the general situation of the application of ringing. This is a case of over-abstraction typical for requirements specifications. Subclasses of the reverting_call class provide exceptional cases to this abstraction. FRORL allows a design strategy in which these exceptions can be ignored initially. Exceptional cases in the LSSGR protocol occur in four-party lines with identifying digits if calling and called parties are on the same side of the line, in which case only the called party should be rung. For a four-party line without an identifying digit, a special reverting ringing code is applied to the called party's line. Using FRORL we can state these exceptions easily by overriding the ring activity as shown below.

Activity: ring(x)
Parts: x: four_party_semisel_iddigit_call
Precond: parties_on_same_side_of_line(x)
Actions: apply_normal_ring(x.callee_id), delay_for_0.5_seconds,
ringing(x)

Activity: ring(x)
  Parts: x: four_party_semisel_nodigit_call
  Actions: apply_normal_ring(x.caller_id), delay_for_0.5_seconds,
  apply_reverting_ring(x.callee_id), delay_for_0.5_seconds,
  ringing(x)

2.5 Developing Requirements Specifications using FRORL

In [352], we presented a methodology to develop FRORL requirements specifications which derives from the object-oriented analysis of Coad and Yourdon [66]. The FRORL development methodology is based on the principles of problem representation to guide users in writing FRORL specifications. It applies top-down design and step-by-step construction to the development of a software system. A system is constructed by dealing with the most general and important concepts in the application domain first, and then proceeding with subsystems through further particularization. Using the FRORL development methodology to construct requirements specifications one can create higher-level frames to represent the main features and use lower-level frames to describe the minute demands. Because FRORL is an executable language, higher-level frames can be directly executed even if their relative lower-level frames have been assigned dummy stubs. Users and developers can understand and validate the main functions of the system at an early stage of software development.

The methodology is also designed to handle changing requirements and problem domains, provide multiple abstract views for specifications, and establish the framework for communication among users and developers. The six major stages of the FRORL development methodology are shown in Fig.2.2.

2.5.1 Identify Themes

In the theme identification stage, the software developers should concentrate solely upon the entities in the problem space. They should try to partition the domain space into several dominating themes. Every such dominating theme becomes a root frame for an object or activity frame hierarchy. The meaning designated by the developers to each root frame (theme) is not allowed to overlap with other themes at this stage. A theme is an aspect of the most primary view of the problem space. Hence the themes will force the developers to follow the "committed" root frames (themes) and construct lower-level frames in their hierarchies to model the problem space.

2.5.2 Define Object Frames

Object frames are used to represent objects of the domain. An object is not restricted to a physically tangible thing. It can also stand for abstract entities such as "ownership," "exam_result," or "grade," etc. Identifying object frames should lead to the representation of the software system closely matching the conceptual model of the

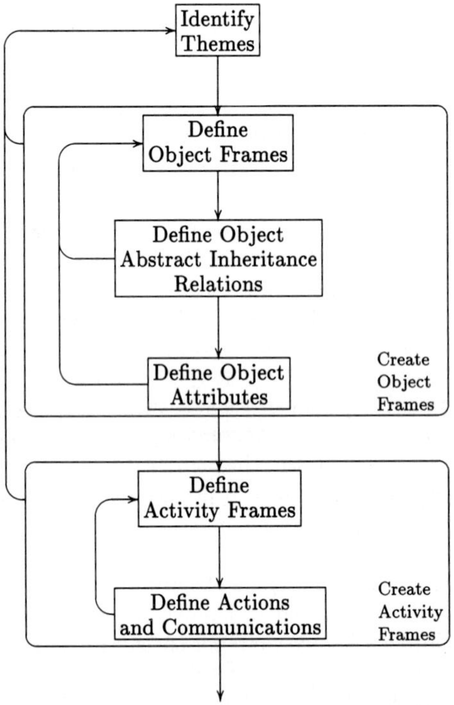

Figure 2.2. FRORL development methodology.

application domain. Object frames provide a relatively stable framework for understanding the problem space and prototyping the requirements specification. At this stage, the developers should not consider the detailed features related to the current object frames. The developers should concentrate solely on the entities of the problem space to be modelled and on how to name the "identified" objects for maximum clarity.

Should the developers find some object frame not belonging to any of the defined themes the problem space must be re-analyzed. If the result indicates the need for a proper theme to enclose the "new" object frame, the developers should return to the theme identification stage to perform the necessary modification of the specification. This iteration continues until every identified object frame belongs to a proper theme in the software system.

2.5.3 Define Object Abstract Inheritance Relations

After identifying the object frames, the developers should define the inheritance relationship for each object frame in the hierarchy. FRORL provides three abstract operators (**a_kind_of**, **a_part_of**, and **an_instance_of**) to represent inheritance among the object frames. At this stage, the developers use the same conceptual definition for object frames as in the previous stage to define abstract inheritance. When naming object frames, they should rely on standard vocabulary for the subject matter of the problem domain. For example, the name of **student-account** would be more natural and self-explanatory for the student account object than **account** alone. Particularly, homophones should be avoided, since they do not allow a consistent interpretation of object frames. When defining a consistent semantic interpretation for an object frame corresponding to the problem space, the developers also define the inheritance relation that this object frame might bear to other entities in the domain. The developers start with the top theme frames and attempts to position the object in a proper theme. Once the root theme is identified, the object frame is examined against the next level child frames of the theme. The developers repeats that process until they find where to position the object frame and what inheritance relation to use for the object frame. If the developers could not identify an appropriate location for the object frame, the stage of identifying themes is revisited.

2.5.4 Define Object Attributes

Attributes serve to describe the characteristics of object frames and to realize what is meant by the names of the object frames. Attributes are either descriptions or definitions. There are four steps to defining the attributes of an object.

1. Justify the proposed attributes and identify the category that each attribute will fall into:

    - description or definition attributes that will potentially be inherited by descendent frames,
    - attributes functionally dependent upon other attributes,
    - time-dependent attributes, and
    - attributes exceptional with respect to the attributes of parent frames.

2. Position the identified attributes (slots).

3. Define the attribute values for the attribute slots.

4. Revise the object frames if necessary.

2.5.5 Define Activity Frames

At this stage, the software developers should start identifying the activities occurring among the identified objects in the problem space.[8] The activities may involve a single object or multiple objects. For example, an activity may only be processing an object or it may be passing messages to other activities and wait for the resulting message to be sent back. The strategy for identifying activity frames has again several steps:

1. Identify activities that add, change, delete, and display data. These activities are used implicitly in all data processing systems.

2. Identify activities which perform computations on data objects. For example, an employee's weekly salary is obtained by multiplying the hourly wage by the number of hours worked.

3. Identify activities which control other activities through sequencing or synchronization. For example, a communication protocol (activity) controls sending and receiving activities between two nodes.

4. Identify activities occurring at time-based functions. For example, the decoding of a dialed digit must be performed within a certain time limit.

5. Identify utility activities such as input-output interfaces, error-handling, mathematical functions, etc.

6. Identify activities that monitor time-critical operations. For example, automated piloting functions need to be constantly monitored for deviations from the planned course.

7. Identify activities modelling the state-event-response in the problem space. For each state, the developers identify external events and the responses required to those events.

2.5.6 Define Actions and Communications

The last stage of defining activity attributes is to complete the activity frames in more specific detail. The attributes of an activity frame consist of the communicated argument, participant, precondition, action, and alternative action. First, the developers should decide which object frame will participate in the processing of this activity. FRORL attempts to increase code reuse by allowing object and activity frames to be shared between development projects. Although there are some differences between object-oriented analysis and the development methodology presented here, since a

[8]The functional requirements of a software system are likely to change during the development of the specification. The effect of change on activity frames is higher than the impact of change on object frames. Therefore, formulation of activity frames is delayed until late in the process.

FRORL requirements specification is leveled, the sharing of frames will not prohibit the application of object-oriented analysis techniques when developing FRORL specifications.

The second step is to define in detail the behavior of the attributes of an action. Activity frames are based on a top-down functional decomposition methodology. Therefore, this stage can take advantage of existing CASE tools for analysis purpose.

1. What primary services should be provided?
2. What are the services of object maintenance (e.g., instance adding, modification, deletion, selection), data computation, data or device monitoring that should be considered?
3. Which of the system's actions are time-event related or require synchronization?
4. Should the activity under consideration be an actively running task?
5. How should each action be decomposed into smaller services and how can the identified services be achieved?
6. Which objects should participate in this activity and what role should each object frame play?
7. What activity frames are available in the specification data base?
8. What inputs are needed; what input and output assertions should be satisfied; what output should be generated?
9. What timing constraints exist and how can they be accomplished?

The third step is to establish the communicated arguments. The developers can either design an argument list of the activity frame or use a message object as communication media between two objects. To be object-oriented, the communication arguments may be defined as an instance of a message object frame. The calling activity frame would instantiate the object frame and send it to the called activity frame which is the destination of the communication. After the called activity frame has achieved the requested task, it shall use an instance of the message object frame to send back the result to the calling activity frame. For real-time applications, the calling activity frame can pose a timing constraint with the message object being passed to the called activity frame.

In the fourth step, the developers should define the precondition for the activity frame which must hold before actions of the frame are triggered. When designing the action, the developers will already have analyzed which input assertions should be satisfied. In this phase, the developers defines the details of the preconditions. At the same time, the developers may define alternative actions triggered if the preconditions are not satisfied. (The alternative actions are not strictly necessary, but avoid duplication of precondition tests.)

3

Nonmonotonic Logic Foundation of the Requirements Specification Language

Informal specification languages raise various problems, such as ambiguities, incompleteness, imprecision, and so on. Whereas some of these are alleviated by formal specification languages, formality alone helps little towards achieving correct systems. In addition, we need to provide a firm semantic foundation to allow the specification to be analyzed for various anomalies. In this chapter, we present the formal foundations of the FRORL requirements specification language; later we will show how these foundations permit verification of the requirements specification.

3.1 The Formal Foundation of FRORL

Informal specifications of systems, while easy to read, tend to be ambiguous, incomplete, imprecise and over-specific. Formal specifications alleviate these problems and may be used to show correctness of the system's implementation and equivalence of different implementations. Formal specifications also allow for the development of verification and validation tools.

However, formality alone is not enough. Formal specifications can be given operational interpretations and can be executed as rapid prototypes. For example, it is easy to develop an operational semantics for FRORL as described in Chapter 2.[1] Witness the many different executable specification languages that have been presented so far. If verification and validation of the requirements specification (beyond watching and instrumenting an executable specification) is desired, we must provide a declarative semantics. In virtue of such a declarative semantics, various properties of the requirements specification may be analyzed. Specifically, features related to the expressive power of the specification language and ease of representation often cause enormous difficulties in verification without a clear semantic understanding.

[1]The requirements specification environment mentioned earlier does rely on such operational semantics to execute FRORL specifications.

In this chapter, we present the foundation of FRORL in terms of a nonmonotonic variant of Horn-clause logic. Nonmonotonicity of the logical foundations provides a semantic characterization of inheritance and exception handling (for a more detailed discussion of the application of nonmonotonic logic to requirements specification refer to [347, 367]). We will later show how the constructs of a FRORL specification can be mapped into the notation of the underlying logic. Chapter 6 shows the analytical capabilities that such a semantic foundation permits.

There have been various attempts to provide a semantic understanding of inheritance within a first-order framework, both of strict inheritance as used in RML [139] and default inheritance (which allows properties asserted of a class to be overridden by instances of that class) [333]. However, these approaches have generally not been computationally feasible.

There have been recent efforts to characterize the semantics of inheritance using abstract data types [128] or feature types [300]. These are specified in many-sorted equational logic and are defined as the initial algebras of their specifications. Inheritance is modelled by subsorting. Such logics have also been used as the underlying logic for programming languages and/or requirements specification languages.

FOOPS [128] is a unification of the functional programming paradigm with the object-oriented programming paradigm. FOOPS supports multiple inheritance for both sorts (for abstract data type values) and classes (for objects), object-valued attributes, generic modules, and module hierarchies.

However, for effective use of specifications with entities standing in hierarchies, their initial algebras need to bear a special relationship to each other: the mapping from the initial algebra of a superclass to the initial algebra of its subclass (more precisely, to the initial algebra of the subclass restricted to the sorts and operations declared in the superclass) should preferably be an isomorphism; at a minimum it must be an injection. But this amounts to strict inheritance, which we argue is insufficient. Indeed, FOOPS obtains its power not through the presence of inheritance, but through the possibility of parameterized programming. The capability of defining *generic* entities, in the sense that some of its operations will have to be specialized before use, allows the combination of entities disregarding the semantic obligations that arise from subclassing.

Goguen hints that FOOPS may be extended to encompass logic programming. Specifically, he indicates that the mechanisms of combining logic programming and functional programming developed in [127] also apply to FOOPS. However, it is unclear what effect such combination will have on inheritance in this combined language.

Feature logic [300] does augment logic programming with inheritance. [300] gives a procedure to unify terms which belong to different classes (feature types). However, the same comments as above apply: that semantics of feature types is described in terms of initial models, and that a model is initial only if (among other things) its ground equations are valid in every model (the *no-confusion rule*). Again, this seems to rule out default inheritance, which typically does introduce such confusion.

The underlying logic of FRORL is nonmonotonic precisely because it allows us to capture inheritance where a subclass may contradict information contained in its superclasses.

Most formal theories of nonmonotonic reasoning show very poor computational behavior and are either intractable or undecidable.[2] In contrast, the purpose of developing the nonmonotonic logic presented here is to enable execution of theories represented in this logic and to prove consequences of those theories (in order to determine whether specifications are correct).

The language of the logic underlying FRORL follows the standard conventions for Horn clauses as described in [199]. A literal may be either a predicate A, or $\P A$. Intuitively, "$\P A$" is read as "it is consistent with the rest of the theory that A." We also make use of the notion of predicate negation: If A is a predicate, then $\overline{A}$ denotes the complement of the extension of A. $\overline{A}$ is also a predicate. Sentences (clauses) are of the form

$$\forall x_1 \ldots x_m(B \leftarrow B_1 \wedge \ldots \wedge B_n),$$

$n \geq 0$, where B is a predicate, each $B_i, 1 \leq i \leq n$, is a literal, and $x_1, \ldots, x_m$ are the variables occurring in $B \leftarrow B_1 \wedge \ldots \wedge B_n$. B is called the *head*, $B_1 \wedge \ldots \wedge B_n$ is called the *body* of the clause. Intuitively, the above clause is read as "if B_1 and ... and B_n then conclude B." The head and/or the body of a clause may be empty. In the following, we adopt the usual convention that clauses are understood as implicitly universally quantified and that the quantifiers are dropped where confusion is unlikely to arise. Note also that a clause with empty body, $B \leftarrow$, will be written simply as B. Such clauses are called facts. A clause with an empty head is called a goal clause. If both head and body are empty we call the clause an empty clause and denote it by "□".[3]

As usual [199], a theory Θ is a set of clauses. Intuitively, a theory is unsatisfiable if the conjunction of the sentences constituting the theory is false in *every* model of the theory. For clauses, however, it suffices to look at a vastly smaller class of models, called *Herbrand models.*

Definition 3.1 *Let Θ be a theory. Let Σ_0 be the set of constants mentioned in Θ; if no constants appear in Θ, let Σ_0 be some arbitrary constant. Let τ_{i+1} be the set of all terms $f(t_1, \ldots, t_n)$ such that f is a function symbol appearing in Θ, and $\{t_1, \ldots, t_n\} \subseteq \Sigma_i$. Then*

$$\Sigma_{i+1} = \Sigma_i \cup \tau_{i+1}$$

[2] Various versions of nonmonotonic logic have been presented in the literature; for an excellent survey, see [207]. [125] is a collection of seminal papers in this area. Recent research results can be found in [264]. It is beyond the scope of this book to compare the various approaches that have been proposed and to relate the logic presented here to those approaches.

[3] Our notion of a clause does not correspond to the notion of Horn clauses, since no restrictions are placed on the form of the literals in the clause.

$$\Sigma_\Theta = \bigcup_i \Sigma_i$$

Σ_Θ is called the Herbrand universe *of Θ.*

Definition 3.2 *Let Θ be a theory. The* Herbrand base *Π_Θ for $\Theta = \{A(t_1, \ldots, t_n) \mid A$ is an n-place predicate symbol mentioned in Θ and $\{t_1, \ldots, t_n\} \subseteq \Sigma_\Theta\}$*

The notions of substitution and unification are as standardly defined.

Given a model (i.e., a nonempty set of objects and an assignment of meaning to the constant symbols, function symbols, and predicate symbols), the meaning of a ground (variable-free) sentence is defined through a set of functions that allows one to calculate the semantic value of that sentence. Due to the semi-decidability of the predicate calculus, a mechanical decision as to the truth of a sentence hinges on the possibility of reducing that sentence to one or more sentences of the propositional calculus. This reduction is not always possible for sentences of first-order predicate logic. However, a clause can be reduced in a systematic way to a countable set of sentences of the propositional calculus. Through Herbrand's theorem [57, p.61], we know that a clause is satisfiable if and only if the countable set of sentences of the propositional calculus, to which it can be reduced, is satisfiable. By an argument similar to Herbrand's, the same property holds in our extended language. Therefore, to test whether a clause is satisfiable, it suffices to consider assignments to variables of the clause with elements drawn from the Herbrand universe. Moreover, it is unnecessary to consider arbitrary models for the symbols in that clause. It suffices to interpret function symbols syntactically, i.e., to consider function symbols as denoting functions from the Herbrand universe to itself. We call such models *Herbrand models.* Note that Herbrand models differ at most on what they assign to predicate symbols. We can, therefore, identify Herbrand models of a theory Θ with subsets of the Herbrand base.

One can easily give a computational procedure which captures the intuitions behind the concept of a derivation as relied upon in FRORL (see Def.3.11). In this section, we are concerned with giving a semantics that corresponds to these intuitions. We explicate this semantics through repeated application of an operator on ground instances (facts) of the clauses contained in a FRORL specification. This operator is chosen so that, after a number of applications (starting with the set of all ground instances of the literals contained in the specification) it eliminates all facts not in a model of the FRORL specification. We call the eliminated facts the *failure set* of the specification. So far, the situation does not differ from standard Horn-clause logic. The key step in making the logic nonmonotonic is to form the nonmonotonic extension of the specification. We take the ground instances of all those literals mentioned in the specification that contain the ¶ operator, whose positive counterparts are contained in the failure set, and add them to the specification. That is, we enrich the specification by adding all potentially exceptional facts consistent with the specification. To determine which facts are contained in the model of a FRORL specification we repeatedly apply the same operator, but this time starting with the empty set and the nonmonotonic extension of the specification.

As informally stated, we explicate the notion of logical consequence in terms of fix-points of a theory operator. To motivate the use of fix-points, see [199, pp.29–32]. Note that if Θ is a theory, then the set of all Herbrand models of Θ (the power-set 2^{Π_Θ} of the Herbrand base Π_Θ) is a complete lattice under the partial order of set inclusion.[4] We then define the theory operator associated with Θ as a map from the set of all Herbrand models to itself.

Definition 3.3 *Let Θ be a theory, π a set of literals, and $\mathcal{M}$ a Herbrand model. Then the theory operator $\mathcal{T}_{\Theta,\pi}$ is a mapping from 2^{Π_Θ} to 2^{Π_Θ}, defined by*

$$\mathcal{T}_{\Theta,\pi}(\mathcal{M}) = \left\{ A \in \Pi_\Theta \;\middle|\; \begin{array}{l} B \leftarrow B_1 \wedge \ldots \wedge B_n \in \Theta, \exists\theta, \text{ such that } A = B\theta \\ \text{and either } B_i\theta \in \mathcal{M} \text{ or } B_i\theta \in \pi, 1 \leq i \leq n \end{array} \right\}$$

Theorem 3.1 *The theory operator $\mathcal{T}_{\Theta,\pi}$ is continuous.*

Proof: We must show, for all directed subsets Γ of Π_Θ, that

$$\mathcal{T}_{\Theta,\pi}(\bigcup \Gamma) = \bigcup \mathcal{T}_{\Theta,\pi}(\Gamma).$$

Let Γ be a directed subset of Π_Θ, let A be an atom in Π_Θ. Note first that $\{B_1, \ldots, B_n\} \in \bigcup \Gamma$ if and only if $\{B_1, \ldots, B_n\} \in \mathcal{M}$, for some $\mathcal{M} \in \Gamma$. (This lemma is shown in the appendix.) $A \in \mathcal{T}_{\Theta,\pi}(\bigcup \Gamma)$ if and only if $B \leftarrow B_1 \wedge \ldots \wedge B_n \in \Theta$, $A = B\theta$, and either $B_i \in \bigcup \Gamma$, or $B_i \in \pi$, $1 \leq i \leq n$ if and only if $B \leftarrow B_1 \wedge \ldots \wedge B_n \in \Theta$, $A = B\theta$, and either for some $\mathcal{M} \in \Gamma$, $B_i \in \mathcal{M}$, or $B_i \in \pi$, $1 \leq i \leq n$ if and only if $A \in \mathcal{T}_{\Theta,\pi}(\mathcal{M})$, for some $\mathcal{M} \in \Gamma$ if and only if $A \in \bigcup \mathcal{T}_{\Theta,\pi}(\Gamma)$. ■

Since the theory operator $\mathcal{T}_{\Theta,\pi}$ is continuous (and therefore, monotonic), by the Knaster-Tarski theorem [322] we know that $\mathcal{T}_{\Theta,\pi}$ has a greatest fix-point and a least fix-point. Next, we define the *approximation from above* to the greatest fix-point of the theory operator in terms of its ordinal powers.

Definition 3.4 *Let Θ be a theory, let $\mathcal{T}_{\Theta,\pi}$ be the theory operator*

(i) $\mathcal{T}_{\Theta,\pi}\downarrow_0 = \Pi_\Theta$

(ii) $\mathcal{T}_{\Theta,\pi}\downarrow_k = \mathcal{T}_{\Theta,\pi}(\mathcal{T}_{\Theta,\pi}\downarrow_{k-1}) =$

$$\left\{ A \in \Pi_\Theta \;\middle|\; \begin{array}{l} B \leftarrow B_1 \wedge \ldots \wedge B_n \in \Theta, A = B\theta, \text{and} \\ B_i\theta \in \mathcal{T}_{\Theta,\pi}\downarrow_{k-1} \text{ or } B_i\theta \in \pi, 1 \leq i \leq n \end{array} \right\}$$

(iii) $\mathcal{T}_{\Theta,\pi}\downarrow_\omega = \bigcap_{k \geq 0} \mathcal{T}_{\Theta,\pi}\downarrow_k$, if ω is the limit ordinal.

$\mathcal{T}_{\Theta,\pi}\downarrow_\omega$ is the approximation from above to the greatest fix-point of the theory operator associated with theory Θ and the set π.

[4] The top element of the lattice is the Herbrand base Π_Θ, the bottom element is $\emptyset$. The least upper bound and greatest lower bound are the union of Herbrand models and their intersection, respectively.

Definition 3.5 *The* failure set *for theory Θ, $\mathcal{F}ail_\Theta$, is defined by*

$$\mathcal{F}ail_\Theta = \Pi_\Theta - \mathcal{T}_{\Theta,\emptyset}\downarrow_\omega .$$

Definition 3.6 *The* nonmonotonic extension *of a theory Θ is the set of literals $\mathcal{N}m(\Theta)$, where*

$$\mathcal{N}m(\Theta) = \{\P A\theta \mid \P A \textit{ is mentioned in } \Theta, A\theta \in \Pi_\Theta, \textit{ and } \overline{A}\theta \in \mathcal{F}ail_\Theta\}.$$

As illustration, consider the example theory Θ_1:[5]

$$\Theta_1 = \left\{ \begin{array}{l} \mathsf{busy\_tone}(x) \leftarrow \mathsf{phone\_call}(x) \wedge \P\mathsf{busy\_tone}(x) \\ \overline{\mathsf{busy\_tone}}(x) \leftarrow \mathsf{three\_way\_call}(x) \\ \mathsf{phone\_call}(x) \leftarrow \mathsf{three\_way\_call}(x) \\ \mathsf{three\_way\_call}(\mathsf{call}_1) \\ \mathsf{phone\_call}(\mathsf{call}_2) \end{array} \right\}$$

The nonmonotonic extension of theory Θ_1 is calculated as follows. We begin with the Herbrand Base Π_{Θ_1} and apply the theory operator $\mathcal{T}_{\Theta,\pi}$ until we approximate the greatest fix-point.

$$\mathcal{T}_{\Theta_1,\emptyset}\downarrow_0 = \Pi_{\Theta_1} = \left\{ \begin{array}{l} \mathsf{busy\_tone}(\mathsf{call}_1) \\ \mathsf{phone\_call}(\mathsf{call}_1) \\ \overline{\mathsf{busy\_tone}}(\mathsf{call}_1) \\ \mathsf{three\_way\_call}(\mathsf{call}_1) \\ \mathsf{busy\_tone}(\mathsf{call}_2) \\ \mathsf{phone\_call}(\mathsf{call}_2) \\ \overline{\mathsf{busy\_tone}}(\mathsf{call}_2) \\ \mathsf{three\_way\_call}(\mathsf{call}_2) \end{array} \right\}.$$

$$\mathcal{T}_{\Theta_1,\emptyset}\downarrow_1 = \left\{ \begin{array}{l} \mathsf{phone\_call}(\mathsf{call}_1) \\ \overline{\mathsf{busy\_tone}}(\mathsf{call}_1) \\ \mathsf{three\_way\_call}(\mathsf{call}_1) \\ \mathsf{phone\_call}(\mathsf{call}_2) \\ \overline{\mathsf{busy\_tone}}(\mathsf{call}_2) \end{array} \right\}.$$

$$\mathcal{T}_{\Theta_1,\emptyset}\downarrow_2 = \mathcal{T}_{\Theta_1,\emptyset}\downarrow_\omega = \left\{ \begin{array}{l} \mathsf{phone\_call}(\mathsf{call}_1) \\ \overline{\mathsf{busy\_tone}}(\mathsf{call}_1) \\ \mathsf{three\_way\_call}(\mathsf{call}_1) \\ \mathsf{phone\_call}(\mathsf{call}_2) \end{array} \right\}.$$

---

[5]Incidentally, the example theory Θ_1 is a translation of the FRORL frames

Object: phone_call
  busy_tone: true

Object: three_way_call
  a_kind_of: phone_call
  busy_tone: false

and the facts "*threeway*"(call_1) and "*phone_call*"(call_2). For the purpose of presentation, we have slightly simplified the translation from that presented in Section 3.3 below.

Thus, we obtain the failure set for Θ_1 as

$$\mathcal{F}ail_{\Theta_1} = \left\{ \begin{array}{l} \mathsf{busy\_tone}(\mathsf{call}_1) \\ \mathsf{busy\_tone}(\mathsf{call}_2) \\ \overline{\mathsf{busy\_tone}}(\mathsf{call}_2) \\ \mathsf{three\_way\_call}(\mathsf{call}_2) \end{array} \right\}$$

The literals in the Herbrand Base Π_{Θ_1} of the shape $\P A$ to consider are $\P\mathsf{busy\_tone}(\mathsf{call}_1)$ and $\P\mathsf{busy\_tone}(\mathsf{call}_2)$. $\overline{\mathsf{busy\_tone}}(\mathsf{call}_1) \notin \mathcal{F}ail_{\Theta_1}$, but $\overline{\mathsf{busy\_tone}}(\mathsf{call}_2) \in \mathcal{F}ail_{\Theta_1}$. Therefore, the nonmonotonic extension of Θ_1 is

$$\mathcal{N}m(\Theta_1) = \{\P\mathsf{busy\_tone}(\mathsf{call}_2)\}.$$

The approximation from above to the greatest fix-point of the theory operator $\mathcal{T}_{\Theta,\pi}$ at ω defines the set of ground sentences that are not logical consequences of a theory. If a literal $\P A$ is mentioned in Θ, and if $\overline{A}\theta$ is not a logical consequence of the theory Θ, then the ground literal $\P A\theta$ is added to the nonmonotonic extension of Θ. The nonmonotonic extension of a theory is the theory plus all the facts of said form. The consideration of the nonmonotonically extended theory, instead of the theory itself, is what makes the logic presented here nonmonotonic.

We define the *approximation from below* to the least fix-point of the theory operator $\mathcal{T}_{\Theta,\pi}$ for a theory Θ.

Definition 3.7 *Let Θ be a theory, let $\mathcal{T}_{\Theta,\pi}$ be the theory operator, then*

(i) $\mathcal{T}_{\Theta,\pi}\uparrow_0 = \emptyset$

(ii) $\mathcal{T}_{\Theta,\pi}\uparrow_k = \mathcal{T}_{\Theta,\pi}(\mathcal{T}_{\Theta,\pi}\uparrow_{k-1}) =$

$$\left\{ A \in \Pi_\Theta \;\middle|\; \begin{array}{l} B \leftarrow B_1 \wedge \ldots \wedge B_n \in \Theta, A = B\theta, \text{ and} \\ B_i\theta \in \mathcal{T}_{\Theta,\pi}\uparrow_{k-1} \text{ or } B_i\theta \in \pi, 1 \le i \le n \end{array} \right\}$$

(iii) $\mathcal{T}_{\Theta,\pi}\uparrow_\omega = \bigcup_{k\ge 0} \mathcal{T}_{\Theta,\pi}\uparrow_k$, if ω is the limit ordinal.

$\mathcal{T}_{\Theta,\pi}\uparrow_\omega$ is the approximation from below to the least fix-point of the theory operator associated with Θ and π. We know that the approximation from below reaches the least fix-point of the theory operator $\mathcal{T}_{\Theta,\pi}$ at ω. $\mathcal{T}_{\Theta,\pi}\uparrow_\omega$ is the least fix-point of the theory operator $\mathcal{T}_{\Theta,\pi}$.[6]

We shall now define the notion of logical consequence in the nonmonotonic logic presented.

Definition 3.8 *A set of clauses Θ and a goal G is unsatisfiable if and only if either*

(i) G contains the ground literal $\leftarrow B$ and $B \in \mathcal{T}_{\Theta,\mathcal{N}m(\Theta)}\uparrow_\omega$,

[6]Note that the same is not true for the approximation from above $\mathcal{T}_{\Theta_1,\emptyset}\downarrow_\omega$. That is, the approximation from above does not reach the greatest fix-point of the theory operator $\mathcal{T}_{\Theta,\pi}$.

(ii) G contains the ground clause $\leftarrow B_1 \wedge \ldots \wedge B_n$ and $\Theta \cup \{\leftarrow B_i\}$ is unsatisfiable, $1 \leq i \leq n$,

(iii) G contains the clause $\leftarrow B_1 \wedge \ldots \wedge B_n$ and $\exists \theta$, such that $B_1\theta, \ldots, B_n\theta$ are ground, and $\Theta \cup \{\leftarrow B_1\theta \wedge \ldots \wedge B_n\theta\}$ is unsatisfiable.

Definition 3.9 *A is a logical consequence of a set of clauses Θ,*

$$\Theta \models^{nm} A \text{ if and only if } \begin{cases} A \neq \P C \text{ and } \Theta \cup \{\leftarrow A\} \text{ is unsatisfiable, or} \\ A \in \mathcal{N}m(\Theta) \end{cases}$$

As illustration, we again consider the example theory:

$$\mathcal{T}_{\Theta_1,\mathcal{N}m(\Theta)}\!\uparrow\! 0 = \emptyset$$

$$\mathcal{T}_{\Theta_1,\mathcal{N}m(\Theta)}\!\uparrow\! 1 = \left\{ \begin{array}{l} \mathsf{three\_way\_call}(\mathsf{call}_1) \\ \mathsf{phone\_call}(\mathsf{call}_2) \end{array} \right\}$$

$$\mathcal{T}_{\Theta_1,\mathcal{N}m(\Theta)}\!\uparrow\! 2 = \mathcal{T}_{\Theta_1,\mathcal{N}m(\Theta)}\!\uparrow\! \omega = \left\{ \begin{array}{l} \mathsf{three\_way\_call}(\mathsf{call}_1) \\ \mathsf{phone\_call}(\mathsf{call}_1) \\ \overline{\mathsf{busy\_tone}}(\mathsf{call}_1) \\ \mathsf{phone\_call}(\mathsf{call}_2) \\ \mathsf{busy\_tone}(\mathsf{call}_2) \end{array} \right\}$$

We want to know whether $\mathsf{busy\_tone}(\mathsf{call}_1)$ is a logical consequence of Θ_1, i.e., whether $\Theta_1 \models^{nm} \mathsf{busy\_tone}(\mathsf{call}_1)$. Since $\mathsf{busy\_tone}(\mathsf{call}_1)$ is ground, this is true only when $\mathsf{busy\_tone}(\mathsf{call}_1) \in \mathcal{T}_{\Theta_1,\mathcal{N}m(\Theta)}\!\uparrow\!\omega$, which it is not. However, $\mathsf{busy\_tone}(\mathsf{call}_2) \in \mathcal{T}_{\Theta_1,\mathcal{N}m(\Theta)}\!\uparrow\!\omega$ and, therefore, $\Theta_1 \models^{nm} \mathsf{busy\_tone}(\mathsf{call}_2)$.

Note again the difference between predicate negation and the negation symbol of standard first-order logic. From Def.3.8 and Def.3.9 one can see that $\Theta \models^{nm} \overline{A}$ if (for a ground literal A), $\overline{A} \in \mathcal{T}_{\Theta,\mathcal{N}m(\Theta)}\!\uparrow\!\omega$, which is obviously different from the claim $\Theta \models^{nm} \overline{A}$ if and only if $\Theta \not\models^{nm} A$ made by standard first-order logic. As far as negation is concerned, FRORL functions just as unaugmented Horn-clause logic.[7]

The semantic notion central to logic programming and reasoning in the Herbrand universe is that of a correct answer substitution. A nonmonotonic correct answer substitution is defined in terms of nonmonotonic logical consequence.

Definition 3.10 *θ is a* nonmonotonic correct answer substitution *for theory Θ and goal $G = \{\leftarrow B_1 \wedge \ldots \wedge B_n\}$ if and only if θ is a (not necessarily ground) substitution for variables in G, and for any substitution θ' of elements of the domain to the remaining variables in G, $\Theta \models^{nm} (B_1 \wedge \ldots \wedge B_n)\theta\theta'$. Let this situation be denoted by $\Theta \models^{nm} \forall((B_1 \wedge \ldots \wedge B_n)\theta)$.*

[7]Negation can be added to our language by forming the completion of the theory Θ. The negation-as-failure rule allows us to deduce negative information closer to the standard first-order meaning. Adding negation follows the arguments given in [10, 60]. However, negation as failure has to be kept distinct from predicate negation.

The nonmonotonic correct answer substitution for theory $\Theta_1 \cup \{\leftarrow \mathsf{busy\_tone}(\mathsf{call}_2)\}$ is the empty substitution, since $\Theta_1 \models^{nm} \forall(\mathsf{busy\_tone}(\mathsf{call}_2))$, whereas Θ_1 together with $\mathsf{busy\_tone}(\mathsf{call}_1)$ does not have a nonmonotonic correct answer substitution.

Note that if $\Theta \cup \{\leftarrow B_1 \wedge \ldots \wedge B_n\} \models^{nm} \Box$, then there exists a substitution θ such that $\Theta \models^{nm} (B_1 \wedge \ldots \wedge B_n)\theta$. Thus, the claim that Θ is a correct answer substitution for the goal G is stronger than the claim that $\Theta \cup G\theta \models^{nm} \Box$. The intuitive idea is that a correct answer substitution replaces those variables of the goal G over which one cannot universally generalize.

3.2 Soundness and Completeness of FRORL

In [366], we showed that one can give a model-theoretic semantics corresponding to above fix-point semantics. For our purposes, it is also important that one be able to define a computational procedure which indicates whether a given clause is a logical consequence of a theory. This computational procedure is the obvious extension of the Horn-clause selection rule as discussed in [199] and is stated in Def.3.11. In this section, we establish soundness and completeness of the logic underlying FRORL relative to that procedure.

3.2.1 Derivations

The syntactic notion of interest is whether a sentence can be derived from a theory.

Definition 3.11 *Let Θ be a theory, $G_i = \{\leftarrow A_1 \wedge \ldots \wedge A_n\}$ a goal, then G_{i+1} is derived from G_i and Θ if A_m is a literal in G_i selected as subgoal, and either*

(i) $A_m \neq \P C$, C_i' is an alphabetic variant of a clause $C_i = B \leftarrow B_1 \wedge \ldots \wedge B_k \in \Theta$ with all new variables, and there is a substitution θ_{i+1} such that $A_m\theta_{i+1} = B\theta_{i+1}$, and $G_{i+1} = \{(\leftarrow A_1 \wedge \ldots \wedge A_{m-1} \wedge B_1 \wedge \ldots \wedge B_k \wedge A_{m+1} \wedge \ldots \wedge A_n)\theta_{i+1}\}$, or

(ii) A_m is a ground literal $\P C$, the attempt to construct a derivation of $\Theta \cup \{\leftarrow \overline{C}\}$ fails after finitely many steps, and $G_{i+1} = \{(\leftarrow A_1 \wedge \ldots \wedge A_{m-1} \wedge A_{m+1} \wedge \ldots \wedge A_n)\theta_{i+1}\}$, where θ_{i+1} is the empty substitution.

It is important that the literal $\P C$ only be selected if it is ground. Consider, for example, the theory $\{A(a) \leftarrow \P B(x), \overline{B}(a)\}$. If we could select unground goals, an attempted refutation for this theory would fail.

Definition 3.12 *A* derivation *of $\Theta \cup G_0$ is a sequence $G_0 G_1 \ldots$ of goals, such that each G_i in this sequence is derived from an earlier goal G_j, $j \leq i$ and Θ.*

A derivation is either an infinite sequence, or it stops after a finite number n of steps. If the last element in the sequence, when the derivation stops, is the empty clause $\Box$, we say the derivation has succeeded. Such a derivation is called a *refutation.*

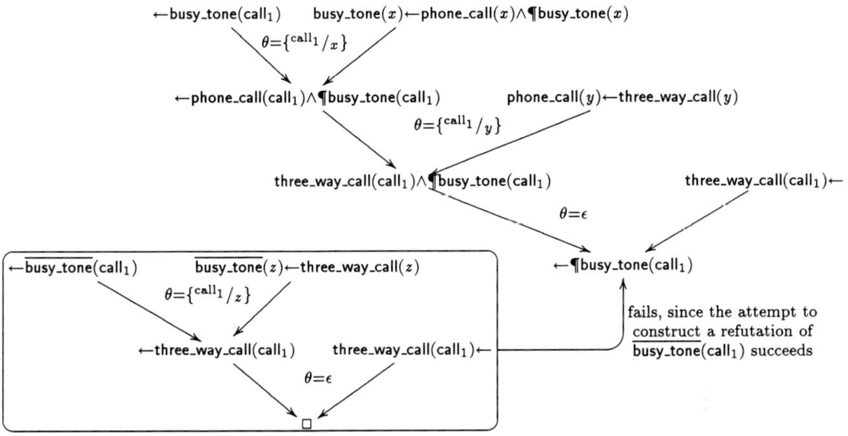

Figure 3.1. Failure of the goal $\{\leftarrow \P\mathsf{busy\_tone}(\mathsf{call}_1)\}$

Otherwise, we say the derivation failed finitely, either because the derivation was unable to continue as defined in Def.3.11(ii), or because no head of a clause $C_n{}'$ unifies with a literal in G_n.

Definition 3.13 *A sequence $G_0 G_1 \ldots G_n$ is a* refutation *of $\Theta \cup G_0$ if and only if every member G_i of this sequence is derived from an earlier member G_j, $j \leq i$ and Θ, $G_n = \Box$, and n is finite.*

If a sentence G, together with a theory Θ, has a refutation, then we say that the goal G can be derived from Θ.

Fig.3.1 and Fig.3.2 exhibit the attempted derivations of $\mathsf{busy\_tone}(\mathsf{call}_1)$ and $\mathsf{busy\_tone}(\mathsf{call}_2)$, respectively, from Θ_1. The refutation of $\Theta_1 \cup \{\leftarrow \mathsf{busy\_tone}(\mathsf{call}_1)\}$ fails, as can be seen in Fig.3.1. The refutation of $\Theta_1 \cup \{\leftarrow \mathsf{busy\_tone}(\mathsf{call}_2)\}$ is successful.

The central notion for logic programming is that of a computed answer substitution.

Definition 3.14 *θ is a nonmonotonic computed answer substitution for theory Θ and goal $G = \{\leftarrow B_1 \wedge \ldots \wedge B_n\}$ if and only if θ is the sequence of most general unifiers $\theta_1 \ldots \theta_n$ used in the refutation of $\Theta \cup G$, restricted to the variables in G.*

3.2.2 Soundness

The soundness result we wish to show is, if a substitution is a computed answer substitution, it is also a correct answer substitution.

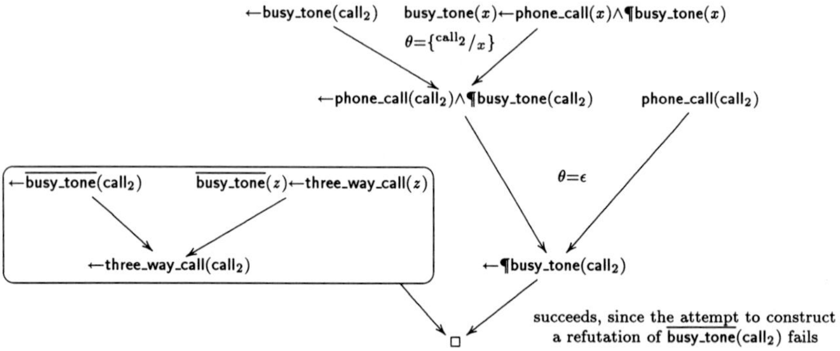

←busy_tone(call2)
busy_tone(x)←phone_call(x)∧¶busy_tone(x)
θ={call2/x}
←phone_call(call2)∧¶busy_tone(call2)
phone_call(call2)
←busy_tone(call2)
busy_tone(z)←three_way_call(z)
θ=ε
←three_way_call(call2)
←¶busy_tone(call2)
succeeds, since the attempt to construct
a refutation of busy_tone(call2) fails

Figure 3.2. Success of the goal $\{\leftarrow \P\text{busy\_tone}(\text{call}_2)\}$

Lemma 3.2 *Let Θ be a theory, G a goal, and θ a substitution. If the attempt to construct a refutation for $\Theta \cup G$ fails with length $\leq n$, then the attempt to construct a refutation of $\Theta \cup G\theta$ fails with length $\leq n$.*

Lemma 3.3 *Let Θ be a theory, let $A_1, \ldots, A_n$ be ground atoms. If the attempt to construct a refutation of $\Theta \cup \{\leftarrow A_1 \wedge \ldots \wedge A_n\}$ fails with length $\leq n$, then for some A_i, $1 \leq i \leq n$, the attempt to construct a refutation of $\Theta \cup \{\leftarrow A_i\}$ fails with length $\leq n$.*

The preceding lemmas are due to Apt [10], where they are established for standard Horn-clause logic. The proofs proceed by induction on the length of the attempted refutations and are omitted.

Lemma 3.4 *If $\Theta \cup \{\leftarrow A\}$ fails finitely, then $A \notin \mathcal{T}_{\Theta,\emptyset}\downarrow_\omega$.*

Proof: Let Θ be a theory. Show by induction on the length n of the attempted refutation that if the derivation of $\Theta \cup \{\leftarrow A\}$ fails with length $\leq n$, then $A \notin \mathcal{T}_{\Theta,\emptyset}\downarrow_n$. But then $A \notin \mathcal{T}_{\Theta,\emptyset}\downarrow_\omega$. Suppose the derivation of $\Theta \cup \{\leftarrow A\}$ fails finitely. Consider $n = 1$, i.e., the derivation of $\Theta \cup \{\leftarrow A\}$ fails with length ≤ 1. Then A is not an instance of the head of any clause in Θ, and so

$$A \notin \mathcal{T}_{\Theta,\emptyset}\downarrow_1.$$

Assume the result holds for all failed derivations of $\Theta \cup \{\leftarrow A\}$ with length $\leq k < n$, and suppose for *reductio* that $A \in \mathcal{T}_{\Theta,\emptyset}\downarrow_n$. Thus, there is a clause $\{B \leftarrow B_1 \wedge \ldots \wedge B_m\} \in \Theta$, such that

$$A = B\theta_1, \text{and } B_i\theta_1 \in \mathcal{T}_{\Theta,\emptyset}\downarrow_{n-1}, 1 \leq i \leq n.$$

By hypothesis, the derivation of $\Theta \cup \{\leftarrow A\}$ fails with length $\leq n$. So, either

(i) the derivation of $\Theta \cup \{\leftarrow B_1\theta \wedge \ldots \wedge B_m\theta\}$ fails with length $\leq n-1$. Now take the substitution θ_2, such that $\theta_1 = \theta\theta_2$. By Lem.3.2 the derivation of $\Theta \cup \{\leftarrow B_1\theta\theta_2 \wedge \ldots \wedge B_n\theta\theta_2\}$ fails with length $\leq n-1$, which means that the derivation of $\Theta \cup \{\leftarrow B_1\theta_1 \wedge \ldots \wedge B_m\theta_1\}$ fails with length $\leq n-1$. Note that θ_1 is a ground substitution. But, then, by Lem.3.3, there is some $B_i\theta_1$ such that the derivation of $\Theta \cup \{\leftarrow B_i\theta_1\}$ fails with length $\leq n-1$. By the induction hypothesis we can conclude that

$$B_i\theta_1 \notin \mathcal{T}_{\Theta,\emptyset}\!\downarrow_{n-1},$$

Otherwise,

(ii) $B \leftarrow B_1 \wedge \ldots \wedge B_m \notin \Theta$, or

(iii) $G \neq B\theta$,

In either case, we can conclude a contradiction. ■

Theorem 3.5 *Let Θ be a theory, $G = \{\leftarrow A_1 \wedge \ldots \wedge A_m\}$ a goal. Then if θ is a nonmonotonic computed answer substitution for $\Theta \cup G$, then θ is correct.*

Proof: By induction on the length n of the refutation of $\Theta \cup G$. Suppose θ is a nonmonotonic computed answer substitution for $\Theta \cup G$, i.e., $\theta = \theta_1 \ldots \theta_n$ is the sequence of most general unifiers used in the refutation of $\Theta \cup G$. Consider $n = 1$; thus, $G = \{\leftarrow A_1\}$. Two cases:

(i) $A_1 \neq \P C$. Since we have a refutation, $\exists C_1{}' \in \Theta$, such that

$$C_1{}' = B \leftarrow \text{and } A_1\theta_1 = B\theta_1.$$

Since $B \leftarrow\, \in \Theta$, $\Theta \models^{nm} \forall(B)$, and also, $\Theta \models^{nm} \forall(B\theta_1)$, and thus $\Theta \models^{nm} \forall(A_1\theta_1)$.

(ii) $A_1 = \P C$. Since A_1 was selected, A_1 is ground. Since we have a refutation, $\Theta \cup \{\leftarrow \overline{C}\}$ failed finitely. So, by Lem.3.4

$$\overline{C} \notin \mathcal{T}_{\Theta,\emptyset}\!\downarrow_{\omega}.$$

But if $\overline{C} \notin \mathcal{T}_{\Theta,\emptyset}\!\downarrow_{\omega}$ and C is ground, then

$$\P C \in \mathcal{N}m(\Theta)$$

and $\Theta \models^{nm} \P C$. Since $\P C$ is ground, $\Theta \models^{nm} \forall(\P C)$.

Now, suppose the result holds for computed answer substitutions from refutations of length $k < n$. Consider a refutation of $\Theta \cup \{\leftarrow A_1 \wedge \ldots \wedge A_m\}$ of length n, where the selected subgoal is A_k. Again, we have to look at the two cases:

(i) $A_k \neq \P C$. Then there must be a clause $C_n{}' = A \leftarrow B_1 \wedge \ldots \wedge B_q$, $C_n{}' \in \Theta$, such that $A_k\theta_1 \ldots \theta_n = A\theta_1 \ldots \theta_n$, and we have a refutation of

$$\Theta \cup \left\{ \begin{array}{c} \leftarrow (A_1 \wedge \ldots \wedge A_{k-1} \wedge B_1 \wedge \ldots \wedge B_q \wedge \\ A_{k+1} \wedge \ldots \wedge A_m)\theta_1 \ldots \theta_{n-1} \end{array} \right\}.$$

By hypothesis $\Theta \models^{nm} \forall((A_1 \wedge \ldots \wedge A_{k-1} \wedge B_1 \wedge \ldots \wedge B_q \wedge A_{k+1} \wedge \ldots \wedge A_m)\theta_1 \ldots \theta_{n-1})$. So, by Def.3.9

$$\Theta \models^{nm} \forall((B_1 \wedge \ldots \wedge B_q)\theta_1 \ldots \theta_n),$$

and also, $\Theta \models^{nm} \forall((A_k)\theta_1 \ldots \theta_n)$, but so $\Theta \models^{nm} \forall((A_1 \wedge \ldots \wedge A_m)\theta_1 \ldots \theta_n)$

(ii) $A_k = \P C$. Then we must have a refutation of

$$\Theta \cup \{\leftarrow (A_1 \wedge \ldots \wedge A_{k-1} \wedge A_{k+1} \wedge \ldots \wedge A_m)\theta_1 \ldots \theta_{n-1}\}.$$

By hypothesis $\Theta \models^{nm} \forall((A_1 \wedge \ldots \wedge A_{k-1} \wedge A_{k+1} \wedge \ldots \wedge A_m)\theta_1 \ldots \theta_{n-1})$. Since A_k was selected, A_k is ground. Since we have a refutation, $\Theta \cup \{\leftarrow \overline{C}\}$ failed finitely. So, by Lem.3.4

$$\overline{C} \notin T_{\Theta,\emptyset}\downarrow_\omega .$$

But if $\overline{C} \notin T_{\Theta,\emptyset}\downarrow_\omega$ and C is ground, then $\P C \in \mathcal{N}m(\Theta)$ and $\Theta \models^{nm} \P C$. But, so also $\Theta \models^{nm} \forall(\P C)$, and $\Theta \models^{nm} \forall((A_k)\theta_1 \ldots \theta_n)$. And so, by Def.3.9,

$$\Theta \models^{nm} \forall((A_1 \wedge \ldots \wedge A_m)\theta_1 \ldots \theta_n).$$

Thus, since $\Theta \models^{nm} \forall((A_1 \wedge \ldots \wedge A_m)\theta_1 \ldots \theta_n)$, $\theta = \theta_1 \ldots \theta_n$ is correct. ■

3.2.3 Completeness

The completeness result states that if a substitution is a correct answer substitution, it is also a computed answer substitution.

Lemma 3.6 *Let Θ be a theory, G a goal, θ a substitution, then if there is a refutation of $\Theta \cup G\theta$, then there is a refutation of $\Theta \cup G$.*

This lemma is also known as *lifting lemma.* A proof can be found in [117, p.88].

Lemma 3.7 *Let Θ be a theory, let A be a ground atom, then if $A \in T_{\Theta,\mathcal{N}m(\Theta)}\uparrow_\omega$, then $\Theta \cup \{\leftarrow A\}$ has a refutation.*

Proof: Suppose that A is a ground atom and $A \in \mathcal{T}_{\Theta,\mathcal{N}m(\Theta)}\uparrow_n$, and show by induction on the approximation from above to the greatest fix-point that $\Theta \cup \{\leftarrow A\}$ has a refutation. Consider $n = 1$. Then $A \in \mathcal{T}_{\Theta,\mathcal{N}m(\Theta)}\uparrow_1$, which means that $A = B\theta$, where $B\theta \leftarrow \in \Theta$, i.e., A is the instance of a fact in Θ. Obviously, $\Theta \cup \{\leftarrow A\}$ has a refutation. Now, assume the result holds for $k < n$. By hypothesis $A \in \mathcal{T}_{\Theta,\mathcal{N}m(\Theta)}\uparrow_n$, so either there is a clause $B \leftarrow B_1 \wedge \ldots \wedge B_m \in \Theta$ such that $A = B\theta$, and $B_i\theta \in \mathcal{T}_{\Theta,\mathcal{N}m(\Theta)}\uparrow_{n-1}$, $1 \leq i \leq m$. By the induction hypothesis $\Theta \cup \{\leftarrow B_i\theta\}$, $1 \leq i \leq m$, has a refutation. Since $B_i\theta$ is ground, these separate refutations can be combined into a refutation of $\Theta \cup \{\leftarrow B_1\theta \wedge \ldots \wedge B_m\theta\}$. But then $\Theta \cup \{\leftarrow A\}$ has a refutation. ∎

Lemma 3.8 *If $\Theta \cup \{\leftarrow A\}$ has a refutation, then $A \in \mathcal{T}_{\Theta,\emptyset}\downarrow_\omega$.*

Proof: Show by induction on the length n of the refutation. Consider $n = 1$. If $\Theta \cup \{\leftarrow A\}$ has a refutation of length 1, then A is an instance of a fact in Θ, and so

$$A \in \mathcal{T}_{\Theta,\emptyset}\downarrow_1 .$$

Suppose, for any refutation of length $k < n$, we know that if $\Theta \cup \{\leftarrow A\}$ has a refutation of length k, then $A \in \mathcal{T}_{\Theta,\emptyset}\downarrow_k$. Now, assume $\Theta \cup \{\leftarrow A\}$ has a refutation of length n. There is a clause $B \leftarrow B_1 \wedge \ldots \wedge B_m \in \Theta$ such that $A = B\theta$, and $B_i\theta$ has a refutation of length $n-1$, $1 \leq i \leq m$. But then, by the induction hypothesis, $B_i\theta \in \mathcal{T}_{\Theta,\emptyset}\downarrow_{n-1}$, $1 \leq i \leq m$. Then, also, $A \in \mathcal{T}_{\Theta,\emptyset}\downarrow_n$. ∎

Lemma 3.9 *If the derivation of $\Theta \cup \{\leftarrow A_1 \wedge \ldots \wedge A_m\}$ is infinite, then the set of all ground instances of A_i is in $\mathcal{T}_{\Theta,\emptyset}\downarrow_\omega$, for $i = 1, 2, \ldots, m$.*

Proof: Let the derivation of $\Theta \cup \{\leftarrow A_1 \wedge \ldots \wedge A_m\}$ be $G_0 G_1 \ldots$, where $G_0 = \{\leftarrow A_1 \wedge \ldots \wedge A_m\}$, let the sequence of most general unifiers used in the derivation be $\theta_1, \theta_2, \ldots$, let $[A]$ denote the set of all ground instances of A. Show by induction on the number $n \in \omega$ of steps in the derivation that for any $i \in \{1, 2, \ldots m\}$, there is a $r \in \omega$, such that $[A_i\theta_1\theta_2 \ldots \theta_r] \subseteq \mathcal{T}_{\Theta,\emptyset}\downarrow_n$. Consider $n = 0$. Obviously, there is a θ_r, such that $[A_i\theta_1\theta_2 \ldots \theta_r] \subseteq \mathcal{T}_{\Theta,\emptyset}\downarrow_0$, namely that θ_r, that makes $A_i\theta_1\theta_2 \ldots \theta_{r-1}$ an instance of the head of the clause $B \leftarrow B_1 \wedge \ldots \wedge B_q \in \Theta$ that was used in this step of the derivation. Assume the result holds for any $k < n$. Now, suppose $A_i\theta_1\theta_2 \ldots \theta_{p-1}$ is the selected literal in goal G_{p-1}.[8] Since the derivation is infinite, there is a clause $B \leftarrow B_1 \wedge \ldots \wedge B_q \in \Theta$, and $A_i\theta_1\theta_2 \ldots \theta_{p-1} = B\theta_p$. Let G_p be $\{\leftarrow B_1\theta p \wedge \ldots \wedge B_q\theta p\}$. By the induction hypothesis, there exists a $s \in \omega$ such that $\{[B_1\theta_{p+1}\theta_{p+2} \ldots \theta_{p+s}], \ldots, [B_1\theta_{p+1}\theta_{p+2} \ldots \theta_{p+s}]\} \subseteq \mathcal{T}_{\Theta,\emptyset}\downarrow_{n-1}$. But then, $\{[A_i\theta_1\theta_2 \ldots \theta_{p+s}]\} \subseteq \mathcal{T}_{\Theta,\emptyset}\downarrow_n$. ∎ (This proof follows that in [199, p.67]).

Lemma 3.10 *Let Θ be a theory, let A be a ground atom. If $A \notin \mathcal{T}_{\Theta,\emptyset}\downarrow_\omega$, then the derivation of $\Theta \cup \{\leftarrow A\}$ fails finitely.*

[8] A_i will eventually be selected. Note that this assumes a fair procedure for selecting literals in goals: for every atom B in the derivation, an instance of B must be selected within a finite number of steps. Lassez [190] characterizes the class of fair selection procedures.

Proof: Show the contrapositive: If either $\Theta \cup \{\leftarrow A\}$ has a refutation or the derivation of $\Theta \cup \{\leftarrow A\}$ is infinite, then $A \in \mathcal{T}_{\Theta,\emptyset}\downarrow_\omega$.

(i) Suppose $\Theta \cup \{\leftarrow A\}$ has a refutation, then by Lem.3.8 $A \in \mathcal{T}_{\Theta,\emptyset}\downarrow_\omega$.

(ii) Suppose the derivation of $\Theta \cup \{\leftarrow A\}$ is infinite, then by Lem.3.9 $[A] \subseteq \mathcal{T}_{\Theta,\emptyset}\downarrow_\omega$. Since A is ground, $A \in [A]$, and $A \in \mathcal{T}_{\Theta,\emptyset}\downarrow_\omega$. ■

It is not possible to prove the exact converse of the soundness result (Thm.3.5), because a computed answer substitution will always be most general. However, we can prove that every correct answer substitution is an instance of a computed answer substitution.

Lemma 3.11 *Let Θ be a theory, A an atom, then if $\Theta \models^{nm} \forall(A)$, then there is a refutation of $\Theta \cup \{\leftarrow A\}$, with $\theta = \epsilon$ as the computed answer substitution.*

Proof: Let $x_1, \ldots, x_n$ be the variables in A, $a_1, \ldots, a_n$ are distinct constants not in Θ or A, and $\theta = \{^{x_1}/_{a_1}, \ldots, ^{x_n}/_{a_n}\}$. Since $\Theta \models^{nm} \forall(A)$, also $\Theta \models^{nm} A\theta$, where $A\theta$ is ground. Consider the two cases:

(i) $A\theta = \P C$. So, by Def.3.9 $\P C \in \mathcal{N}m(\Theta)$, and thus,

$$\overline{C} \notin \mathcal{T}_{\Theta,\emptyset}\downarrow_\omega,$$

and thus, by Lem.3.10, $\Theta \cup \{\leftarrow \overline{C}\}$ does not have a refutation. $\P C$ succeeds and we have a refutation of $\Theta \cup \{\leftarrow A\theta\}$.

(ii) $A\theta \neq \P C$. Then by Def.3.8

$$A\theta \in \mathcal{T}_{\Theta,\mathcal{N}m(\Theta)}\uparrow_\omega,$$

and so by Lem.3.7 $\Theta \cup \{\leftarrow A\theta\}$ has a refutation.

Since a_i is neither in Θ nor A, $1 \leq i \leq n$, we can transform this refutation into a refutation of $\Theta \cup \{\leftarrow A\}$, and thus, the computed answer substitution θ is the empty substitution. ■

Theorem 3.12 *If θ is a correct answer substitution for $\Theta \cup G$, then there exist substitutions θ_1 and θ_2, such that θ_1 is the computed answer substitution for $\Theta \cup G$, and $\theta = \theta_1\theta_2$.*

Proof: Let $G = \{\leftarrow A_1 \wedge \ldots \wedge A_n\}$. By hypothesis θ is correct, so

$$\Theta \models^{nm} \forall((A_1 \wedge \ldots \wedge A_n)\theta),$$

and $\Theta \models^{nm} \forall(A_i\theta)$, $1 \leq i \leq n$, and each $A_i\theta$ is ground. By Lem.3.11 $\Theta \cup \{\leftarrow A_i\theta\}$ has a refutation. We can combine these individual refutations into a refutation of

$\Theta \cup G\theta$. By Lem.3.6 we also have a refutation of $\Theta \cup G$, although θ may not be a most general unifier. ∎

Lem.3.11 established that we can combine individual refutations at the ground level. After combining these refutations into a single refutation, we apply the lifting lemma to obtain a refutation for the nonground case. It is important to perform the combination of the refutations at the ground level to ensure the consistency of substitutions across the individual refutations.

3.3 Representing FRORL Constructs

The modeling constructs of FRORL have to be expressed in terms of the logical machinery described above. The FRORL syntax presented in Chapter 2 is only the surface syntax; reasoning about specifications, as well as program transformation, are performed at the level of nonmonotonic Horn-clause logic. Here we show how the constructs of the FRORL surface syntax can be translated into the underlying logic. (This translation is performed automatically. The users of FRORL encounter their specifications only in terms of FRORL's rule and frame notation.) As previously mentioned, FRORL uses *object frames* and *activity frames* to distinguish *objects* and *activities* in the modeled domain. Object frames represent the entities of the domain. Each object has its own attributes or properties. The objects and activities of FRORL, as well as their attributes or properties, are represented in the underlying logic through predicates. For example,

$$\mathsf{phone\_call}(\mathsf{call}_1) \leftarrow \tag{3.1}$$

indicates the membership of the object call_1 in the class phone_call. It could also indicate that object call_1 has the property phone_call, or—although with a bit of linguistic abuse—it could describe an activity phone_call. The point is that various concepts of the FRORL surface syntax are expressed in terms of predicates of nonmonotonic Horn-clause logic. Objects in FRORL usually stand in a hierarchy. That one class is a subclass of another can be stated by conditionally qualifying statement (1):

$$\mathsf{phone\_call}(x) \leftarrow \mathsf{three\_way\_call}(x) \tag{3.2}$$

(2) states that objects which are three_way_call are also phone_call. By virtue of being a member of a given kind, objects will have a set of properties or attributes. For example, statement (3) asserts that any objects of the kind three_way_call will have the property busy_tone.

$$\mathsf{busy\_tone}(x) \leftarrow \mathsf{three\_way\_call}(x) \tag{3.3}$$

Statement (3) asserts the property of busy_tone unconditionally for any object of type three_way_call. Typically, in object hierarchies, we may override certain properties at lower levels of the hierarchy. We use the "¶" operator to permit exceptions to rules.

$$\mathsf{busy\_tone}(x) \leftarrow \mathsf{three\_way\_call}(x) \wedge \P\mathsf{busy\_tone}(x) \tag{3.4}$$

3.3.1 Object Frames

We will now show how the surface syntax of FRORL (which relies on the use of object and activity frames) is mapped onto its underlying logic. Consider the following FRORL object frame.

Object: phone_call
caller_id:
line_type: two_parties

Object: three_way_call
a_kind_of: phone_call
line_type: three_parties

Object frames are implicitly universally quantified sentences, with the attributes relativized to inheritance of the relevant object type. In the underlying logic, three_way_call is represented through several clauses.

$$\mathsf{phone\_call}(x) \leftarrow \mathsf{three\_way\_call}(x) \tag{3.5}$$

$$\mathsf{line\_type}(x, \mathsf{three\_parties}) \leftarrow \mathsf{three\_way\_call}(x) \wedge \P\mathsf{line\_type}(x, \mathsf{three\_parties}) \tag{3.6}$$

$$\overline{\mathsf{line\_type}}(x, y) \leftarrow \mathsf{reverting\_call}(x) \wedge y \neq \mathsf{three\_parties} \tag{3.7}$$

Attribute slots represent particular properties of an object. For example, objects of the type two_party_call are initiated from a line shared by two parties. Attributes are inherited from the parent object. Attributes may also have activities attached which determine the value of that attribute. Note how attributes that may be overridden further down the hierarchy allow for exceptions due to the use of the ¶ operator. Generally, object frames have the form

Object: K
a_kind_of: $\mathsf{K}_1, \mathsf{K}_2, \ldots, \mathsf{K}_n$
A_1
A_2
⋮
A_m

$\mathsf{K}_1, \mathsf{K}_2, \ldots$ are parent classes of an object; $\mathsf{A}_1, \mathsf{A}_2, \ldots$ are attributes. The translation into the base logic is

$$\mathsf{K}_1(x) \leftarrow \mathsf{K}(x)$$

$$\mathsf{K}_2(x) \leftarrow \mathsf{K}(x)$$

$$\vdots$$

$$\mathsf{K}_n(x) \leftarrow \mathsf{K}(x)$$
$$\mathsf{A}_1(x, val_1) \leftarrow \mathsf{K}(x) \wedge \P\mathsf{A}_1(x, val_1)$$
$$\overline{\mathsf{A}_1}(x, y) \leftarrow \mathsf{K}(x) \wedge y \neq val_1$$
$$\mathsf{A}_2(x, val_2) \leftarrow \mathsf{K}(x) \wedge \P\mathsf{A}_2(x, val_2)$$
$$\overline{\mathsf{A}_2}(x, y) \leftarrow \mathsf{K}(x) \wedge y \neq val_2$$
$$\vdots$$
$$\mathsf{A}_m(x, val_m) \leftarrow \mathsf{K}(x) \wedge \P\mathsf{A}_m(x, val_m)$$
$$\overline{\mathsf{A}_m}(x, y) \leftarrow \mathsf{K}(x) \wedge y \neq val_m$$

Class membership and attributes are both expressed through predicates in the base logic. Attributes may be overridden, as indicated by presence of the ¶ operator. On the other hand, class membership is asserted without exceptions. For each attribute of a class, any object not belonging to that class has the complement of that attribute (asserted through predicate negation). This assertion blocks the inference that such an attribute holds in a class (when in fact it is overridden).

3.3.2 Activity Frames

Relations between objects are described by activity frames. That certain propositions hold for objects of a given type, provided that certain conditions are met, is again represented through conditional assertion of predicates.

Activity frames are initiated with values as arguments. Uninstantiated variables, which receive values as the result of performing an activity, may be passed to activity frames. Variables may be also instantiated to lists [65], as discussed earlier. For example,

Activity: initiate_busy_tone(x)
  Parts: x: reverting_call
  Actions: apply_busy_tone(x.caller_id), wait_for_disconnect(x)

When the initiate_busy_tone activity is performed for a reverting_call, two further actions (i.e., apply_busy_tone and wait_for_disconnect) occur. The precise action taken in these activities is determined by the type of the arguments. For example, there may be different wait_for_disconnect activities defined for phone_call and reverting_call.

The representation in the underlying logic is not as straightforward as for object frames. For one, we must provide for separate inheritance of precondition slots, action slots, and alternative action slots. Another complication is introduced by the fact that activities lower down the hierarchy may either augment actions inherited from their superclasses (as indicated by the presence of the keyword **super**) or override them.

To deal with the former, a clause is introduced which mediates the inheritance of the component slots of an activity. For example, the frame above becomes

$$\begin{aligned}&\mathsf{initiate\_busy\_tone}(x) \leftarrow\\&\quad \mathsf{reverting\_call}(x)\\&\quad \wedge\mathsf{precond}(\mathsf{initiate\_busy\_tone}, y_1, x)\\&\quad \wedge\P\mathsf{action}(\mathsf{initiate\_busy\_tone}, \mathsf{reverting\_call}, x)\\&\quad \wedge\mathsf{action}(\mathsf{initiate\_busy\_tone}, \mathsf{reverting\_call}, x)\\&\quad \wedge\mathsf{alt\_action}(\mathsf{initiate\_busy\_tone}, y_2, x)\end{aligned}$$

Then clauses are generated for the individual actions:

$$\begin{aligned}&\mathsf{action}(\mathsf{initiate\_busy\_tone}, \mathsf{reverting\_call}, x) \leftarrow\\&\quad \mathsf{reverting\_call}(x)\\&\quad \wedge\mathsf{apply\_busy\_tone}(x.\mathsf{caller\_id})\\&\quad \wedge\mathsf{wait\_for\_disconnect}(x)\end{aligned}$$

$$\begin{aligned}&\overline{\mathsf{action}}(\mathsf{initiate\_busy\_tone}, y, x) \leftarrow\\&\quad \mathsf{reverting\_call}(x) \wedge y \neq \mathsf{reverting\_call}\end{aligned}$$

In addition, where overriding of an action (instead of augmenting an inherited action) is intended, the complement of that activity is asserted, similar as in the case of attribute inheritance for object frames. The example above also shows the clauses generated when augmentation semantics is intended, as is the case for its precondition slots and alternative action slots. As can be seen, the translation into the base logic differs. We do not check, through the ¶ operator, for the possibility of the slot being overridden and any inherited predicate for that slot is executed unconditionally in addition to the predicates stated for the activity. The same type of translation is performed in the presence of the keyword **super**.

The general schema for an activity is

Activity: $\mathsf{K}(t_1, \ldots, t_n)$
  Parts: $t_1 \colon \mathsf{K}_1, \ldots, t_n \colon \mathsf{K}_n$
  Precond: $\mathsf{A}_1, \ldots, \mathsf{A}_m$
  Actions: $\mathsf{B}_1, \ldots, \mathsf{B}_p$
  Alt_Actions: $\mathsf{C}_1, \ldots, \mathsf{C}_q$

Transformation into the base logic results in the following clauses:

$$\begin{aligned}&\mathsf{K}(t_1, \ldots t_n) \leftarrow\\&\quad \mathsf{K}_1(t_1) \wedge \ldots \wedge \mathsf{K}_n(t_n)\\&\quad \wedge\langle\text{translation of precondition slot}\rangle\\&\quad \wedge\langle\text{translation of action slot}\rangle\end{aligned}$$

$$\begin{aligned}&\mathsf{K}(t_1, \ldots t_n) \leftarrow\\&\quad \mathsf{K}_1(t_1) \wedge \ldots \wedge \mathsf{K}_n(t_n)\\&\quad \wedge\overline{\mathsf{A}_1} \wedge \ldots \wedge \overline{\mathsf{A}_m}\\&\quad \wedge\langle\text{translation of alternative action slot}\rangle\end{aligned}$$

For example, the action slot is translated as

$$\vdots$$
$$\mathsf{action}(\mathsf{K}, var_1, \ldots, var_n, t_1, \ldots, t_n) \wedge$$
$$\vdots$$

(where $var_1, \ldots, var_n$ are new variables) or

$$\vdots$$
$$\P\mathsf{action}(\mathsf{K}, \mathsf{K}_1, \ldots, \mathsf{K}_n, t_1, \ldots, t_n) \wedge$$
$$\mathsf{action}(\mathsf{K}, \mathsf{K}_1, \ldots, \mathsf{K}_n, t_1, \ldots, t_n) \wedge$$
$$\vdots$$

depending on whether the slot is intended to augment inherited slots (if there is no information present for that slot or the keyword **super** is included as one of the conjuncts in that slot) or it is intended to override any inherited slot. Except for the slot name used as predicate, the translations are the same for precondition and alternative action slots. An additional clause is then generated for each defined slot, for example

$$\begin{aligned}&\mathsf{action}(\mathsf{K}, \mathsf{K}_1, \ldots, \mathsf{K}_n, t_1, \ldots, t_n) \leftarrow \\ &\quad \mathsf{K}_1(t_1) \wedge \ldots \wedge \mathsf{K}_n(t_n) \wedge \mathsf{B}_1 \wedge \ldots \wedge \mathsf{B}_p\end{aligned}$$

for the action slot. Where overriding of the inherited information is intended, we also generate the clause

$$\begin{aligned}&\overline{\mathsf{action}}(\mathsf{K}, var_1, \ldots, var_n, t_1, \ldots, t_n) \leftarrow \\ &\quad \mathsf{K}_1(t_1) \wedge \ldots \wedge \mathsf{K}_n(t_n) \wedge var_1 \neq \mathsf{K}_1 \wedge \ldots \wedge var_n \neq \mathsf{K}_n\end{aligned}$$

(in the example of the action slot). In the discussion above, $\mathsf{A}_1 \ldots \mathsf{A}_n$, $\mathsf{B}_1, \ldots, \mathsf{B}_p$, $\mathsf{C}_1, \ldots, \mathsf{C}_q$ are predicates ranging over some of the variables $t_1 \ldots t_n$.

4

A Requirements Specification Language for Real-Time Distributed Software Systems

As it stands, FRORL does not provide sufficient mechanisms to meet the specific demands of real-time distributed software systems development. In this chapter, we augment FRORL with constructs specifically geared to the specification of real-time distributed systems. FRORL, thus enhanced, relies on the surface syntax of frames and production rules plus some additional mechanisms presented here. The semantics of FRORL is defined through nonmonotonic Horn-clause logic. Temporal properties of the specification are described by sentences that are given its meaning through temporal logic. The temporal logic will be presented in more detail in Chapter 5. Using FRORL, timing constraints, temporal properties, and other concurrent distributed features of real-time distributed systems can be specified easily.

4.1 Characteristics of Real-Time Distributed Software Systems

Real-time distributed systems are quite different from conventional computer systems. The following characteristics of real-time distributed systems make specifying such systems more difficult than specifying conventional software systems.

- *Multiple processes and process communication* — A real-time distributed system is made up of a collection of processes which communicate with one another through shared variables and/or by message passing over a communication channel. With each process, a set of state variables and a set of events are associated. An event is modeled by a predicate which describes how the values of the network's state variables changed from false to true or vice versa. The predicate embodies specifications of both the event's enabling conditions and resultant actions.

- *Multiple processors* — The processes that compose the distributed system can be running on different physical processors in parallel. Since processes on different processors can execute in parallel, the state of the whole system is the union of the states of all processors.

- *Inter/intra-process timing constraints* — The correctness of a real-time distributed system depends not only on the logical result of the computation, but also on the time at which the results are produced. Often, the processes composing a real-time distributed system are coupled to processes or events of the environment. The response-time of a real-time distributed system depends on the performance of the underlying processors. Its correctness hinges also on meeting the timing constraints imposed by the environment. A timing constraint defined among several processes is called an inter-process timing constraint; that defined within a single process is called an intra-process timing constraint.

- *Unpredictable communication delays* — The processors on which the distributed system is running can be geographically dispersed. Therefore, the inter-process communication delays become non-negligible. Difficulties in synchronization among the processes on different processors will result from the introduction of unpredictable communication delays.

- *Nondeterministic execution behavior* — For a sequential program, one can usually guarantee reproducible execution by supplying the same input each time the program is executed. A distributed system is often characterized by race conditions between their processes. Because of the concurrent nature of real-time distributed systems, a re-execution of the program does not guarantee the same behavior.

In this chapter, we augment the FRORL specification language by constructs specifically geared to the specification of real-time distributed systems. Again, the representational constructs introduced are merely elements of a surface syntax which is explicated in terms of an underlying logical framework.

4.2 Demands on Requirements Specification Languages for Real-Time Distributed Systems

Most real-time systems, such as process control programs or telephone switching systems, never terminate (or better, are not intended to terminate under ordinary circumstances). They are not executing to obtain a final result, but to maintain interaction with their environment. Hence, a real-time system requires the ability to respond to external stimuli within an allotted time-frame. Real-time systems usually consist of two parts: the controlled system and the controlling system. The controlled system consists of hardware devices which interface with the environment. The controlling system consists of the software elements together with their associated processing hardware. A system is said to operate in "real-time" if its response time is regarded as instantaneous. The response time of a system is the time the system needs to react to a change in or a stimulus from its environment. Beyond the demands on a requirements specification language for conventional systems, as discussed in Section 2.1, the unique aspects of real-time distributed systems impose further considerations.

4.2.1 Real-Time Processes Modeling

A real-time system can be seen as a system that carries out a set of activities. From a software point of view, each activity is modeled as a process and interaction between processes may exist. A process that has associated timing constraints and whose correctness depends on satisfying those constraints is called a *real-time process.* The timing constraints of a process may be defined on the whole process or on parts of the process. Requirements for real-time processing should specify when and for how long a given process has to execute and how quickly it needs to respond to the triggering situation.

The two commonly distinguished types of real-time processes, *periodic processes* and *sporadic processes* [158], require different timing constructs. (Lee [192] also defines a third type of process, a *communicating process*, for synchronization and communication.) A periodic process becomes ready at regular intervals as opposed to a sporadic process which becomes ready at a predefined time. A periodic process requires actions to be taken at fixed intervals; it usually performs a cyclic function, such as collecting data values at predetermined times or performing routine maintenance chores. Sporadic processes typically respond to external stimuli or events. Their behavior is not necessarily periodic or predictable. They occur because the real-time computer system must interact with its environment, such as commands from human operators or changes in a monitored sensor's value. A real-time communication process specifies the timing constraints associated with inter-process communication. It indicates how soon a message should be received and how quickly the receiving process should respond to that message after it is sent. It also determines how long a sending process is willing to wait for a reply after a message has been sent. The length of time a receiving process is willing to wait for a message may need to be specified. The time needed for a receiving process to respond to a message after it has been received may need to be limited.

4.2.2 Timing Constraints Modeling

A timing constraint may derive from the process itself, from a communicating process, or from the external environment. Timing constraints set time limits between events. An event is considered to be either a stimulus to the system from its environment or an externally observable response that the system makes to its environment. *Performance constraints* set time limits on the response time of the system. *Behavioral constraints* set time limits on the rates at which stimuli are applied to the system.

Following Dasarathy [76], we classify timing constraints into maximum timing constraints (no more than a certain length of time may elapse between the occurrence of two events), and minimum timing constraints (no more than a given length of time may elapse between two events). Dasarathy also distinguishes durational timing constraints which set time limits on how long an event should last.[1]

When modeling timing constraints, we describe the system's response should behavioral constraints be violated by the external environment. We must also commit to the system's speed in responding to external stimuli.

4.2.3 Real-Time Concurrent Distributed Features Modeling

In addition to the constructs required for modeling real-time systems, there are several other mechanisms needed specifically for modeling the concurrent distributed features in real-time distributed systems. Among these features are concurrency constructs, nondeterminism, communication mechanisms, synchronization mechanisms, and real-time communication.

4.3 Languages to Formulate Real-Time Requirements Specifications

Real-time programs are programs which must satisfy both functional correctness and strict timing demands. They are required to respond to external stimuli and generate results within a fixed time deadline [339]. In designing a real-time distributed system, there are two fundamental concerns: producing correct results and producing those results within the allotted time. Specification of real-time distributed systems must incorporate the means to represent such concerns.

Many formalisms have been proposed to specify real-time distributed systems. Again, we only present the broad categories of approaches that have been proposed along with some typical examples. We are particularly focusing on those formalisms which, in addition to specifying a real-time distributed system, provide for mechanisms to verify at least some critical aspects of such systems. Note that we, therefore, specifically exclude all those systems that fall under the broad heading "data flow diagram techniques," which have become the basis for the CASE tools currently prevalent in industry. These systems typically lack formal foundations precise enough to allow for verification surpassing pure syntactic checks (a noteworthy exception is state-charts [144], the specification language of the STATEMATE system [145]).

[1]We will, however, consider events to be instantaneous and express durational timing constraints as constraints between a starting event and a stopping event.

4.3.1 Temporal Logic

Temporal logic is an extension of classical logic (either of propositional or of predicate logic) with temporal operators for reasoning about situations that change over time. The semantics of temporal logic distinguishes between the static aspect of a situation (a state) and the dynamic aspect (the relation over time between states). Temporal operators are used to describe the evolution of a system over time.

Temporal logic has been used extensively for the specification and verification of concurrent systems. It was found especially useful in proving properties of concurrent programs [210, 213, 243, 253], describing systems at any level of abstraction, and for compositional reasoning. Different systems of temporal logic use different modalities and notations. However, they generally rely on either linear or branching time logics. In a linear time logic, the temporal modalities are defined with respect to a single path which the program follows. Typical linear time operators include "always," "sometimes," "next," and "until." Properties expressed by branching time logics include "inevitably," (for all futures, sometime) "potentially," (for some future, sometime) and "invariably" (for all futures, always). With temporal logic based frameworks, it is difficult to specify notions of absolute time. Generally, only relative orderings between processes can be stated.

Along with timed transition models, RTTL [242] is a powerful framework using an explicit-clock linear logic. The timed transition model associates a lower and upper time bound with transitions. Firing of an enabled transition (i.e., a transition with true guard) is delayed for the specified amount of time. If the upper bound is reached without the transition having fired, firing is enforced. Timed transition models represent systems. Properties of systems are specified using RTTL sentences. RTTL allows first-order quantification over time variables. In addition, a special clock variable t refers to the current time (of the local clock). Arithmetic operations may be used to specify timing constraints. RTTL is very expressive (even allowing reference to absolute time) but undecidable.

The logic of RTTL may be restricted to yield decidable fragments. [185] describes a logic in which references to time are restricted to bounds on the temporal operators. Since no explicit references to a clock are allowed, this approach is referred to as hidden-clock logic. Hidden-clock logic can relate only adjacent temporal contexts. Henzinger [152] introduced freeze quantification to overcome this limitation. A freeze quantifier binds its associated variable to the time of the current temporal context.

Ostroff has presented verification techniques for timed transition models to determine whether properties stated in RTTL hold of a model [240, 241]. A deductive proof system for RTTL is presented in [239]. Alur and Henzinger [8] compared logics capable of expressing real-time constraints with respect to decidability and complexity of verification algorithms.

RTL (Real-Time Logic) [158], is designed primarily to analyze timing behavior of systems with respect to absolute time. Given the specification of a system and safety assertions to be analyzed either the safety assertion is a theorem derivable from the system's specification or the safety assertion is unsatisfiable under certain conditions. RTL uses an event-action model to model real-time systems. Time is expressed through occurrence functions which assign time values to event occurrences. The specification of a system in the event-action model is mechanically transformed into a set of sentences of RTL. The RTL sentences are then transformed into predicates of Presburger Arithmetic [291]. Uninterpreted integer functions and existing procedures are used to determine whether a given safety assertion is a theorem derivable from the system's specification. RTL is based on a first-order theory and has no modal operators. Time is captured by an occurrence function which assigns time values to event occurrences. A safety property is established if there is no mapping of event occurrences to time values consistent with the negation of the safety property. RTL cannot concisely specify certain concurrency properties, such as fairness, since it does not provide temporal operators. A visual formalism has been developed for the decidable subset of RTL [159] which can be analyzed by testing computation graphs for the presence of cycles. Automated verification of modular RTL specifications has been reported in [209].

4.3.2 Petri Nets

Petri nets model a system by a five-tuple $\langle P, T, I, O, M\rangle$. P is a finite set of places representing conditions. Places may contain tokens; the distribution of tokens over the net is referred to as marking. M is the initial marking of the net. A marking represents the state of the system at a given moment. T is a finite set of transitions representing events. I and O are functions from transitions to (input and output) places. A transition is enabled if for any input arc there is a token at the originating place. An enabled transition may fire, in which case one token is removed for each arc from the corresponding input place, and a token is put in each output place. To model values communicated between places, colored Petri nets assume that tokens may have values.

Ramchandani [261] derived Timed Petri nets from classical Petri nets by associating a finite firing duration with each transition of the net. A transition in a Timed Petri net fires as soon as possible, but firing is delayed for the associated period after a transition becomes enabled. Timed Petri nets are capable of specifying timing requirements for the components of a system, representing a fixed execution time (or time delay) [72, 386], and modeling minimum, maximum, and random firing times associated with transitions [215, 220, 243]. To date, analytical results of Timed Petri nets have been mainly confined to performance evaluation using computer simulation. Timed Petri nets cannot explicitly describe certain basic properties of concurrent systems, such as eventuality and fairness.

Time Petri nets [219, 220] assert both a lower and an upper bound of the firing of each transition. Time Petri nets have proven very convenient in expressing temporal constraints. Berthomieu [29] proposed an enumerative analysis technique for time Petri nets to model their behavior and analyze properties (undecidability and boundedness) of timed systems. His technique is derived from reachability analysis for classical Petri nets [167].

Suzuki [313] introduced temporal Petri nets to incorporate both temporal operators and Petri nets. In temporal Petri nets, certain constraints of a net are represented by sentences containing temporal operators, such as $\Diamond$ (eventually) and $\Box$ (henceforth). Temporal Petri nets can describe clearly and compactly temporal relationships between the events of a system including eventuality and fairness. A shortcoming of temporal Petri nets is that they require both the semantics of Petri nets and of temporal operators. There is no unique boundary between those aspects of a system that must be represented by Petri nets and those that have to be represented by temporal operators.

4.3.3 Process Algebra

Process Algebras, such as CCS [224, 225], CSP [154], or ACP [13], are powerful mechanisms to express concurrent, distributed systems (Milner is generally credited with initiating the axiomatic study of the mathematical objects comprising a theory of concurrency). Programs are specified in algebraic languages providing sequential and parallel composition of processes, nondeterministic choice, hiding, and recursion. Labeled transition systems provide the semantics for process algebra specifications, where the states are process expressions, and the labels are actions or communications between processes. We can view process algebras as descendents of automata theory. However, instead of examining the execution traces of a single automaton, process algebras are interested in the behavior of systems of communicating automata. The most distinguishing feature of process algebras is a calculus for reasoning about processes based on equations. The algebraic laws of these calculi define the actions of operators and allow transformation of one system into another. Lastly, process algebras define various notions (of increasing strength) of equivalence of systems (bisimulation, trace-equivalence, observational equivalence, failure-equivalence, etc.). Properties of process algebra specifications can be verified through reasoning in the corresponding calculus or by analysis of the labeled transition system that is the model of a specification. An implementation can be shown correct relative to a specification by proving that the proper congruence or equivalence holds between them. Properties of a specification may also be stated and proven in terms of a modal logic (such as Hennessy-Milner logic [151]).

Process algebras have been extended to include the notion of time (a survey can be found in [237]) by allowing labels to be taken from the time domain. In a timed system, a process changes state by either executing some atomic action assumed to take no time or by letting time pass. Time passes only if all component processes accept to do so. Several tools have been developed to verify systems specified in terms of temporal process algebras (e.g., CWB [227]). Temporal process algebras provide operators such as time-lock, delay, urgency, time-out, and watchdog timers .

4.3.4 Automata and State Transition Systems

Alpern [7] specifies temporal properties as boolean combinations of deterministic Büchi automata. A Büchi automaton accepts or rejects infinite sequences of input symbols; every nondeterministic Büchi automaton can be expressed as a boolean combination of deterministic Büchi automata. Procedures exist to translate sentences of propositional temporal logic into Büchi automata where state transitions are defined in terms of atomic sentences. [7] shows how proof obligations are extracted from these automata. Proof obligations generalize the invariant used to prove partial correctness and termination and define verification conditions that must hold for any program satisfying the temporal property described by the Büchi automaton. The verification conditions can be formulated as sentences of predicate logic and Hoare logic, so temporal properties can be proved without reasoning in temporal logic.

If a program has a finite-state space it can also be viewed as a Büchi automaton [331, 358]. From this automaton and the one recognizing sequences satisfying the negation of the temporal property one is trying to establish for the program, a combined Büchi automaton can be constructed. The decision procedure for the emptiness of this combined automaton can then be used to determine if the program satisfies the property. If the computation sequence recognized by the combined automaton is empty, the property holds for the program. This procedure is algorithmic, but only applicable to finite-state programs. In contrast, Alpern's [7] method is not limited to finite-state programs, but is undecidable for the general case.

Shyamasundar [292] expands on the compositional semantics of CSP to derive properties of real-time distributed programs. He uses the maximum parallelism model to provide a static characterization of real-time systems and then proceeds to develop two proof systems for establishing correctness. His emphasis is on timing and communication synchronization rather than on performance. His systems are also based on Büchi automata to derive properties such as persistence and recurrence.

PAISLey [379, 381] is designed to enable the development of an executable model accompanied by specification methods, analysis techniques, and software tools. PAISLey combines formal representations of both data manipulation and control. Along with general functional programming features PAISLey uses cyclic processes and exchange functions to specify real-time systems. In PAISLey, processes are specified by the set of all possible states together with a successor function on those states. The successor function defines the successor state for each state. Processes are cyclic (the successor function describes their natural cycle). PAISLey verifies timing properties through two notions: timing assumption and timing assertion. A timing assumption is a property that is directly enforceable through implementation decisions. A timing assertion is a timing requirement that is not directly enforceable. The goal of validation is to establish that the timing assumptions imply the timing assertions. Timing constraints are part of the PAISLey syntax and semantics: Timing assumptions and assertions are specified as upper and lower bounds on function evaluation time. To test a timing assertion is to simulate the performance of the specified system and to check whether the assertion holds. Timing assumptions are inconsistent when the lower bound of a function is greater than the upper bound of the function that calls it.

4.4 Modeling Mechanisms for Concurrent Distributed Systems

FRORL provides various representational mechanisms enabling us to specify concurrently executing processes and inter-process communication. Note however that these constructs are representational tools to construct a specification. The constructs of the requirements specification do not determine how concurrency and communication will be *implemented.*

4.4.1 Concurrency Constructs

Concurrency may be realized in one of two ways: *Or-parallelism* attempts to solve a single goal in several ways concurrently. *And-parallelism* reduces several goals in parallel and hence, solves these goals simultaneously.

FRORL provides for or-parallelism as a parallel search for a matching activity when attempting to evaluate a goal. And-parallelism evaluates preconditions, actions and alternative actions of activities in parallel. Two preconditions, actions, etc., may be evaluated in parallel by conjoining them with the explicit parallelism operator "||."[2]

4.4.2 Don't-care Nondeterminism

We can also distinguish two types of nondeterminism, *don't-care nondeterminism* and *don't know nondeterminism.*[3] In don't-know nondeterminism, all applicable actions are performed by sequential search and backtracking (sequential Prolog adopts this mode of nondeterminism). In don't-care nondeterminism, only actions committed to (that is, choices which do not lead to failure because some preconditions are not fulfilled) are performed. The latter strategy is adopted by, e.g., concurrent Prolog, PARLOG, and the guarded Horn-clause approaches of the Fifth Generation Computer Project.

FRORL also espouses don't-care nondeterminism. Execution of an activity proceeds by finding all activity frames that define the given activity (i.e., all the activity frames matching the given activity and applicable due to their parts description). The precondition slots of the activity frames defining the activity are evaluated and every activity frame with a successfully evaluated precondition becomes a candidate frame. One of

[2]The || operator is only used to indicate the presence of and-parallelism between two actions. It is not a logical construct and will not appear in the translation of the FRORL specification into the base logic. However, it is an important signal for both verification through executing the specification, and for code generation.

[3]Sometimes, don't-care nondeterminism is referred to as *indeterminacy*, and don't-know nondeterminism is called *nondeterminism.*

the candidate frames is then committed to and no backtracking into the preconditions occurs (backtracking may occur, however, within the evaluation of the preconditions or within the evaluation of actions and alternative actions). This behavior is termed don't-care nondeterminism, since one does not care which of the candidate predicates is committed to. Note that variables in the clause head are bound only after commitment to a clause, thus making it unnecessary for variable bindings in the clause head to be withdrawn.

4.4.3 Communication Mechanisms

Processes may need to share information between each other. Two standard abstract models of communication are prevalent: information exchange through shared variables (i.e., shared memory locations) or through the passing of messages between the processes.

At surface syntax level FRORL provides communication through message passing through the following predicates:[4]

- **send**(*channel*, *message*) sends a message on a given channel.
- **receive**(*channel*, *message*) receives data on a channel. The receiving process will suspend until data is available on the channel. Note that if **receive** is called with an instantiated variable *message*, it will only succeed in reading data from the channel, if the data present on the channel can be unified with the contents of the variable *message*. Otherwise **receive** acts as if there were no data on the channel, and continues waiting for incoming data.

The communication between processes is asynchronous. The sending process need not wait for the receiving process to send a message. (FRORL provides two additional message passing predicates which give us synchronous message passing, as shown below.)

4.4.4 Synchronization Mechanisms

Synchronization is a constraint on the execution order in which operations are carried out. A synchronization rule can, for example, specify the precedence, priority, or mutual exclusion in time of a given set of operations. FRORL provides the following built-in predicates which can be used to specify various synchronization constraints:

- **mutex**($event_1$, $event_2$) ensures that $event_1$ and $event_2$ do not occur simultaneously.

---

[4]Again, selection of the message-passing communication model does not prejudice implementation. Implementation of the message passing mechanism may be through shared variables. As far as the users are concerned, however, FRORL provides synchronous and asynchronous communication through messages.

- **synch**($event_1$, $event_2$) ensures that the execution of $event_1$ will not occur before $event_2$ does or vice versa.
- **send_wait_ack**(*channel*, *message*) sends a message then waits for an acknowledgment from the receiver.
- **receive_ack**(*channel*, *message*) sends an acknowledgment to the sender upon receipt of the message. Otherwise it functions just as the asynchronous **receive** statement.

4.4.5 Real-Time Communication

A real-time communication is an inter-process communication with associated timing constraints (these include, e.g., how soon a message is received by a process after being sent). These timing constraints are expressed in the same way as other timing constraints that might be imposed on activities (see Section 4.5.2). Sending and receiving processes need to set deadlines and initiate exception routines if those deadlines are not met.

Example 4.1 A standard producer/consumer process pair is easily described in FRORL. We begin by showing a simple producer process.

> **Activity:** producer()
> **Precond:** create(*the_item*)
> **Actions:** **send_wait_ack**(*control*, [ ]), **send**(*channel*, *the_item*), producer()

An activity constitutes a long-lived process if it is formulated tail-recursive (as the above producer process). The produced variable is sent on the channel. Immediately prior to communicating a newly generated variable, the producer synchronizes to avoid overwriting a communicated variable (should the receiver have had no chance to read the previously communicated value). A simple matching receiver process could be described as follows.

> **Activity:** consumer()
> **Precond:** **receive_ack**(*control*, *ctrl_msg*), **receive**(*the_item*)
> **Actions:** operate_on(*the_item*), consumer()

We create both a producer and a consumer process in parallel:

> **Activity:** producer_consumer()
> **Actions:** producer() || consumer()

Example 4.2 A more asynchronous version of the producer/consumer process pair is specified in FRORL just as easily. We begin by modeling an unbounded buffer over which the two processes may exchange information:

Activity: buffer($state$)
  Precond: $state = [\,]$, **receive**($chnl, x$)
  Actions: buffer($[x]$)

Activity: buffer($state$)
  Precond: $state = [y \mid S]$, **receive**($chnl, x$)
  Actions: buffer($[x, y \mid S]$)

Activity: buffer($state$)
  Precond: $state = [y \mid S]$
  Actions: **send_wait_ack**(out_chnl, y), buffer(S)

An empty buffer can only receive data which comes in over the communication channel *chnl*. The buffer can receive more incoming values, and forward them, one item at a time, on the outgoing channel *out_chnl*. The producer and consumer processes are similar to above.

Activity: producer()
  Precond: create(the_item)
  Actions: **send**($chnl, the\_item$), producer()

Activity: consumer()
  Precond: **receive_ack**(out_chnl, the_item)
  Actions: operate_on(the_item), consumer()

Activity: producer_consumer()
  Actions: producer() || consumer() || buffer([ ])

4.5 Modeling Constructs for Real-Time Processes, Timing Constraints, and Temporal Properties

The modeling primitives of the real-time distributed aspects of FRORL are also based on object frames and activity frames. Each entity of the domain is modeled as an object. Changes occurring in the domain are represented in the requirements model as activities. The frame representation of each object and activity is augmented to state associated properties, assumptions, or constraints. A periodic process becomes ready at regular intervals as opposed to a sporadic process which becomes ready at some predetermined time. A periodic process requires actions to be executed at fixed intervals. A sporadic process is triggered by the occurrence of external stimuli which correspond to events in the environment. The occurrence of events (and therefore, the execution of sporadic processes) is not necessarily periodic or predictable. Timing constraints are classified into maximum, minimum, and durational maximum/minimum timing constraints. To represent timing constraints, we introduce a new type of activity frame called a *time-activity frame* and define several new built-in functions which express the various real-time aspects of processes.

4.5.1 Periodic Processes

To ensure the repetitive nature of a periodic activity, we associate a cyclic value with a time activity to represent its period. A time-activity frame expresses periodic processes in an external manner (rather than expressing the period as internal to the activity) to ensure that the timing constraints of periodic activities are enforced by the system and do not depend on the execution of the processes themselves. Therefore, even if a periodic activity misses its period, it will still be scheduled properly, although the time elapsed or periods missed cannot be determined. A time-activity frame is specified as follows:

TimeActivity: ⟨activity-name⟩(⟨variable⟩, ⟨variable⟩, ...)
Parts: ⟨variable⟩: ⟨object-name⟩, ⟨variable⟩: ⟨object-name⟩, ...
Period: ⟨value⟩
Precond: ⟨activity-desc⟩, ⟨activity-desc⟩, ...
Actions: ⟨activity-desc⟩, ⟨activity-desc⟩, ...
Alt_Actions: ⟨activity-desc⟩, ⟨activity-desc⟩, ...

Note that actions or alternative actions might represent a single process or a set of processes. In this case, the periodic timing constraint will constitute a single deadline for the specified composite task.

4.5.2 Timing Constraints for Sporadic Processes

Sporadic time activities are initiated like nontimed activities and do not contain a period attribute. Because the timing constraints of sporadic processes are more varied and complex than those of periodic processes, built-in operations are required to express such constraints conveniently.

Timing constraints are classified into maximum and minimum timing constraints. These timing constraints can be modeled in FRORL with the help of specialized activity frames which adhere to the following schema:

⟨activity-type⟩**Activity:** ⟨activity-name⟩(⟨variable⟩, ⟨variable⟩, ...)
Parts: ⟨variable⟩: ⟨object-name⟩, ⟨variable⟩: ⟨object-name⟩, ...
Time_constraint: ⟨value⟩
From: ⟨starting-event⟩
To: ⟨stopping-event⟩
Precond: ⟨activity-desc⟩, ⟨activity-desc⟩, ...
Actions: ⟨activity-desc⟩, ⟨activity-desc⟩, ...
Alt_Actions: ⟨activity-desc⟩, ⟨activity-desc⟩, ...

These activity frames describe various timing constraints. We will distinguish here between activities subject to a maximum timing constraint (**MAXActivity**) and activities with a minimum timing constraint (**MINActivity**). These activities are constrained regarding the time lag allowed between the occurrence of the event designated by the **From** slot (⟨starting-event⟩) and the event designated by the **To** slot (⟨stopping-event⟩). For a maximum timing constraint, no more than t length of time may elapse between the occurrences of two events. No less than t length of time may elapse between the occurrence of two events in minimum timing constraints. Note that the starting event or the stopping event (or both) may be left unspecified. If the starting event is missing, then the timing constraint holds from the moment of the initial invocation of this activity. If the stopping event is missing, the time activity functions as a pure time-out operation: After expiration of the associated timer the clause representing this time activity will always generate the alternative actions specified.

Durational timing constraints [76] are modeled by maximum and minimum timing constraints. For durational timing constraints, the time between the starting event of a task and the stopping event of a task is constrained.

4.5.3 Predicates to Express Temporal Properties of the Specification

FRORL provides various built-in operators to allow the assertion of temporal properties of real-time distributed systems. These timing assertions can be used during verification to ensure that certain important timing-related requirements of the specification are met. The constructs themselves do not have computational impact.

- **next**(*assertion*) states that *assertion* holds after the current state.
- **henceforth**(*assertion*) states that *assertion* holds from the current state on.
- **eventually**(*assertion*) states that *assertion* holds eventually.
- **until**($assertion_1$, $assertion_2$) states that $assertion_1$ holds until the state in which $assertion_2$ holds.
- **precede**($assertion_1$, $assertion_2$) states that $assertion_1$ holds before $assertion_2$ holds.

5

Temporal Logic Foundation of the Real-Time Distributed Requirements Specification Language

The semantics of FRORL, as presented in Chapter 3, does not permit us to express the temporal aspects of a FRORL requirements specification. In this chapter, we present a temporal logic to both describe timing-related information and reason about it. We then show how the timing-related constructs of a FRORL specification can be translated into sentences of this temporal logic.

Standard temporal logic cannot specify absolute time, as in maximum or minimum timing constraints, but only the relative orderings between processes [186]. Message passing systems usually impose timing constraints on send/receive commands (e.g., time-out). The temporal logic presented in this chapter is specifically geared to specifying timing constraints.

5.1 The Temporal Fix-Point Calculus

To specify and validate real-time distributed systems, we need to extend our specification language by adding the concept of time. Temporal logic is a language for both describing sequences of situations over time and for reasoning about them. In this context, we consider sequences of situations as representing the successive states a program runs through during its execution. This interpretation allows us to use temporal logic to specify and verify time-dependent programs.[1]

It is difficult to implement real-time distributed systems correctly. However, an incorrectly executing real-time program might have grave consequences. Verification of real-time programs has received much attention and consequently, many different approaches to the verification of such systems have been presented in the literature. For an overview of the use of temporal logic in the specification and verification of

[1]This was first pointed out by Pnueli [254], where he argued that the then *en vogue* notions of predicate transformers could not handle real-time distributed systems which do not have a final state.

real-time distributed systems, see [256, 376], but in particular the excellent survey by Emerson in [89].

Temporal logic allows, along with the standard vocabulary of first-order logic, the use of temporal modalities to form sentences, such as (provided that P and Q are sentences) $\bigcirc P$, $\Diamond P$, $\Box P$, or $P \mathcal{U} Q$. Intuitively, "$\bigcirc P$" means that "P holds at the next time," "$\Diamond P$" means that "P will eventually hold," "$\Box P$" is read as "P will hold from now on" (or "P always holds," but note that this operator looks only into the future and does not extend into the past). Lastly, "$P \mathcal{U} Q$" means that "P will hold until Q holds." Depending on the types of situations we interpret the sentences of temporal logic over, we get different types of temporal logics. Linear-time temporal logic considers modalities to be defined only over a single sequence of situations, or alternatively, over a single computation path [255]. In linear temporal logic, we consider each situation as having only one next situation. If we consider modalities over all computation paths, we are operating in branching-time temporal logic. In branching-time temporal logic, we allow several successor situations for each situation. Typical modal operators for branching-time temporal logic include notions such as "inevitably P" (i.e., P will eventually hold in all futures), "potentially P" (in some future, P will eventually hold), or "invariably P" (in all futures, P will henceforth hold). As one can see from the intuitive readings of these modalities, branching-time temporal logic quantifies over futures, or computation sequences [90, 91]. In dynamic logic, the modalities correspond to computation sequences of *different* programs [188]. The previously mentioned modal operators are relativized to sets of programs. For example, we could assert that "after the execution of either program α or program β, chosen nondeterministically, P will henceforth hold."

Note that all the temporal logics mentioned have been presented from the viewpoint of time being made up of discrete points, looking only into the future. Other ontologies are possible, such as time being made up of intervals [284], or dense points [21], or time also including the past [360]. However, most research focuses on the former models of time.[2] Furthermore, these approaches rely on propositional temporal logic.[3]

The logic presented in this chapter takes a yet different track. It is an extension of the modal μ-calculus first presented by Kozen [187], who took a modal logic with labels and added a least fix-point operator, so that $\mu z \cdot P[z]$ is intended to be the least fix-point of P, considered as a functional on its free propositional variable z. The introduction of fix-point operators enriches the language allowed by the above modal systems in important ways: Standard branching-time temporal logic cannot express certain fairness assumptions crucial for real-time systems [91]. Standard temporal logics cannot express certain modular properties of concurrent programs (e.g., "P holds at all even moments") [374]. Furthermore, the modal approaches deal with temporal

[2]The latter models of the nature of time may have applications, but often allow merely for simpler representation [360] at the cost of more complicated semantics.

[3]Allowing quantification over points of time makes the logic undecidable. Also, it raises grave complications regarding the identity of individuals over time. For a fascinating study of these issues refer to [140].

aspects of a system purely from a qualitative viewpoint. Quantitative aspects, such as the demand that a system respond to an event within a certain fixed time, have only been dealt with in an *ad hoc* manner. Such qualitative claims are crucial for real-time systems. The extension to the modal μ-calculus presented in this chapter allows us to reason about such quantitative aspects as well.

We refer to our extension of the modal μ-calculus as $\text{RT}\mu$. Sentences in $\text{RT}\mu$ are formed in the standard way. We assume an infinite supply of propositional constants P, Q, etc., and propositional variables x, y, and so on. Provided that P and Q are sentences, $\neg P$, $\bigcirc P$, and $P \wedge Q$ are sentences. As explained earlier, the intuitive reading of "$\bigcirc P$" is that "P holds at the next time." Furthermore, if P is a sentence and z a propositional variable, then $\mu z \cdot P[z]$ is a sentence, where by "$P[z]$" we mean that z occurs free in P, and k is a natural number. We pose the additional restriction that $P[z]$ must be syntactically monotonic in the propositional variable z, i.e., all free occurrences of z in $P[z]$ must fall under an even number of negations. Intuitively, "$\mu z \cdot P[z]$" represents the least fix-point of $P[z]$.

Other operators are introduced by definition: $P \vee Q = \neg(\neg P \wedge \neg Q)$, $P \Rightarrow Q = \neg P \vee Q$, and $\nu z \cdot P[z] = \neg \mu z \cdot \neg P[^z/_{\neg z}]$; the latter denotes the greatest fix-point (as usual $P[^x/_{x'}]$ means that all free occurrences of z in $P[z]$ have been replaced by z').

We consider some examples of sentences containing fix-points. Take the following two sentences:

$$\mu z \cdot P \vee \bigcirc z$$
$$\nu z \cdot P \wedge \bigcirc z$$

Intuitively, the first sentence means that either P holds now, or at the next state, P holds, or ..., up to the fix-point. This sentence says that P will eventually hold. The second sentence expresses the meaning of "always": P holds now, and at the next state, P holds, and so on. The above sentences express the meaning of $\Diamond P$ and $\Box P$ of standard temporal logic. One may wonder here why one formulation uses the least fix-point whereas the other formulation uses the greatest fix-point. The former requires P to be true in some finite time whereas the latter is concerned with infinite behavior (P is required to hold along infinite computations). $P \,\mathcal{U}\, Q$ is just as easily expressed:

$$\mu z \cdot Q \vee (P \wedge \bigcirc z).$$

We consider the three sentences presented above as abbreviations of the corresponding sentences of standard temporal logic. A sentence that cannot be expressed in standard temporal logic is

$$\nu z \cdot P \wedge \bigcirc\bigcirc z,$$

which is the formulation of "P holds every other time" of [374]. For a final, more complicated example, consider

$$\nu z \cdot \mu x \cdot (P \vee \bigcirc x) \wedge \bigcirc z$$

Let the above sentence be abbreviated by Φ. If we unfold the fix-point, we obtain

$$(P \vee \bigcirc\mu z \cdot (P \vee \bigcirc z) \wedge \bigcirc\Phi) \wedge \bigcirc\Phi$$

The second conjunct tells us that the next state must again satisfy Φ. Concerning the first conjunct, either P holds, or $\mu z \cdot (P \vee \bigcirc z) \wedge \bigcirc\Phi$ holds at the next time. In the latter case, we can unfold the fix-point. Since we are dealing with a least fix-point, this sentence must be true in a finite length of time. Thus, P must eventually hold. Taken together, Φ expresses that P eventually holds, and that it will do so infinitely often, i.e., that P holds infinitely often.

The temporal operators discussed so far allow qualitative claims regarding the temporal aspects of a theory. For example, $\Diamond P$ says that *eventually* P will hold. None of the modalities presented thus far can state, for example, that P will hold after a certain length of time (after a certain number of computation steps). We add an operator that allows us to express precisely that type of claim: $\mu^{\leq k} z \cdot P[z]$ expresses the claim that $P[z]$ will hold after a length of time k (where k is a natural number). Intuitively, k corresponds to the maximum number of applications of the functional corresponding to $P[z]$. Again, we can define the dual $\nu^{\leq k} z \cdot P[z]$. (We could also relativize the abbreviations $\Diamond$, $\Box$, and $\mathcal{U}$ to k in a similar way.)

Let us again illustrate this modality with a few examples:

$$\Box(\neg P \vee \mu^{\leq k} z \cdot Q \vee \bigcirc z)$$

states that P always results in Q within a bounded length of time k. This sentence could be used to assert that a system must respond to an event P within a certain length of time k with the action Q.[4] Now, consider a group of processes $P_1 \ldots P_n$ required to satisfy the property of k-bounded fairness, i.e., each process must be scheduled for execution at least once every k steps of the overall computation of the system. This property can be expressed as

$$\bigwedge_{i=1}^{n} \mu^{\leq k} z \cdot P_i \vee \bigcirc z \wedge \bigwedge_{i=1}^{n} \Box(P_i \;\Rightarrow\; \bigcirc\mu^{\leq k\text{-}1} z \cdot P_i \vee \bigcirc z).$$

The first group of conjuncts states that each process will be executed at least once within the allotted k time-steps, whereas the second group of conjuncts states that once a process has been executed it will again be scheduled within k time-steps.

We now give the semantics for RTμ. We are provided with a set of propositional constants *Prop*, and a set of propositional variables *Var*. We are also given some finite, nonempty set $\mathcal{S}$. Let $\mathcal{L}$ be a mapping from $Prop \times \mathcal{S}$ into the set $\{\text{true}, \text{false}\}$. $\mathcal{L}$ gives an assignment of truth values to each proposition, for each state of the system's computation. Note that we can also view this mapping as going from $\mathcal{S}$ into *Prop* into the truth values, i.e., as a sequence of choices of truth values for the propositional constants in the theory. We rely on the latter view, and take $\mathcal{L}$ to map $\mathcal{S}$ into 2^{Prop}.

---

[4] This and the following example are taken from [93], where a similar extension is presented for Emerson's CTL branching-time logic.

Furthermore, let a valuation be a mapping from *Var* into $2^{\mathcal{S}}$. A valuation assigns a set of states to each propositional variable. Lastly, we have a transition function $\mathcal{R}$ from $\mathcal{S}$ into $2^{\mathcal{S}}$. $\mathcal{R}$ tells us which states can be reached in a step of the computation from each given state. We call the triple $\langle \mathcal{S}, \mathcal{R}, \mathcal{L} \rangle$ a model.

We define a mapping from $\mathcal{S}$ to $\mathcal{S}$:

Definition 5.1 *Let $\mathcal{M}$ be a model, $\mathcal{V}$ be a valuation, and Φ a sentence of* RTμ, *possibly containing the free propositional variable z, then the* temporal theory operator *$\mathcal{T}_{\mathcal{M},\mathcal{V},\Phi}$ is a mapping from $\mathcal{S}$ to $\mathcal{S}$, defined by*

$$\mathcal{T}_{\mathcal{M},\mathcal{V},\Phi}(s) = \Phi_{\mathcal{M}}^{\mathcal{V}[z:=s]}$$

for $s \in \mathcal{S}$.

(By $\mathcal{V}[z := s]$ we mean the valuation that agrees with $\mathcal{V}$, except that it assigns s to z.)

The power set of states, $2^{\mathcal{S}}$, forms a complete lattice under the partial order of set inclusion.[5] The temporal theory operator is monotonic, due to the restriction on the fix-point operator that it must be syntactically monotonic in its free variable. Therefore, by the Knaster-Tarski fix-point theorem (see Appendix C) we know that a greatest lower bound and a least upper bound exist for this functional.

Next, we define the *approximation from below* to the least fix-point of the temporal theory operator in terms of its ordinal powers.

Definition 5.2 *Let $\mathcal{M}$ be a model, $\mathcal{V}$ be a valuation, and Φ a sentence of* RTμ, *possibly containing the free propositional variable z. Let $\mathcal{T}_{\mathcal{M},\mathcal{V},\Phi}$ be the temporal theory operator. The approximation from below to the least fix-point of the temporal theory operator is defined as*

(i) $\mathcal{T}_{\mathcal{M},\mathcal{V},\Phi}\uparrow_0 = \emptyset$

(ii) $\mathcal{T}_{\mathcal{M},\mathcal{V},\Phi}\uparrow_k = \mathcal{T}_{\Theta,\pi}(\mathcal{T}_{\mathcal{M},\mathcal{V},\Phi}\uparrow_{k-1}) = \Phi_{\mathcal{M}}^{\mathcal{V}[z:=\mathcal{T}_{\mathcal{M},\mathcal{V},\Phi}\uparrow_{k-1}]}$

(iii) $\mathcal{T}_{\mathcal{M},\mathcal{V},\Phi}\uparrow_\omega = \bigcup_{k\geq 0} \mathcal{T}_{\mathcal{M},\mathcal{V},\Phi}\uparrow_k$, if ω is the limit ordinal.

The approximation from below reaches the least fix-point at the limit. We interpret sentences of RTμ relative to a model $\mathcal{M} = \langle \mathcal{S}, \mathcal{R}, \mathcal{L} \rangle$ and a valuation $\mathcal{V}$.

Definition 5.3 *Let Φ be a sentence of* RTμ *possibly containing free propositional variables. Given a model $\mathcal{M} = \langle \mathcal{S}, \mathcal{R}, \mathcal{L} \rangle$ and a valuation $\mathcal{V}$, the semantic value of Φ, $\Phi_{\mathcal{M}}^{\mathcal{V}}$ is defined as*

[5]The top element is the set of states, the bottom element is the empty set; union and intersection form the upper and lower bounds, respectively.

$$\begin{aligned}
\Phi^{\mathcal{V}}_{\mathcal{M}} &= \{s \in \mathcal{S} \mid \Phi \in \mathcal{L}(s)\}, \text{ if } \Phi \in \mathit{Prop} \\
\Phi^{\mathcal{V}}_{\mathcal{M}} &= \mathcal{V}(\Phi), \text{ if } \Phi \in \mathit{Var} \\
\Phi^{\mathcal{V}}_{\mathcal{M}} &= \phi^{\mathcal{V}}_{\mathcal{M}} \cup \psi^{\mathcal{V}}_{\mathcal{M}}, \text{ if } \Phi \text{ is } \phi \wedge \psi \\
\Phi^{\mathcal{V}}_{\mathcal{M}} &= 2^{\mathit{Prop}} - \phi^{\mathcal{V}}_{\mathcal{M}}, \text{ if } \Phi \text{ is } \neg\phi \\
\Phi^{\mathcal{V}}_{\mathcal{M}} &= \{s \in \mathcal{S} \mid \exists t \in \phi^{\mathcal{V}}_{\mathcal{M}} \cdot t \in \mathcal{R}(s)\}, \text{ if } \Phi \text{ is } \bigcirc\phi
\end{aligned}$$

The semantic value for the μ operator is given in terms of the fix-point of $\Phi^{\mathcal{V}[z:=s]}_{\mathcal{M}}$:

$$\Phi^{\mathcal{V}}_{\mathcal{M}} = \mathrm{glb}\{s \in \mathcal{S} \mid \mathcal{T}_{\mathcal{M},\mathcal{V},\phi} s \subseteq s\}, \text{ if } \Phi \text{ is } \mu z \cdot \phi$$

We define the semantic value for $\mu^{\leq k} z \cdot P[z]$ in terms of the ordinal powers of the earlier mentioned functional.

$$\Phi^{\mathcal{V}}_{\mathcal{M}} = \mathcal{T}_{\mathcal{M},\mathcal{V},\phi}\uparrow_k, \text{ if } \Phi \text{ is } \mu^{\leq k} z \cdot \phi, 1 \leq k < \omega$$

Definition 5.4 *A (closed) sentence P of* RTμ *is true in model $\mathcal{M} = \langle \mathcal{S}, \mathcal{R}, \mathcal{L} \rangle$ in state s*

$$\mathcal{M}, s \models P \textit{ if and only if } s \in P^{\mathcal{V}}_{\mathcal{M}},$$

for some valuation $\mathcal{V}$. We call a model $\mathcal{M}$ that meets this condition a model of P.

5.2 Model Checking

Given a sentence P of RTμ, we want to be able to determine whether this sentence holds. There are two possible questions one may ask here. One question is: Given a particular model $\mathcal{M}$, is $\mathcal{M}$ a model of P, i.e., is there a state $s \in \mathcal{S}$ such that $\mathcal{M}, s \models P$? Alternatively, one may ask whether there exists a model for P. In line with standard terminology, we refer to the former as *model checking* and to the latter as determining the *satisfiability* of a sentence.[6]

Algorithm 5.1 below determines whether a given model $\mathcal{M}$ is a model for a sentence P.

Our algorithm proceeds in stages. For each subsentence of P, we determine whether it holds in a state of the model. We begin by examining the propositional constants in P. These are true at all states in the model in which they are contained. We then straightforwardly apply the rules given in Def.5.3. After considering the finitely many subsentences of P, we have obtained the set of states at which P holds in the model. If this set is empty, the model is not a model for P.

The treatment of sentences of the form $\mu z \cdot P[z]$ and $\mu^{\leq k} z \cdot P[z]$ relies again on the Knaster-Tarski fix-point theorem and Kleene's proof that ordinal approximations to the greatest lower bound and least upper bound, respectively, do in fact, reach the fix-points (Thm.C.3), i.e.,

$$\mu z \cdot P[z]^{\mathcal{V}}_{\mathcal{M}} = \mathrm{lub}\{\mu^{\leq n} z \cdot \Phi^{\mathcal{V}}_{\mathcal{M}} \mid n < \omega\}$$

[6]In this book, we are not concerned with satisfiability checking.

Algorithm 5.1 (Model checking)

input model $M = \langle \mathcal{S}, \mathcal{R}, \mathcal{L} \rangle$, sentence Φ
output set of states in which Φ holds
types S', S'', S_z: set of states
case syntactic form of Φ **in**
  P (constant): $S' \leftarrow \{s \in S \mid P \in L(s)\}$
  z (variable): $S' \leftarrow S_z$
  $\neg P$: $S' \leftarrow S -$ Model checking(P)
  $P \wedge Q$: $S' \leftarrow$ Model checking$(P) \cap$ Model checking(Q)
  $\bigcirc P$: $S'' \leftarrow$ Model checking(P)
    $S' \leftarrow \{s \in S \mid \exists t \in S'' \cdot t = R(s)\}$
  $\mu z \cdot P[z]$: $S_z \leftarrow \{\}$
    repeat
      $S' \leftarrow S_z$
      $S_z \leftarrow$ Model checking$(P[z])$
    until $S' = S_z$
  $\mu^{\leq k} z \cdot P[z]$: $count \leftarrow k;\ S_z \leftarrow \{\}$
    repeat
      $S' \leftarrow S_z$
      $S_z \leftarrow$ Model checking$(P[z])$
      $count \leftarrow count - 1$
    until $S' = S_z \vee count = 0$

The algorithm above is similar to one presented by Emerson and Lei [92]. They have shown, for a slightly different version of the μ-calculus, that the complexity of this algorithm is a polynomial of a degree related to the alternated nesting of μ and ν operators.[7] It is important to note that most (or all) modalities that have proven useful for discussing real-time computer programs can be expressed by nesting depths of degree 1 or 2. Therefore, the above model checking algorithm has a small polynomial time complexity.[8]

[7] For details and the precise definition of the notion of alternate nesting refer to [92].

[8] Emerson [92, 93] has pointed out that the performance of model checking can be improved further by relying on memoization when constructing the set of states in which a property holds (obviously, identical subsentences need to be checked only once). Furthermore, the propositional variables bound by fix-point operators induce simultaneous monotonicity. They also show that the number of iterations necessary to evaluate the fix-point operator is bounded by the number of states in the model.

5.3 Expressing the Temporal Aspects of a FRORL Specification

In Section 3.3, we presented object and activity frames, and their translations into the underlying logic. In this section, we show how the temporal constructs of FRORL are converted into constructs of the RTμ calculus presented above. In Chapter 6, we show how one uses the model checking algorithm to determine important properties regarding the time-dependent behavior of a specification.

We distinguish between two aspects of a FRORL specification: Parts of a specification are concerned with producing the functionality of the specified system. Other parts of a specification are concerned with stating constraints imposed on the system, due to its being embedded into a real-time environment and its need to exchange information with other processes. We refer to the former as the functional aspects of a specification, and to the latter as the time-related aspects of the specification.

Translation of the time-dependent constructs yields, on one hand, sentences of the base logic of FRORL representing the functional behavior of the time-dependent constructs. These are used along with the rest of the specification both for execution as a prototype and for validation. On the other hand, we obtain assertions in temporal logic used in verification of the time-dependent behavior of the specification. Where translation of the functional aspects into constructs of the base logic is obvious it is omitted from the examples below.

The functional aspects of the specification are given their semantics through the nonmonotonic logic presented in Chapter 3. The translation of the functional aspect of the specification into the base logic is performed as described above. However, we distinguish (to ease later analysis) between literals in the base logic derived from preconditions of an object or activity frame, and those literals deriving from either actions or alternative actions. This distinction is made purely for convenience and has no logical meaning. We indicate the distinction by using the special conjunction symbol "|" between the literals derived from preconditions and the literals derived from actions. The conjunction symbol "|" has the same logical meaning as the standard conjunction symbol.[9]

The theory obtained from the functional aspects of the specification is used to validate the requirements through executing the specification. For execution purposes we allow special operators indicating parallel execution of literals, mutual exclusion between events, etc. Again, none of these is given any logical meaning.

The time-related aspects of the specification receive their meanings from the temporal logic presented in Section 5.1. Time-dependent information is extracted from the specification and expressed in a form amenable to formal verification techniques, such as the model checking approach described above.

In addition to the constructs presented in the formal presentation of RTμ above,

[9] If no conjunction symbol of the form "|" occurs in a sentence of the base logic, then there were no preconditions in the corresponding activity from which this sentence has been derived.

we make free use of defined modalities relativized to bounds on their defining fix-point. For example, "$P\ \mathcal{U}^{\leq k}\ Q$" means that P will hold until Q holds, which will happen within k time steps. Other defined operators are extended in analogous ways. In addition, we rely on the complementary notions $\mu^{=k}z \cdot P[z]$ and $\mu^{\geq k}z \cdot P[z]$ to the bounded fix-point operator introduced above. Intuitively, the former states that P will be true after precisely k time steps, whereas the latter states that P will be true no earlier than k time steps.[10]

We assume, in a real-time distributed system, each processor has a physical local clock which produces "tick" interrupts. Every process has a software timer which has access to the time of the local clock associated with the underlying processor. In FRORL, we use three built-in operations – **start**(), **alarm**(), and **delay**() to interface with these local timers and to specify timing constraints. These built-in operations can be used in any time-activity frame where time is a critical component.

Note again that the following constructs and the notion of a local software timer are only constructs concerned with executing the specification.

- **alarm**(*timer_name*) is used to access the timer *timer_name* to determine whether the timing constraint, specified by either **start**(*timer_name*, *time_length*) or **delay**(*timer_name*, *time_length*), is violated. An exception is raised if a timing violation is revealed.

- **start**(*timer_name*, *time_length*) initiates a timer *timer_name* with a specified length *time_length* of time. The operation **alarm**(*timer_name*) becomes true if the timer so initiated has expired.

- **delay**(*timer_name*, *time_length*) initiates a timer *timer_name* with a specified length *time_length* of time. The operation **alarm**(*timer_name*) becomes true when the timer is accessed within the allotted length of time.

5.3.1 Time-Activity Frames

A time activity expresses a timing constraint for periodic processes. The general schema for a time-activity frame is shown on p.82 as

TimeActivity: $\mathsf{K}(t_1, \ldots, t_n)$
  Parts: t_1: $\mathsf{K}_1, \ldots, t_n$: K_n
  Precond: $\mathsf{A}_1, \ldots, \mathsf{A}_m$
  Period: p
  Actions: $\mathsf{B}_1, \ldots, \mathsf{B}_p$
  Alt_Actions: $\mathsf{C}_1, \ldots, \mathsf{C}_q$

[10]The extensions used here are introduced merely for representational convenience and do not alter the semantics of RTμ.

Let p be the time period associated with the time activity K, and $t_1 \ldots t_n$ be arguments to time activity K. The time activity is converted into the following sentence of the RTμ calculus.

$$(\mu^{=p} z \cdot \mathsf{K}(t_1 \ldots t_n) \vee \bigcirc z) \wedge \Box(\mathsf{K}(t_1 \ldots t_n) \Rightarrow \bigcirc \mu^{=p-1} z \cdot \mathsf{K}(t_1 \ldots t_n) \vee \bigcirc z)$$

The first conjunct states that time activity K is executed in exactly p time-steps. The second conjunct states that each time K has been executed, it will again be scheduled to execute in exactly p time-steps.

As far as the functional aspect is concerned, the time activity represents a periodically scheduled process. Preconditions, actions, and alternative actions are translated as usual. An additional conjunct is added to both actions and alternative actions representing the spawning of the next occurrence of the time activity:

$$\vdots$$
$$\langle\text{translation of (alternative) action slot}\rangle \parallel \textbf{start}(\mathit{new\_timer}, p) \wedge \mathsf{K}(t_1 \ldots t_n)$$
$$\vdots$$

This expression simply states that after the timer with period p expires, a copy of the time activity K is executed.

5.3.2 Sporadic Processes

The schema for sporadic processes is

$\langle$activity-type$\rangle$**Activity:** $\mathsf{K}(t_1, \ldots, t_n)$
  Parts: $t_1 : \mathsf{K}_1, \ldots, t_n : \mathsf{K}_n$
  Precond: $\mathsf{A}_1, \ldots, \mathsf{A}_m$
  Time_constraint: p
  From: E_1
  To: E_2
  Actions: $\mathsf{B}_1, \ldots, \mathsf{B}_p$
  Alt_Actions: $\mathsf{C}_1, \ldots, \mathsf{C}_q$

Maximum timing constraints are expressed by a **MAXActivity** frame. The translation of the functional aspects remains as shown in Chapter 3. We add the spawning of a timer process, corresponding to the stated timing constraint, to the preconditions of the frame. An additional process is created which watches for a violation of the timing constraint by the timer.

$\mathsf{K}(t_1, \ldots t_n) \leftarrow$
  $\mathsf{K}_1(t_1) \wedge \ldots \wedge \mathsf{K}_n(t_n)$
  $\wedge\langle$translation of precondition slot$\rangle \mid \mathsf{E}_1 \parallel \textbf{start}(\mathit{new_timer}, \mathsf{p})$
  $\wedge\langle$translation of action slot$\rangle \wedge \mathsf{E}_2$

$$\mathsf{K}(t_1, \ldots t_n) \leftarrow$$
$$\overline{\mathbf{alarm}(new\_timer, \mathsf{p})} \mid \langle\text{translation of alternative action slot}\rangle$$

A third clause is created should the evaluation of the precondition fail as described in Chapter 3. Successful evaluation of the preconditions causes execution of the starting event E_1 and simultaneous spawning of a timer with duration p. An additional clause detects the timeout generated by the timer and leads to execution of the alternative actions (as it would if the preconditions of the activity had failed). If the timing constraint is not violated, the actions are executed as usual.

A maximum timing constraint also generates a timing assertion which is expressed in RTμ as

$$\mathsf{E}_1\, \mathcal{U}^{\leq \mathsf{p}}\, \mathsf{E}_2$$

(where E_1 and E_2 are the events between which the maximum timing constraint is asserted). This sentence of RTμ states that E_1 holds now but E_2 will become true within p length of time.

The situation is analogous for minimum timing constraints. Instead of creating a timer that raises an alarm upon timeout, we create a timer which raises an alarm if accessed before the timeout period.

$$\begin{aligned}
&\mathsf{K}(t_1, \ldots t_n) \leftarrow \\
&\quad \mathsf{K}_1(t_1) \wedge \ldots \wedge \mathsf{K}_n(t_n) \\
&\quad \wedge\langle\text{translation of precondition slot}\rangle \mid \mathsf{E}_1 \parallel \mathbf{delay}(new_timer, \mathsf{p}) \\
&\quad \wedge\langle\text{translation of action slot}\rangle \wedge \mathsf{E}_2
\end{aligned}$$

The accompanying timing assertion generated by a minimum timing constraint is

$$\mathsf{E}_1\, \mathcal{U}^{\geq \mathsf{p}}\, \mathsf{E}_2.$$

5.3.3 Built-In Temporal Operators

The various temporal operators **next**, **henceforth**, **eventually**, **until** and **precede** have a straightforward conversion into RTμ, as shown below.

next(*assertion*)	$\bigcirc$*assertion*
henceforth(*assertion*)	$\Box$*assertion*
eventually(*assertion*)	$\Diamond$*assertion*
until(*assertion*$_1$, *assertion*$_2$)	$assertion_1\, \mathcal{U}\, assertion_2$
precede(*assertion*$_1$, *assertion*$_2$)	$\neg(\neg assertion_1\, \mathcal{U}\, assertion_2)$

6

Verification of Requirements Specifications

Various properties of a specification, like reachability, reversibility, liveness, and consistency, etc., are of interest to the specification designer. Once a specification has been constructed using the FRORL requirements specification language, it may be subject to analysis tools which attempt to determine whether such properties hold for a given specification. In this checking process, the users, with the aid of the system, go through a sequence of iterations of specification modification and verification until the specification is assumed to be correct.

FRORL employs various strategies when analyzing requirements specifications, namely (i) resolution refutation (for reachability, reversibility, liveness, consistency, synchronic distance, and bounded fairness), (ii) model checking in temporal logic, and (iii) graph-theoretical algorithms for the determination of the consistency of timing constraints. Note that analysis is performed at the level of the underlying logic, rather than at the level of the FRORL surface syntax of frames and rules. Throughout this chapter, we assume (unless otherwise noted) we are dealing with the requirements specification as translated into a theory of the underlying logic. We speak, for example, of clauses of a specification, by which we mean "clauses of the theory obtained by translating the requirements specification into the base logic." Also, when considering requirements specifications translated into the language of the underlying logic, we are concerned with the nonmonotonically extended theory.

6.1 Analysis through Resolution Refutation

As far as logic-based reasoning is concerned, to analyze a specification for dynamic properties [352] (i.e., functional properties that arise from the execution of the specification) one can rely on either a state-space strategy or a problem-reduction strategy. The state-space strategy is based on data-driven/bottom-up reasoning. This reasoning employs two sets of entities. The first set is a collection of *states*, where each state reflects the condition/status of the problem at each stage on the way to its solution. The other is a collection of *operators* which help to transform the problem from one state to another. The problem-reduction strategy is based on goal-directed/top-down reasoning, which again involves two sets of entities: A collection of *goals/subgoals* which describe the problem, and a collection of *operators* which convert a goal/subgoal into more refined, or detailed, conjunctive subgoals. It can be shown [231] that the problem-reduction strategy of a problem is logically equivalent to a state-space strategy of the same problem.

The development of a FRORL specification is based on an object-oriented top-down design methodology, and hence, FRORL essentially relies on a problem-reduction strategy. In modeling a system composed of a set of processes, FRORL creates a conjunctive goal (a top level activity), with each goal modelling a specific process in the system. The state of a system process is assumed to be the sum of the values of its goal arguments. Each process is decomposed into several subprocesses, and likewise, each goal is refined into many subgoals (lower-level activities). The state of a system is thought to be the union of the states of its component processes, which corresponds to conjunction of its goal arguments. The sole operator employed is the resolution rule.

In the following, we discuss several dynamic properties of software specifications which have been presented elsewhere from a state-space point of view. For example, Murata [230] introduced reachability, reversibility, liveness, synchronic distance, bounded fairness, etc., of Petri nets. In Petri nets, reachability and reversibility are defined upon markings; liveness and consistency are properties of the whole net; synchronic distance and bounded fairness are properties of transitions. We describe analogous properties of a FRORL specification. In FRORL, reachability and reversibility are properties of goals; liveness and consistency are properties of a complete specification; synchronic distance and bounded fairness are properties of individual activities of the specification.

Definition 6.1 *A goal G is said to be* reachable *from a theory Θ if there is a sequence of clause selections $\sigma = c_1 c_2 \ldots c_n$ that transforms G to an empty clause by the resolution rule, i.e., $c_1 = G$, and $c_n = \Box$, and each c_j was obtained from earlier clauses in the sequence by the application of the resolution rule.*

The set of all possible goals reachable from a theory Θ is denoted by $\mathcal{R}^*(\Theta)$. Thus, a goal G is reachable if $G \in \mathcal{R}^*(\Theta)$. We extend this concept to reachability between two goals.

Definition 6.2 *In a theory Θ, if G is a reachable goal from Θ, a subgoal G' is said to be* reachable *from G if there is a sequence of clause selection $\sigma = c_1 c_2 \ldots c_k$ that transforms G' into G ($c_1 = G'$, $c_k = G$).*

All the dynamic properties of the specification discussed in this section are verified through the construction of resolution refutations from the theory derived from the specification and a chosen goal clause.

- *Reversibility* — Determines whether an *initial goal* of a specification can always be resumed. Again, we extend this concept to arbitrary goals, to confirm whether a *specific goal* can be resumed.

  A goal G is said to be *reversible* if, for each reachable goal G' in $\mathcal{R}^*(\Theta)$, G is reachable from G'.

- *Liveness* — Ensures that every goal in a specification is resumable from any other reachable goal.

  A theory is said to be *live* if, independent of the goal reached, it is possible to reach any other goal of the theory by progressing through some clause selection sequence. That is, each goal $G \in \mathcal{R}^*(\Theta)$ can be reached from any other reachable goal $G' \in \mathcal{R}^*(\Theta)$. Note that if a specification is live, then all reachable goals in the specification are also reversible.

- *Consistency* — Consistency analysis determines whether contradictions occur between the clauses of a FRORL specification.

  In practice, we prefer a slightly stronger notion of inconsistency: Let G and G' be two literal goals, where $G = A(t_1, \ldots, t_n)$, $G' = \overline{A}(t'_1, \ldots, t'_n)$, for some predicate A, such that for all i, there is a substitution θ and either $t_i = t'_i\theta$ or $t_i\theta = t'_i$. A theory Θ of the underlying logic is said to be *inconsistent* if for G and G', either (i) there exist resolution refutations for both G and G'; (ii) there exists a resolution refutation of G, but there exists a sequence of clause selections $\sigma = c'_1 c'_2 \ldots c'_k \ldots$ that results in an infinite recursion; (iii) vice versa; or (iv) there exist sequences of clause selections from both G and G' that enter infinite recursion. A theory Θ is then said to be consistent if it is not inconsistent.

- *Synchronic Distance* — In testing and debugging a requirements specification, it is helpful to know the mutual dependence among clauses of the specification. *Synchronic distance* measures the correlation between two clauses, i.e., their relevancy to one another.

  Synchronic distance is a metric closely related to the degree of mutual dependence between two selected clauses C_i and C_j in a theory, and is defined by

  $$d_{i,j} = max_\delta \mid \delta(C_i) - \delta(C_j) \mid$$

  where δ is a clause-selection sequence starting at any goal G in $\mathcal{R}^*(\Theta)$ and $\delta(C_i)$ is the number of times the clause C_i, $i = 1, 2$ is selected in δ.

- *Bounded Fairness* — Two clauses R_i and R_j of a FRORL specification are in a *bounded-fair* relation, if there is a bound on the number of times one is invoked while the other is not.

6.2 Model Checking

In Chapter 5, we presented a temporal logic framework to model the time-dependent aspects of a specification. We also gave a method for determining whether a model is a model *for* a given sentence of the temporal calculus (Section 5.2), i.e., whether a given sentence is true in a model. To verify a program through model checking treat the specification as a transition system as described below. Then determine whether this transition system is a model for sentences of RTμ that express a desired property of the specification. As illustrated in Section 5.2, the procedure for determining whether a transition system is a model of RTμ has acceptable time-complexity. Model checking gives us a powerful mechanism to determine the correctness of our specification with respect to a wide variety of temporal properties.

In this section, we first show how a specification can be interpreted as a transition system that could be a model for a sentence of RTμ. We then give examples of interesting specification properties and of how they can be formulated in the temporal calculus.

6.2.1 *Specifications as Models*

We can view a specification as a transition system: Given a set of states of the computation, the specification tells us for each state, which other states we can reach by a single step of the computation. If we assign labels to the computation steps and interpret each step as a transition, we obtain a transition system from our specification. In the following, we show in more detail how a specification is converted into a transition system. We then give a procedure to convert a transition system into a model.

A transition system is a triple $A = \langle \Sigma_A, \mathcal{S}_A, \mathcal{R}_A \rangle$, where Σ_A is the alphabet of the transition system, $\mathcal{S}_A$ is a set of states, and $\mathcal{R}_A$ is a function from $\mathcal{S}_A \times \Sigma_A$ to $2^{\mathcal{S}_A}$. Each transition has an associated label (a member of the alphabet Σ_A). $\mathcal{R}_A$ tells us which states one can reach from a given state, by a transition with a given label. To convert a specification into the corresponding transition system, create a new state for each unique action (or alternative action) and precondition in the specification. Let the alphabet Σ_A of the transition system be the set of actions, preconditions, etc., of the specification. Then, for every two states that correspond to two actions or preconditions in the specification connected by a conjunction, create a transition between these two states labelled by the first action/precondition.

Note that we are here only concerned with time-related aspects of the specification. We can, therefore, collapse any sequence of states, which do not contribute to the time-dependent behavior of the specified system, into a single state (and remove the corresponding transitions). This procedure is best illustrated by an example.

Example 6.1 We represent a simple system of two processes implementing Peterson's protocol [249] ensuring mutual exclusion between two processes. Consider one such process P. The FRORL specification for P is

Activity: P()
 $\mathsf{NCS_P}(), \textbf{send}(in_p, \mathsf{t}), \textbf{send}(turn, \mathsf{q}), \mathsf{doCS_P}$

Activity: $\mathsf{doCS_P}()$
 Precond: $\textbf{receive}(in_q, x), x \neq \mathsf{t})$
 Actions: $\mathsf{CS_P}(), \textbf{send}(in_p, \mathsf{f}), \mathsf{P}()$
 Alt_Actions: $\mathsf{doCS_P}()$

Activity: $\mathsf{doCS_P}()$
 Precond: $\textbf{receive}(turn, \mathsf{p})$
 Actions: $\mathsf{CS_P}(), \textbf{send}(in_p, \mathsf{f}), \mathsf{P}()$
 Alt_Actions: $\mathsf{doCS_P}()$

We have already collapsed those aspects of the specification that are not time-dependent into the actions $\mathsf{NCS_P}()$, the actions performed by process P outside the critical section, and $\mathsf{CS_P}()$, which represents those activities of this process that must be performed under mutual exclusion.[1] Process P is described as a long-lived process through the use of tail-recursion. Peterson's protocol requires that a process first announces its request to enter the critical region, and leave a "key" (expressed by the variable *turn*) behind for the other process to enter the region. It can, however, only enter the critical region if no other process is in the critical region, or if the other process has handed over the "key."

When constructing the transition system corresponding to the above specification, it is easiest if we unfold the definitions of $\mathsf{doCS_P}$ within the body of P. The alphabet of the transition system is (we abbreviate $\textbf{send}(var, val)$ by $var \leftarrow val$, and $\textbf{receive}(var, val)$ by $var = val$)

$$\Sigma_{\mathsf{P}} = \left\{ \begin{array}{l} \mathsf{NCS_P}(), in_p \leftarrow \mathsf{t}, turn \leftarrow \mathsf{q}, \neg in_q = \mathsf{t}, \\ \mathsf{CS_P}(), in_p \leftarrow \mathsf{f}, turn = \mathsf{p}, \end{array} \right\}$$

Fig.6.1(a) shows the transition system resulting from the translation of process P. The unfolding of the recursion is possible since the calculus of RTμ makes use of fix-point operations. The specification also includes a process Q symmetric to P, with the variable in_p being replaced by in_q, and the statement $\textbf{send}(turn, \mathsf{q})$ in place of the corresponding statement of P. Fig.6.1(b) shows the transition system resulting from process Q.

In this example, the two processes P and Q are assumed to exchange information through the variables in_p, in_q, and *turn* which represent communication channels. A key idea in the construction of a transition system from the specification is that channels, as well as shared variables essential to the concurrent behavior of a system,

---

[1]Note that FRORL provides a higher level construct to express the mutual exclusion of processes, **mutex()**. So, typically, when using FRORL to specify a system one would not write above specification. However, it is possible to describe and verify algorithms at this level, if so desired.

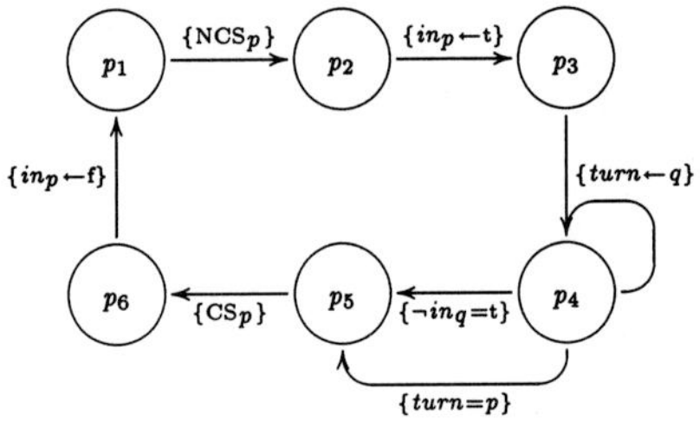

(a) process P

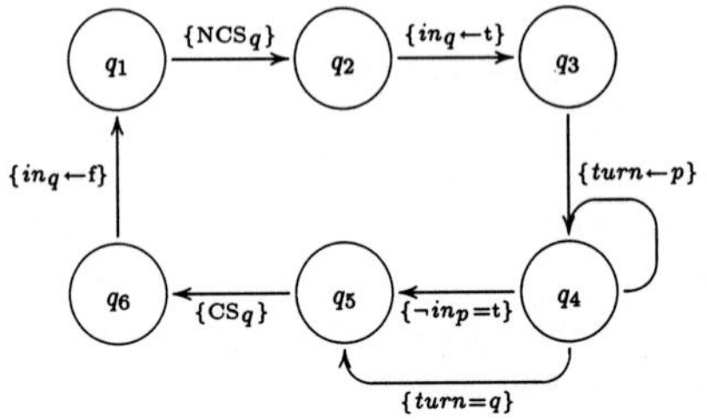

(b) process Q

Figure 6.1. The transition systems for processes P and Q

are also modelled as processes. The states of these processes are the possible values of the variable. Assignments to the variable result in state changes. In cases where the value of variables is not affected, there are looping transitions for all states. Fig.6.2 shows the resulting transition systems. The alphabets for these systems are formed in the obvious way. For example, the alphabet for the transition system corresponding to the variable in_p is

$$\Sigma_{in_p} = \left\{ \; in_p \leftarrow \mathsf{t}, in_p = \mathsf{t}, \neg \; in_p = \mathsf{t}, in_p \leftarrow \mathsf{f} \; \right\}$$

So far, we only considered these processes in isolation. However, the timing- and concurrency-related aspects of the system, as well as problems resulting from them, arise only if the processes are concurrently executed. For example, our specification above might include the following activity which executes both P and Q in parallel,

Activity: Peterson()
  Precond: **send**(in_p, f), **send**(in_q, f), **send**($turn$, p)
  Actions: P() || Q()

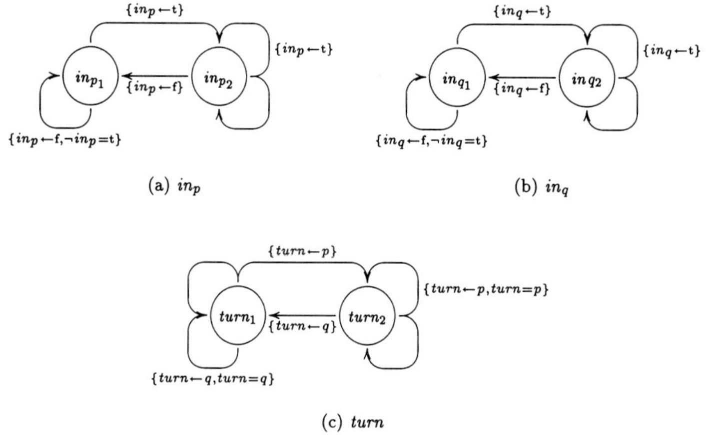

Figure 6.2. The transition systems for variables in_p, in_q, and *turn*

as explained in Chapter 4. We give an arbitrary initial assignment to the "key" variable *turn*.

When several processes execute concurrently, each state of the execution is a combination of the states of the individual processes. To form a transition system representing the concurrent execution of the component transition systems, we form the product of the component transition system. A transition in the combined system is then due to a transition in one of the component transition systems. We add, however, a constraint on transitions in the combined system. There are situations requiring two actions of component systems to be executed simultaneously. For example, when process P assigns a value to the variable in_p (i.e., executes the transition labelled $in_p \leftarrow \mathbf{t}$, say), the transition system representing the variable in_p must perform the matching transition. If this constraint is met by the product of two transition systems, we call the resulting system synchronized. (The notion of a synchronized transition system is derived from a similar notion for automata stated in [331].)

Definition 6.3 *Given transition systems* $A_1 = \langle \Sigma_1, \mathcal{S}_1, \mathcal{R}_1 \rangle, \ldots, A_n = \langle \Sigma_n, \mathcal{S}_n, \mathcal{R}_n \rangle$, *the* synchronized product *of* $A_1, \ldots, A_n$ *is the transition system* $A = \langle \Sigma, \mathcal{S}, \mathcal{R} \rangle$, *where*

(i) $\Sigma = \bigcup_{i=1}^{n} \Sigma_i$

(ii) $\mathcal{S} = \mathcal{S}_1 \times \ldots \times \mathcal{S}_n$

(iii) $\prod_{k=1}^{n} v_k \in \mathcal{R}(\prod_{k=1}^{n} u_k, \alpha)$, for any $1 \leq i, j \leq n$, and $i \neq j$, either

- $\alpha \in \Sigma_i \cap \Sigma_j$ and $v_i \in \mathcal{R}_i(u_i, \alpha) \wedge v_j \in \mathcal{R}_j(u_j, \alpha)$
- $\alpha \in \Sigma_i - \Sigma_j$ and $v_i \in \mathcal{R}_i(u_i, \alpha) \wedge v_j = u_j$.

(let $\prod_{k=1}^{n}$ denote the formation of an n-tuple).

Note that the synchronized product of transition systems is both associative and commutative [331]. We could also express it as an operation over two transition systems and obtain the product of several transition systems through repeated product formation.

From the synchronized product of the processes under consideration, we construct the model for the sentences of the temporal calculus to be tested.

Definition 6.4 *Let A be the transition system $\langle \Sigma_A, \mathcal{S}_A, \mathcal{R}_A \rangle$; then the model $\mathcal{M} = \langle \mathcal{S}, \mathcal{R}, \mathcal{L} \rangle$ corresponding to A is*

(i) $\mathcal{S} = \mathcal{S}_A$

(ii) $\mathcal{R}$ is a function from $\mathcal{S}$ to $2^{\mathcal{S}}$, such that $t \in \mathcal{R}(s)$ if for some label $\alpha \in \Sigma_A$, $t \in \mathcal{R}_A(s, \alpha)$

(iii) $\mathcal{L}$ is a function from $\mathcal{S}$ to 2^{Σ_A}, such that if there exist states $s, t \in \mathcal{S}_A$ and a label $\alpha \in \Sigma_A$, and $t \in \mathcal{R}_A(s, \alpha)$, then $\alpha \in \mathcal{R}(t)$.

Note that the set of propositional constants of the model is the set of labels of the corresponding transition system.

6.2.2 Data Independence of a Specification

The procedure for constructing a transition system from a specification or program presented above suffers one important limitation: Variables are translated as processes, with a state for each value the variable can take. If the variable were to take an infinite range of values, the resulting system would not be finite-state, and our model checking algorithm would not be applicable. Indeed, it is impossible to deal with systems where variables can take values from an infinite domain within propositional temporal logic.[2] Typically, infinite domains of variables have been handled by ignoring the difference between the data values. Of course, this approach is not suitable for stating properties where data does matter, such as "each value input gets output exactly once."

Example 6.2 The following property states that if two input values d_j and d_i are read exactly once, and if d_i is read before d_j, then d_j and d_i are output exactly once, and d_i is output before d_j (where D is the domain of the data values, $\mathtt{in}d_i$ means that d_i is input, $\mathtt{out}d_i$ means that d_i is output):

---

[2]Thus propositional temporal logic cannot describe the behavior of an unbounded buffer, for example. In [184], it is shown that even uninterpreted first-order temporal logic cannot specify unbounded buffers.

$$\bigwedge_{i,j \in D} ($$
$$(\Diamond \mathsf{in}\,d_j \wedge \Box(\mathsf{in}\,d_j \Rightarrow \bigcirc\Box\neg\mathsf{in}\,d_j) \wedge$$
$$\Diamond \mathsf{in}\,d_i \wedge \Box(\mathsf{in}\,d_i \Rightarrow \bigcirc\Box\neg\mathsf{in}\,d_i) \wedge \neg\mathsf{in}\,d_j\,\mathcal{U}\,\mathsf{in}\,d_i) \Rightarrow$$
$$(\Diamond \mathsf{out}\,d_j \wedge \Box(\mathsf{out}\,d_j \Rightarrow \bigcirc\Box\neg\mathsf{out}\,d_j) \wedge$$
$$\Diamond \mathsf{out}\,d_i \wedge \Box(\mathsf{out}\,d_i \Rightarrow \bigcirc\Box\neg\mathsf{out}\,d_i) \wedge \neg\mathsf{out}\,d_j\,\mathcal{U}\,\mathsf{out}\,d_i))$$

Wolper [375] has pointed out that the fact that we are dealing with infinite data values is often irrelevant to the correctness of the specified system. For example, a protocol should treat each message identically, independent of the cardinality of the domain from which the messages are taken. Wolper introduced the notion of *data independence* and shows that if we can establish that the behavior of the specification or program is independent of its data (in a sense to be made precise), we can then utilize propositional temporal logic to reason about specifications or programs stated over infinite data domains. This is a very powerful result because it makes the model checking approach presented earlier applicable to a much broader class of systems. As long as we can partition our variables into data and control variables, and show that the specification is data-independent of the data variables, then the cardinality of the domain of the data variables is irrelevant. Intuitively, a specification or program is data-independent if, should we change the input data variables only the data variables output should change correspondingly. We can, therefore, view the *behavior* of a specification or program simply as an infinite sequence of input and output events of data variables (and treat the rest of the specification/program as a "black box").

Definition 6.5 *A specification or program P is* data-independent *if for all data domains D and functions f from D into D', σ is a possible behavior of P for input $d \in D$ if and only if $f(\sigma)$ is a possible behavior of P for input $f(d)$.*

In general, it is arbitrarily hard to decide whether a given specification or program is indeed data-independent. However, in practice it is usually easy to separate the specification/program into data variables and control variables, where the system's actions are only dependent upon the control variables. One can give syntactically checkable conditions sufficient for the specification or program to be independent of the data variables (for example, if a system only reads a variable from a channel, copies the variable, and writes the variable to a channel, clearly the specification or program is independent of the value of the variable).

[375] shows that properties of data-independent specifications or programs can be specified over different data domains. It is possible to replace a property specified over an infinite data domain by a property specified over a finite data domain. In the following discussion, we concern ourselves only with properties dealing with data variables. Such properties are made up of propositions involving input and output events of data d, where d is taken from some domain D. We denote such a property

by Φ_D. A property Φ_D is satisfied by a specification/program P if it is satisfied by all possible input/output behaviors of P over the domain D.

Theorem 6.1 *Given a data-independent specification or program P and a surjective function f from D into D', then P satisfies a property $\Phi_{D'}$ over the data domain D' if and only if P satisfies $\Phi_{f^{-1}(D')}$.*

$f^{-1}(D')$ is a mapping from D' into 2^D with $d \in f^{-1}(d')$ if and only if $f(d) = d'$, for a mapping f from D into D'; $\Phi_{f^{-1}(D')}$ is a property over D' where each proposition of the form $\phi(d')$ is replaced by the (possibly infinite) disjunction $\bigvee_{d \in f^{-1}(d')} \phi(d)$.
Proof: One needs to prove that all input/output behaviors of P over D' satisfy $\Phi_{D'}$ if and only if all input/output behaviors of P over D satisfy $\Phi_{f^{-1}(D')}$. From the assumption of data independence it follows that if P has a behavior σ over D, it also has behavior $f(\sigma)$ over D'. Because f is surjective, if the specification or program has a behavior σ' over D', then it also has a behavior σ over D such that $\sigma' = f(\sigma)$. It is therefore sufficient to prove that a behavior σ satisfies $\Phi_{f^{-1}(D')}$ if and only if $f(\sigma)$ satisfies $\Phi_{D'}$. This claim is established by a straightforward structural induction on the sentence stating the property Φ (for details refer to [375]). ∎

Wolper established further results for properties of data-independent specifications or programs which involve only finite subsets D_0 of D (let such properties be denoted by $\Phi_{D_0 \subset D}$).

Theorem 6.2 *Given a data-independent specification or program P and a mapping f from D to D' that is one-to-one over D_0, then $\Phi_{D_0 \subset D}$ holds if and only if $\Phi_{f(D_0 \subset D)}$.*

We can obtain a corollary to Thm.6.2 stating that to show that a given property holds for all finite subsets of the data domain of a fixed cardinality, it is sufficient to show that it holds for one such subset.

Theorem 6.3 *Given a data-independent specification or program P and a mapping f from D to D' that is one-to-one over some finite subset D_0 of D, then $\Phi_{D_0 \subset D}$ holds for every finite subset D_i of D such that $|D_i| = |D_0|$ if and only if $\Phi_{f(D_0 \subset D)}$.*

Note that we can, therefore, replace any sentence describing a property over a finite subset D_0 of the domain D by a sentence describing a property over a data domain containing only $|D_0|+1$ elements (we map all elements of $D - D_0$ into a single element of D').

Example 6.3 Ex. 6.2 expresses a property over a subset of cardinality 2 of a potentially infinite data domain D. Thm.6.3 instructs us that to prove this property it is sufficient to prove a corresponding property over a data domain D' containing only 3 elements (let $D' = \{d_1, d_2, d_3\}$).

$$(\Diamond \mathsf{in}\,d_2 \wedge \Box(\mathsf{in}\,d_2 \Rightarrow \bigcirc\Box\neg\mathsf{in}\,d_2) \wedge$$
$$\Diamond \mathsf{in}\,d_1 \wedge \Box(\mathsf{in}\,d_1 \Rightarrow \bigcirc\Box\neg\mathsf{in}\,d_1) \wedge \neg\mathsf{in}\,d_2\,\mathcal{U}\,\mathsf{in}\,d_1) \Rightarrow$$
$$(\Diamond \mathsf{out}\,d_2 \wedge \Box(\mathsf{out}\,d_2 \Rightarrow \bigcirc\Box\neg\mathsf{out}\,d_2) \wedge$$
$$\Diamond \mathsf{out}\,d_1 \wedge \Box(\mathsf{out}\,d_1 \Rightarrow \bigcirc\Box\neg\mathsf{out}\,d_1) \wedge \neg\mathsf{out}\,d_2\,\mathcal{U}\,\mathsf{out}\,d_1)$$

6.2.3 Temporal Properties of a Specification

Sentences of the temporal calculus RTμ express properties of computation sequences. If a given specification or program is a model for such a sentence Φ of RTμ, we say that the specification or program has the property Φ. In Section 5.2, we gave an algorithm to determine whether a specification or program is indeed a model for a sentence of RTμ. In this section, we survey properties of particular interest.[3]

Safety properties intuitively assert that "nothing bad happens" during the computation. Less colloquially, a safety property states that a finite prefix of a computation (the computation may be infinite) satisfies some condition. Typically safety properties have the form $\Box\phi$, where ϕ specifies the condition that has to be met within a finite prefix of the computation, and the modal operator $\Box$ ensures that ϕ holds of all finite prefixes. The following are examples of safety properties.

- *Partial correctness* — We say that a specification or program is partially correct with respect to a precondition ϕ and a postcondition ψ if, provided that it starts to execute in a state satisfying the precondition, it will terminate in a state satisfying the postcondition, should it terminate. In the following, let ℓ denote some specification/program state (with ℓ_0 being singled out as the initial state of the specification or program, and ℓ_t the state in which the specification or program terminates), then partial correctness is stated in RTμ as

  $$\ell_0 \wedge \phi \Rightarrow \Box(\ell_t \Rightarrow \psi)$$

- *Invariance* — That a property ϕ holds throughout the execution of the specification or program is simply described by

  $$\Box\phi$$

  Local invariance claims that this property holds locally at certain states:

  $$\Box(\ell \Rightarrow \phi)$$

- *Mutual Exclusion* — The requirement that several processes be mutually exclusive with respect to a critical region is expressed as

  $$\Box\neg\bigwedge_i CS_i,$$

  where CS_i indicates that process i is in the critical region.

---

[3] For a detailed discussion of specification/program properties see [189]. However, Kröger discusses program verification from a manual theorem-proving point of view.

- *Deadlock freedom* — A set of processes is said to be deadlocked, if no process is enabled to continue. If we let $enabled_i$ mean that process i is enabled, freedom from deadlock can be stated in the following way.

$$\Box \bigvee_i enabled_i$$

Roughly speaking, *liveness properties* assert that "something good will eventually happen." They require that for some element of a finite prefix of a computation some condition hold.

- *Total correctness* — A specification or program is said to be totally correct with respect to its precondition ϕ and postcondition ψ if it is partially correct and the specification or program terminates:

$$\ell_0 \wedge \phi \;\Rightarrow\; \Diamond(\ell_t \wedge \psi)$$

- *Guaranteed accessibility* — for a process states that if a process reaches a certain state in the computation, it will eventually reach some other state:

$$\ell \;\Rightarrow\; \Diamond \ell'$$

  This property is sometimes referred to as absence of starvation. (Starvation freedom also refers to properties such as guaranteed granting of requested resources, etc.)

Precedence properties often arise in connection with resource allocation. More generally, they express that some temporal order exists for certain events. The following examples deal with resource allocation, where req_i means that process i requests a resource, and $grant_i$ means that the process is granted the resource. Of particular interest here is the fair behavior of the resource allocation mechanism.

- *Absence of unsolicited response* — No resource is granted unless previously solicited.

$$\bigwedge_i \neg grant_i \;\Rightarrow\; (\neg grant_i \,\mathcal{U}\, req_i)$$

- *Fair handling of requests* — A simple mechanism to guarantee that all requests are handled is to grant them in a "First come, first served" manner:

$$req_i \wedge (\bigwedge_{j \neq i} \neg req_j) \;\Rightarrow\; (\bigwedge_{j \neq i} \neg grant_j) \,\mathcal{U}\, grant_i$$

  A slightly more liberal strategy is to allow some limited number of overtaking. For example, one process may be handled before another which had already requested a resource (but only a bounded number of times). 1-bounded overtaking is expressed by the following sentence of RTμ:

$$req_i \wedge (\bigwedge_{j \neq i} \neg req_j) \;\Rightarrow$$

$$(\bigwedge_{j \neq i} \neg grant_j) \,\mathcal{U}\, ((\bigwedge_{j' \neq i} grant_{j'}) \,\mathcal{U}\, ((\bigwedge_{j'' \neq i} \neg grant_{j''}) \,\mathcal{U}\, grant_i))$$

Intuitively speaking, *fairness* gives every process the chance to make some progress in its computation, independent of the relative speeds of the individual processes. Various fairness properties of different strengths have been proposed. Among them are (again let $enabled_i$ mean that process i is enabled; $execute_i$ shall mean that process i is executed):

- *Unconditional fairness* — Every process is executed infinitely often, as expressed by

$$\bigwedge_i \nu z \cdot \mu x \cdot (execute_i \vee \bigcirc x) \wedge \bigcirc z$$

(The details of the fix-point formulation of "infinitely often" were explained on p.86.)

- *Weak fairness* — Every process that is enabled almost everywhere is executed infinitely often.

$$\bigwedge_i (\nu z \cdot \mu x \cdot (enabled_i \wedge \bigcirc x) \vee \bigcirc z \;\Rightarrow\; \nu z \cdot \mu x \cdot (execute_i \vee \bigcirc x) \wedge \bigcirc z)$$

- *Strong fairness* — Every process enabled infinitely often is executed infinitely often.

$$\bigwedge_i (\nu z \cdot \mu x \cdot (enabled_i \vee \bigcirc x) \wedge \bigcirc z \;\Rightarrow\; \nu z \cdot \mu x \cdot (execute_i \vee \bigcirc x) \wedge \bigcirc z)$$

The properties listed above are templates of how one would express fairness, mutual exclusion, etc., for a concurrent specification. These must be adjusted to the individual case, as shown below for Peterson's protocol of Ex. 6.1.

Example 6.4 Mutual exclusion states that no two processes may be in the critical region simultaneously. In RTμ, this situation is expressed for process P as follows

$$\Box(\mathsf{CS_p} \;\Rightarrow\; \neg\mathsf{CS_q}\,\mathcal{U}\,\textbf{send}(in_p, \mathsf{f}))$$

and symmetrically for process Q:

$$\Box(\mathsf{CS_q} \;\Rightarrow\; \neg\mathsf{CS_p}\,\mathcal{U}\,\textbf{send}(in_q, \mathsf{f}))$$

We also want to establish that Peterson's protocol satisfies the liveness property. This condition asserts that once a process announces its interest to enter the critical section, it will, eventually, be allowed to enter the critical section (i.e., no process idles infinitely in the trying region before the critical section). The corresponding RTμ statements are

$$\Box(\textbf{send}(in_p, \mathsf{t}) \;\Rightarrow\; \Diamond\mathsf{CS_p})$$

and

$$\Box(\textbf{send}(in_q, \mathsf{t}) \;\Rightarrow\; \Diamond\mathsf{CS_q}).$$

Algorithm Alg.6.1 determines whether a given property Φ holds for a specification P.

Algorithm 6.1 (Verify temporal property)

/*Model checking (Alg.5.1) is performed on a global model M*/
input property Φ, specification P
Convert P into the corresponding model M
if Model checking(Φ) $\neq \{\}$
then report P satisfies Φ
else report failure

As pointed out earlier, model checking is of polynomial time-complexity, where the polynomial is of a degree dependent on the model of the sentence to be checked (note that the specification itself does not contain temporal modalities). Emerson [89] mentions that systems with up to 10^5 states can currently be handled by model checking techniques. However, it should be pointed out that the size of the transition system corresponding to the specification or program grows exponentially with the number of processes. Note that many concurrent systems are (at least partially) composed of many copies of identical processes (for example, Peterson's protocol above is such a case). An important research topic is the development of techniques that avoid this exponential blowup at least for systems composed of such identical processes [64].

6.2.4 Fairness Hypothesis

Proving the stronger temporal properties above is often impossible without assuming concurrent processes are executed fairly. That is, we have to assume any process eventually executes some action. One could add such an assumption in terms of a sentence of RTμ. However, it is often more convenient to represent the fairness assumption as inherent in the specification or program modelled.

Fairness amounts to assuming the transitions taken by the transition system representing the specification are chosen independent of the individual processes. For example, a scheduler might pick which of the possible transitions is taken, and this scheduler is blind to the processes involved. We can easily represent such an assumption by conjoining a "scheduler" transition system to the synchronized product obtained from the transition systems representing the processes. The scheduler for Peterson's protocol of Ex. 6.1 is shown in Fig.6.3.

The fairness hypothesis is represented by a transition system with one state for each process plus one central state. There are transitions from that central state to each of the states representing processes. The transitions back to the central state are labelled with the possible actions of each process and are thus synchronized with the action of the process. In an infinite execution sequence of this transition system,

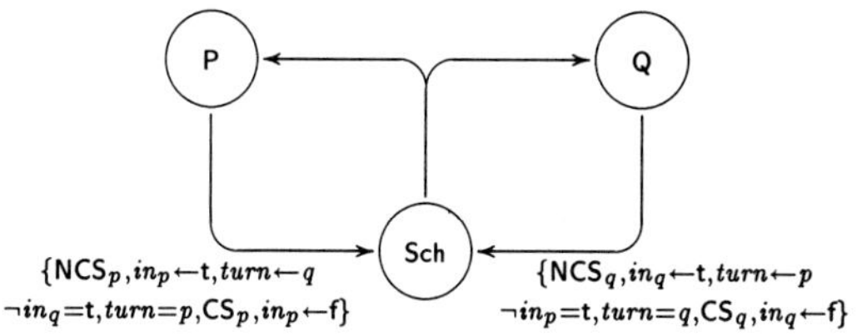

Figure 6.3. Fairness hypothesis for Peterson's protocol.

every state is visited infinitely often (and thus, every process executes infinitely often if it can execute at all). Note that the fairness hypothesis does not entail that a specification or program is indeed fair. It only means that the execution of enabled processes does not depend on those processes.

6.3 Timing Constraints Consistency Analysis

A real-time system is thought to be composed of two subsystems, a controlling subsystem and a controlled subsystem. The controlling subsystem is a real-time program that manages and coordinates activities. The controlled subsystem is the environment with which the real-time program interacts. The timing constraints of a real-time system can be classified into performance constraints and behavior constraints. Performance constraints set the response-time limits on the controlling subsystem whereas behavior constraints make demands on the rates at which the controlled subsystems provides stimuli to the controlling subsystem.

The correctness of a real-time system depends not only on the logical result of the computation, but also on the time at which the results are produced. An important aspect of the correctness of a real-time system is the consistency of the various timing constraints imposed on the individual components of a system. The system will not function correctly if even two of the timing constraints cannot jointly be met.

Timing constraints consistency analysis is concerned with real-time related aspects of the specification only. We may, therefore, safely omit all those clauses of a specification not related to stating timing-specific requirements (as discussed on p.98).

Step 1: Generate directed timing constraints graph (DTCG) and the corresponding directed timing constraints matrix (DTCM)

Based on the timing related parts of a FRORL specification, we create a DTCG by letting the vertices be the events mentioned in the specification, and the arrows (with their associated weights) be the timing constraints that hold between two events. The arrows point in the direction of the timing constraint (e.g., for a maximum timing constraint between event e_1 and event e_2 the arrow goes from e_1 to e_2, and vice versa for a minimum timing constraint).[4]

Algorithm 6.2 (Create Directed Timing Constraints Graph, DTCG)

/*Let minact(e_m, e_n, tc) be the activity with minimum timing constraint tc between events e_m and e_n, and similarly for maxact, durminact, and durmaxact.*/
for each activity act with associated timing constraint
  if act = minact(e_m, e_n, tc) $\vee$ act = durminact(e_m, e_n, tc))
  then if $\exists e_i \cdot e_m$ is unifiable with event e_i
    then $e_{to} \leftarrow e_i$
    else $e_{to} \leftarrow e_m$
      create vertex for e_m
      label e_m
    if $\exists e_i \cdot e_n$ is unifiable with event e_i
    then $e_{from} \leftarrow e_i$
    else $e_{from} \leftarrow e_n$
      create vertex for e_n
      label e_n
  if act = maxact(e_m, e_n, tc) $\vee$ act = durmaxact(e_m, e_n, tc))
  then if $\exists e_i \cdot e_m$ is unifiable with event e_i
    then $e_{from} \leftarrow e_i$
    else $e_{from} \leftarrow e_m$
      create vertex for e_m
      label e_m
    if $\exists e_i \cdot e_n$ is unifiable with event e_i
    then $e_{to} \leftarrow e_i$
    else $e_{to} \leftarrow e_n$
      create vertex for e_n
      label e_n
    $tc \leftarrow -tc$
  draw an arrow from event e_{from} to event e_{to}
  $tc_{m,n} \leftarrow tc$ /*label the arrow tc*/

The directed timing constraints graph is then converted into the directed timing constraints matrix DTCM by letting the cells in the matrix hold either the weight of the arrow between two events, or 0, if there is no arrow between two events. Thus, the size of the graph is reduced by eliminating redundant arrows and vertices.

---

[4]We assume there is no timing constraint on events, so the DTCG is a directed graph with n vertices and no looping edges.

Algorithm 6.3 (Create Directed Timing Constraints Matrix, DTCM)

```
/*Let e_1 ... e_n be the events mentioned in the specification.*/
types DTCM: e_1 ... e_n × e_1 ... e_n → int
for i = 1 to n
    for j = 1 to n
        if there is an arrow from e_i to e_j
        then DTCM_{i,j} ← tc_{i,j}
```

Detection of inconsistencies between timing constraints relies on the following theorem (which is an application of basic inequality reasoning).

Theorem 6.4 *For a cycle in a directed timing constraints graph (*DTCG*), if the sum of the weights of the arrows in the cycle is positive, then the timing constraints in the cycle are inconsistent.*

Proof: Given a DTCG, and a timing constraint $tc_{i,j}$ between two events e_i and e_j, the weight of the arrow between these events can be represented by the inequality

$$e_i + tc_{i,j} \leq e_j. \tag{6.1}$$

Assume the events $e_1, e_2, \ldots, e_k$ form a cycle with the sum of the weights of all arrows being positive, where each vertex v_i corresponds to an event e_i. Repeatedly applying formula (1) for each timing constraint and taking the conjunction of all the inequalities, we obtain

$$\begin{array}{l} e_1 + tc_{1,2} \leq e_2 \wedge \\ e_2 + tc_{2,3} \leq e_3 \wedge \\ \quad\vdots \\ e_k + tc_{k,1} \leq e_1 \end{array}$$

This conjunction can be collapsed into

$$tc_{1,2} + tc_{2,3} + \cdots tc_{k,1} \leq 0$$

which is a contradiction, since by assumption the sum of the weights of the edges in the cycle formed by $e_1, e_2, \ldots, e_k$ is positive. ∎

Step 2: Transform DTCM to canonical form

Based on Thm.6.4, we shall locate all the cycles in a DTCG and compute the timing constraints on the cycles. First, we eliminate all events and arrows from the DTCG which cannot contribute to a cycle, i.e., all events (and their connected arrows) from which either no arrow originates or at which no arrow ends.

The next algorithm obtains the canonical form of the directed timing constraints matrix by noticing that rows or columns with only 0 entries indicate that at that event either no arrow originates or no arrow ends.

Algorithm 6.4 (Convert DTCM to canonical form)

```
n ← |DTCM_1|
rm-list ← { }
for i = 1 to n
    for j = 1 to n
        if i = j
        then continue /*with next iteration*/
        if DTCM_{i,j} ≠ ε
        then break /*from this loop*/
        if j = n
        then rm-list ← rm-list ∪ {i}
            if i = n
            then for each k ∈ rm-list
                        remove row k and column k from DTCM
n ← n − |rm-list|
rm-list ← { }
for j = 1 to n
    for i = 1 to n
        if i = j
        then continue /*with next iteration*/
        if DTCM_{i,j} ≠ ε
        then break /*from this loop*/
        if i = n
        then rm-list ← rm-list ∪ {i}
            if j = n
            then for each k ∈ rm-list
                        remove row k and column k from DTCM
if rm-list ≠ { }
then call "Convert DTCM to canonical form"
```

Step 3: Locate timing constraints contradictions

Now find cycles with the sum of the weight of the contained arrows being positive, and compute the overall timing constraints values. The following algorithm is based on Tiernan's algorithm [332] and its modification in [82].

Alg.6.5 outputs all directed cycles in the timing constraint detection matrix and their corresponding sums of the weights associated with each cycle. According to Thm.6.4, we locate the cycles with positive overall weights to detect inconsistent timing constraints in a requirements specification.

Algorithm 6.5 (Timing Constraints Detection, TCD)

/*Let $e_1, \ldots, e_n$ be the events in a specification, let $sumtc$ be an accumulator for the overall weight of the cycle through the canonicalized DTCG.*/
types $path$: **list** event
$start \leftarrow 1$
(i) $F \leftarrow 0$
(ii) $i \leftarrow start + 1$
(iii) **if** $i > n$
    then goto (v)
    else if $\exists i \leq n \cdot tc_{\mathsf{last}(path), e_i} = 0$
        then goto (iv)
        else if $e_i \in path$
            then goto (iv)
            else if e_i is forbidden from last($path$)
                then goto (iv)
                else $k \leftarrow k + 1$
                    $path \leftarrow path \cup e_i$
                    $sumtc \leftarrow sumtc + tc_{\mathsf{last}(path), e_i}$
                    goto (ii)
(iv) $i \leftarrow i + 1$
    goto (iii)
(v) **if** $tc_{\mathsf{last}(path), start} \neq 0$
    then $sumtc \leftarrow sumtc + tc_{\mathsf{last}(path), e_i}$
        report weight of $path$ is $sumtc$

    else if $k = 1$
        then goto (vi)
        else clear the list of vertices forbidden from last($path$)
            make last($path$) forbidden from one_but_last($path$)
            remove last($path$) from $path$
            $k \leftarrow k - 1$
            goto (ii)
(vi) $start \leftarrow start + 1$
    $path \leftarrow path \cup e_{start}$
    if $start = n$
    then goto (v)
    else if $start < n$
        then goto (i)

1. A call should be initiated (i.e., required resources should be allocated within the exchange) no earlier than 4 sec. and no later than 7 sec. after the subscriber terminal goes off-hook.
2. The subscriber shall dial the first digit within 5 sec. after going off-hook.
3. If the call cannot be attempted the subscriber should receive a congestion tone no later than 8 sec. after going off-hook.
4. Dialing should be completed within 20 sec. after dialing the first digit.
5. The first digit should be dialed no earlier than 2 sec. after the call has been initiated.
6. The system should attempt to connect the call within 8 sec. after the last digit had been dialed and a ringing tone should be applied to the called party's line.
7. If an attempt to connect cannot be made (e.g., due to traffic on the line, or the called party's terminal being off-hook, etc.), the subscriber terminal should receive a busy-tone within 8 sec. after dialing the last digit.
8. Ringing should be applied to the called party's line no earlier than 15 sec. after initiating the call.
9. The called party shall go on-line within 120 sec. after the ringing tone is first applied to the line.
10. The subscriber terminal shall go on-hook within 20 sec. after receiving either a congestion tone or a busy tone.

Figure 6.4. Timing requirements for Ex. 6.5.

Example 6.5 The timing constraints for parts of a telephone switching system are shown in Fig.6.4. We show the timing constraints consistency analysis of this specification step by step (we omit presenting the FRORL specification).

Step 1: Generate DTCG and the corresponding DTCM

After forming the FRORL specification and abstracting the timing-related information we label the events in the system as follows: off_hook (e_1), initiate_call (e_2), first_digit (e_3), last_digit (e_4), ringing (e_5), on_line (e_6), busy_tone (e_7), congestion_tone (e_8), on_hook (e_9), and on_line (e_{10}).

The DTCG and DTCM are given in Fig.6.5 and Fig.6.6, respectively.

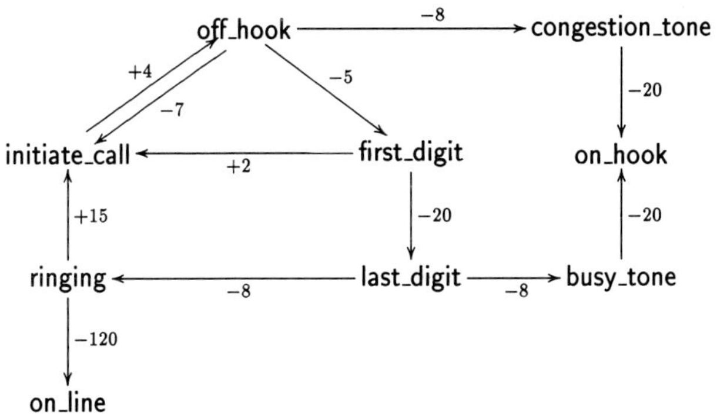

Figure 6.5. Generated directed timing constraints graph (DTCG).

	off_hook	initiate_call	first_digit	last_digit	ringing
off_hook		+4			
initiate_call	−7		+2		+15
first_digit	−5				
last_digit			−20		
ringing				−8	

Figure 6.6. The canonical form of the directed timing constraints matrix (DTCM).

Step 2: Transform DTCM to canonical form

Step 3: Locate timing constraints contradictions

The timing constraints detection algorithm unveils the following cycles among the timing constraints of the canonical DTCM.

1. $e_1 e_3 e_4 e_5 e_2 e_1$. Overall timing constraint on this cycle $= -15$.

2. $e_1 e_3 e_2 e_1$. Overall timing constraint on this cycle $= +1$.

According to Thm.6.4, the cycle $e_1 e_3 e_2 e_1$ points to inconsistencies in the timing constraints for the requirements specification of Fig.6.4. Returning to the specification, we notice that the maximum timing constraint (2) is inconsistent with the minimum timing constraints (5) and (1).

7

Development, Specification, and Verification of Knowledge-Based Systems

Knowledge-based systems model human know-how and attempt to solve problems in areas where algorithmic solutions are not readily available. Knowledge-based systems can be developed following the same techniques as when developing conventional systems. Because their execution mechanisms are based on formal foundations, various verification techniques have been proposed to aid in the development of knowledge-based systems.
In this chapter, we argue that static analysis algorithms as well as dynamic techniques proposed so far fall short of satisfying the needs of knowledge engineers. We present a novel dynamic approach, potential-conflict backtracking, to the verification of knowledge bases. Potential-conflict backtracking does not pose unreasonable and limiting assumptions on the rule base and can aid the knowledge engineer in the initial development of the rule base.

7.1 Difficulties in Verifying Knowledge-Based Systems

Knowledge-based systems (expert systems) are software systems attempting to imitate the know-how of human experts. They store and use human knowledge (instead of algorithms) and apply to areas where algorithmic solutions are not available.

Various representation methods have been developed and relied upon to codify human knowledge, although heuristic rules are the most frequently used representation. (Most well-known systems, e.g., MYCIN [51], are rule-based expert systems.) Rules are processed by treating them as logical implications and applying inference rules to them, to derive new information. The preconditions of the rules consist of a (possibly empty) list of facts that must be satisfied to execute its actions. The actions consist of, or produce, new facts that may fire other rules, resulting in chains of inference.[1]

[1]Typically the inference engine processing rules and facts can protocol its inference steps, to explain obtained results to the users. Answers can be given to "Why result R?" or "Why not the result R'?"-questions.

Recently, additional representational mechanisms have become available for the development of expert systems. *Objects* (derived from Smalltalk [131]) and *frames* [32] are data structures that can be created during runtime and inherit properties (fields) from its specified class. Repertory grids (e.g., KSSO [290]) form hierarchical, decision-table-like arrays representing weighted relationships between influence factors and results. Demons (e.g., BABYLON [59]) and methods (e.g., NEXPERT OBJECT ([234]) are (small) procedures activated and processed at predefined events, such as object creation, object property fetches or changes.

Originally, expert systems existed as small laboratory prototypes; they were easy to handle and the developers had no difficulty managing their structure and behavior. During recent years, expert systems have grown from laboratory prototypes to large and complex applications for use under real-life conditions. With the increase in complexity and problem solving capabilities, the systems became harder to understand, and all the negative phenomena of the software life-cycle were encountered. Today's expert systems require strategies for correctness testing just as "conventional" software systems do. However, during the verification of knowledge-based systems difficulties beyond the verification problems of conventional software development arise [36, 115, 136, 281].

- The development of knowledge-based systems often starts with vague requirements so that it becomes difficult to determine the system's tasks and whether it performs them correctly. Requirements specifications are often nonexistent, imprecise, or rapidly changing.

- Whereas individual rules are often unstructured, the rules of a knowledge-based system are heavily interdependent. This makes it difficult to determine the execution sequence from a static examination of the knowledge base.

- The logical relationships between data structures are quite complex. With the added effects of rules and demons, it is very difficult to maintain an understanding of the system's functionality.

- Development of expert systems by teams can easily lead to contradictions, redundancies, and missing information in the knowledge base. Similar problems arise when attempting to enhance or modify the expert system's performance through the addition of rules.

A knowledge engineer's task is to acquire knowledge from the human expert and model it on the computer. The difficulties faced by a knowledge engineer with respect to software engineering issues can be appreciated if one looks at DEC's XCON which configured VAX computer systems. Whereas originally replacing 75 system configuration specialists, soon more than 150 knowledge engineers were needed to keep the system up-to-date and correct.

Still, little software engineering support is given to the developers of knowledge-based systems. [36, 136, 297] presented knowledge-based system development frameworks conforming to the traditional waterfall life-cycle. Geissman [115] proposed a development methodology employing an iterative prototyping process to elicit feedback from developers and users, and modifying the intermediate product to achieve satisfactory performance. Research has mainly focused on verification methodologies [73, 121, 198, 216, 236, 257, 281, 312] without a proper framework for knowledge-based system development, and on knowledge acquisition support (e.g., MACAO [12], KSSO [290], or CLASSICA [112]).

7.2 Correctness Problems in Knowledge Bases

According to development strategy, language idioms, inference strategy, and degree of automation, a wide collection of correctness problems in knowledge-based systems have been identified, often with overlapping (and even disagreeing) definitions. In the following, we present several examples of such properties, with "definitions" obtained by forming the union of various proposals by different authors.

In a knowledge-based system, a *conflict* occurs if the inference process generates several different solutions where only one is intended. Conflicts may occur either explicitly (as $A \wedge \neg A$) or mediated through an equational calculus ($v = val_1 \wedge v = val_2 \wedge val_1 \neq val_2$).

"Definition" 7.1 A knowledge base contains *conflicts* if either

(i) the propositional symbols can be interpreted such that a logical contradiction arises [121]

(ii) two rules can fire in the same situation and conclude logically contradictory results [56, 121, 221, 235, 268, 311]

(iii) two rules can fire in the same situation and single-valued parameters are assigned different values [221, 235]

(iv) a semantic contradiction (specified by constraints) can be inferred [56, 221]

(v) the preconditions of two rules are not mutually exclusive but conclude different/contradictory results [56, 252, 268]

(vi) a contradiction is derivable from a noncontradictory initial fact base [270]

(vii) it contradicts test cases or test results [56, 123]

Redundancies and *subsumption* are not strictly logical problems and ordinarily do not affect the inference process. However, they often lose their redundant status; for example, in languages containing uncertainty measures, rules having different certainty factors, but otherwise identical, *do* affect the inference process.

"Definition" 7.2 A knowledge base contains *redundancies* if either

(i) one rule can be derived from another [121]

(ii) rules fire in the same situation and conclude the same results [95, 311]

(iii) rules have unifiable preconditions and conclusions [121, 235, 303]

(iv) the precondition of a rule can be unified with the subset of the preconditions of another rule and the rules have unifiable conclusions [235, 268, 311]

(v) a conjunct occurring in the precondition of a rule appears negated in the precondition of another rule [235]

(vi) it contains rules the presence or absence of which do not affect the results [56, 311]

From a logical viewpoint, *rule cycles* represent equivalences and should present no problems for a "knowledge" base. However, knowledge in an expert system is processed by interpretation. If circular inference chains are possible, the inference process may end up in a loop (note though that not all equivalences lead to cycles).

"Definition" 7.3 A *rule cycle* occurs if either

(i) the conclusion of a rule directly or indirectly causes the precondition of the same rule to be satisfied [235, 268]

(ii) a conjunct in the precondition of a rule occurs in the derivation path of the same rule [95]

If there are input combinations possible that do not meet the preconditions of any rule (*noncovered inputs*) in the knowledge base, the system will be unable to respond to that particular situation. *Dead-ends* are intermediate results computed by the inference process, not covered by any rule in the knowledge base, and thus, not allowing for computation of further results.

"Definition" 7.4 A knowledge base is *incomplete* if either

(i) any (intermediate) goal clause is unreachable [56, 235, 311]

(ii) the precondition of a rule is unsatisfiable [56, 235, 268]

(iii) the conclusion of a rule does not match a precondition of any other rule [56, 268]

(iv) input values are possible that do not match the precondition of any rule [56, 235]

7.3 Approaches to the Verification of Knowledge-Based Systems

Various techniques and tools have been developed to support the development of correct knowledge-based systems. They either try to gain a program that can correctly replay sets of test cases, or they check an existing knowledge base for internal correctness. The approaches differ vastly in their underlying concepts of correctness (e.g., absence of certain phenomena, correctness with respect to test cases, or even logical correctness). Furthermore, they are specific to a particular set of language idioms to represent knowledge and a particular inference strategy.

Several authors (e. g., [172]) rely on a concept of correctness derived from the logical concepts of consistency and/or completeness. These approaches typically allow only languages that are formal but weak with respect to their expressive power (production rules without function symbols). Inference mechanisms are usually restricted (e.g., monotonic inference, rules may fire only once, all facts have to be given initially, etc.). The allowed representations and the assumptions placed on the inference mechanisms prove inappropriate for most realistic application.

Most approaches select a particular representational mechanism and inference procedure and define, for this particular representation/interpreter combination, a set of properties the absence of which is assumed to constitute correctness of a knowledge-based system. That is, no attempt is made to relate the applied concept of correctness to the logical concepts of consistency and completeness of the knowledge base. Instead, it is assumed that a knowledge base is correct if certain structural or functional properties (e.g., "conflict," "cycle," "disagreement with case data,", etc.) are absent from the knowledge base [201]. The properties selected to constitute incorrectness vary from approach to approach, and are closely related to the representational and inferential mechanisms addressed. Although they are intended to "approximate" the related logical concepts, usually no attempt is made to justify the claim that the sum of these properties indeed amounts to the logical concept.

7.3.1 Algorithmic Checking

Algorithmic checkers consider knowledge bases as decision tables and provide algorithms to determine the presence/absence of above mentioned properties.

ONCOCIN [311] is a development tool for medical therapy selection based on the formalisms of MYCIN (rules, contexts [51]). After every change or insertion of a rule into the knowledge base the system checks for conflicts, redundancies and missing rules (a situation exists in which a particular inference is required but no rule succeeds).

A table is constructed representing all combinations of variables in the preconditions of the rules together with the values assigned to the variables in actions. This table is algorithmically checked for conflicts, redundancies, subsumptions and missing rules. ONCOCIN assumes every combination of variables and values needs a rule. According to this assumption, the system proposes rules for combinations not previously covered.

CHECK [236] is intended to be applied to existing knowledge bases. The knowledge base is assumed to contain only rules with certainty factors. The system supports a backward chaining interpreter that tries to prove some specified goal clauses.

In a table, rules are compared with each other to detect dependencies between the preconditions and conclusions of each rule, as well as dependencies between rules and goal clauses. Algorithms are also included to check for cycles, missing rules (every attribute-value combination must be covered), unreachable clauses, and dead-end clauses.

The Expert Systems Validation Associate [56] is a wide-range rule base checking system containing algorithms that can be applied to existing knowledge bases developed with expert system shells such as ART, CLIPS, OPS5, or KEE. It checks rule bases extended by meta-knowledge pertaining to constraints and object structures.

Apart from the standard algorithms for table comparison, EVA relies on a wide range of meta-knowledge for judging potential sources of conflicts and incompleteness. By specifying meta-knowledge as constraints, the users can transfer semantic information about the application domain to the system. The users define relations among predicates by meta-predicates such as "*synonymous*," "*incompatible*," "*inverse*," "*transitive*," or "*reflexive*." Similarly, relationships between objects and classes of objects may be defined.

COVADIS [270] is applicable to developed knowledge bases specified in rule format. Constraints are used for specifying contradictions. COVADIS assumes the rules of the knowledge base to be activated in forward chaining fashion, starting with the initially supplied fact base.

During the inference process, the following additional assignments are made: to each derived fact the system assigns a "context" (a set of input facts necessary to infer the particular fact). These contexts are propagated through the chains of inference. The system stops if either a constraint is fired or saturation is reached. Firing a constraint means that a contradiction has occurred. The system then displays the contexts of the involved facts to the users who are required to identify them as significant or not. The inference chain is shown for debugging or for the assertion of additional constraints.

7.3.2 Graph-Based Checking

Tools in this category construct ATMS-like causal graphs, Petri Nets, etc., from the knowledge base. Checking algorithms are then applied to the graphs.

INDE [252] is applied to existing rules bases. The rules are specified in a variable-value formalism where variables can be bound to only one value. Rules are assumed to be activated by forward chaining.

The rules in the knowledge base are collected into maximally large rule clusters (referred to as "concepts"), such that the members of any concept are mutually exclusive to the members of any other concept. If two rules are mutually exclusive, they cannot fire simultaneously. Then concepts are transformed into Petri Nets in which variables are represented as places and rules as transitions. Inconsistencies are identified by places having arcs leading to them from transitions that represent rules assigning different values to the variable. For the rule-based system this corresponds to a situation where the same attribute is assigned different values by several rules contained in the same concept. The rule base is determined incomplete if all rules that assign a value to a given attribute are not in the union of all concepts. Rules not in the union of all concepts are considered unsatisfiable.

KB-REDUCER2 [121, 123] checks existing knowledge bases for consistency. It assumes all input facts are available and rules are specified in a first-order form. Inference is assumed to progress by forward chaining under the "negation as failure" assumption.

A graph is constructed with nodes representing facts and edges representing rules. Starting with the input facts ("inference level 0") the rules, whose preconditions match the input facts, form edges to facts of inference level 1, and so on until no rule is applicable. During graph formation every fact is assigned an "environment," i. e. the set of all (minimal) input facts entailing it.

A rule is redundant if its deletion causes no change in the set of derived facts. Inconsistencies are detected by facts declared as contradictories (by way of meta-language constraints) but have unifiable clauses in their environments.

Meseguer's system [221] checks knowledge bases formulated in the language of propositional logic with conjunctive normal form preconditions and literals as conclusions. Monotonic forward chaining is used assuming all input facts are initially available and consistent. Meta-language constraints specify contradictory facts.

The checking process begins by identifying subsets of rules which lead to contradictions (should unfavorable input conditions arise). Each such rule set is translated into a Petri Net where facts and rules are mapped to places and transitions, respectively. Next, the system attempts to find a maximal consistent set of facts that results in a contradiction when given as input to the selected rule set. If no such consistent input assignment is found, the rule base is assumed consistent.

KET [95] is a frame-based system whose checking abilities are applied to existing knowledge bases. The system assigns the frame slots in a backward chaining fashion. Values of slots are either derived by rule application or entered by the users (a slot assigned by user input is called an "ask slot").

A graph is constructed connecting frame slots; the leaves of the graph are ask slots. For each rule, there is a "path" in this graph traversing the set of slots necessary for firing that rule. The graph is checked for slots with missing or contradictory assignment rules. Rules are identified as inconsistent (redundant) if they have the same preconditions and assign different (same) values to a slot. A cycle is detected if a rule "path" contains the resulting slot itself.

Furthermore, KET identifies overlap (redundancies) in the frame structure. If frames are found with overlapping slots, a higher-level frame is created and the overlapping slots are moved there. The overlapping frames become descendents of the newly formed frame.

Riedesel's approach [268] applies to existing rule bases specified in an attribute-value formalism with abstract set formers (quantifiers over sets).

The checking algorithm works in steps, each involving a check for a certain consistency/completeness property. First, the rule base is converted into an ATMS network. Then a sequence of checking modules reasoning over the ATMS structure are called, detecting conflicts, cycles, noncovered inputs, and dead-ends. Furthermore, the structure of the knowledge base is examined to improve efficiency by clustering. These checks assume monotonicity of facts, typed variables, and provided mode specifications of variables (as input, intermediate, or output variables).

7.3.3 Knowledge-Base Refinement

Statistical, heuristic, or user-defined methods are applied to a knowledge base to decrease the differences between the knowledge base evaluations and provided case data.

MORE/MOLE [96, 163] uses heuristics for generating refinement measurements in causal networks processed in both forward- and backward-chaining direction.

The users can enter three kinds of assertions: symptoms, prior-conditions and qualifying conditions. A symptom is a condition that leads to a hypothesis if it is satisfied. A prior-condition makes a hypothesis only more probable or less probable; a qualifying condition influences the evidence of a symptom or a prior-condition. The knowledge base is constructed as a network with weighted vertices, with the edges constituting causal relationships. MORE processes the network in the direction of the hypotheses and compares support values with a preset threshold. Only hypotheses with values above this threshold are accepted; intermediate candidates that do not contribute to the explanation of a symptom are also rejected.

MOLE provides added refinement heuristics. It assumes each symptom has an explanation and for each explanation as few hypotheses as possible should be used. MOLE requires the users to input "core symptoms," for which the explaining hypotheses are found using heuristics. Additional heuristics are used to detect inconsistencies (ambiguities) and incompleteness in the network. By comparing the resultant system evaluations with test cases, missing knowledge and further ambiguities are detected.

SEEK2 [124] supports the refinement of rule bases processed through backward chaining. SEEK2 understands consistency and completeness as correspondence of the system-generated results with test cases.

An initial knowledge base is run on several test cases. Based on collected performance statistics, proposals for changes in the rules are generated. Suggestions include generalizing or specializing the preconditions of a rule. SEEK2 also provides an "Automatic Pilot," which applies the refinement heuristics and attempts to optimize the knowledge base using hill-climbing search. SEEK2 supports a meta-language allowing the users to formalize refinement heuristics.

AQUINAS [39] supports the refinement of weighted decision tables ("repertory grids") by comparing its results with test cases.

A repertory grid is a table in which columns hold influence factors ("traits") and possible solutions are entered in rows. The relationships between traits and solutions and between traits are weighted. The repertory grids of a knowledge base form hierarchical modules. AQUINAS detects analogies in the rows of the tables and helps in eliminating redundancies. The users define constraints to provide meta-language information. AQUINAS varies grid values and trait weights, records changes, and tries to obtain agreement with test cases by applying a hill-climbing search. Various heuristic rules are provided for selecting the grid values or trait weights to refine.

INDE[2] [329] is applied to existing knowledge bases represented as a domain model with shallow rules specified in a Prolog-like formalism where each variable holds only one value. Rules are assumed to be processed in a forward chaining manner.

Given the domain theory and test cases, INDE constructs a Prolog-like proof for each test case. From the proof, shallow rules are generated which are usually too general. Each shallow rule is individually checked against the test data. If the result is incorrect, one or more theory rules applied in the proof are responsible. The debugger must find the theory rule(s) which have propagated the error to the shallow rules. In a meta-theory, the possible errors "clause error" (rules are too general/restrictive) and "value error" (a numeric value is outside its valid range) are defined.

Furthermore, the meta theory computes relations between the errors ("same error," "opposite error"). These relations form a graph; if a shallow rule generates an erroneous result, this error is propagated throughout the graph. The domain theory rules are further evaluated by error indicators measuring how frequently they are causing errors.

LAPS [86] allows the expert to input single case solutions and supports their depth-first refinement. LAPS translates resultant decision tables to data-driven rules for expert system shells like M.1 or CLIPS.

LAPS drives the development process in three "sessions." First, the expert enters and solves example case data. In session 2, these example case data are elaborated to an initial model with heuristics, explanations and intermediate hypotheses. In session 3, the examples are further developed and refined to decision tables. These decision tables are then checked for consistency and completeness using algorithmic methods.

[2]A different system from the earlier mentioned graph checker.

7.4 Dynamic Verification

In this section, we discuss a novel approach to the verification of knowledge-based systems. This approach begins by identifying potential manifestations of problems in the knowledge base. The system then tries to reason backwards to determine whether the problem can indeed occur. Reasoning backwards by way of symbolic execution is flexible to adapt to the various types of knowledge representation mechanisms relied upon in modern expert systems.

7.4.1 The Importance of System Context

In current knowledge-based system development projects, a wide range of different expert knowledge representations and interpretation methods are used.

To represent the expert knowledge naturally, a variety of formalisms have been developed. In knowledge-based systems, multiple formalisms are often applied which differ in their basic idioms. "Production systems" ("facts" and "rules"), decision tables, causal graphs (the state of one node in the graph influences the state of another node) and frame models (object frames with inheritance) are most frequently used. The chosen knowledge representation method influences the correctness concept of a knowledge base and consequentially, the techniques applicable to determine its correctness. For example, if a language allows only propositions, a simple conflict may be a sentence $A \wedge \neg A$ whereas otherwise, the notion of "conflict" would have to be extended to include equality ($v = val_1 \wedge v = val_2$, where $val_1 \neq val_2$). Similarly, multiple assignments to the same variable may either indicate a conflict, or be legitimate means of expressing a collection of data.

In knowledge-based systems, new information is derived by applying inference rules to available facts. Various inference strategies have been proposed (such as SLD-resolution, universal instantiations, modus ponens, etc.). Often, more than one rule of the knowledge base may be applicable. An inference strategy decides which of the applicable rules will be used to derive new information. For example, inference may be monotonic (the set of the known facts in the knowledge base must not be reduced) or nonmonotonic; selective (not all applicable rules are fired, instead one is selected, e. g. "first rule," "most specialized rule") or not; rules are allowed to fire only once, or whenever applicable; applicable rules may be searched for in a depth-first manner (a problem branch is first refined and followed into detail and then the next problem branch is processed); the order of the rules may be relevant for their semantics and processing; negation may be handled by the "closed-world assumption," or a third truth-value (e.g., "unknown") may be available; and so on. Again, the notion of correctness of a rule base depends heavily on the particular inference strategy supported.

Example 7.1 Consider a knowledge base containing the following two rules:

Rule-1: determine_action

Precond: $light = \mathsf{red}$
Actions: $action \leftarrow$ slow_shutdown

Rule-2: determine_action
Precond: $light = \mathsf{red} \wedge temp > 95$
Actions: $action \leftarrow$ fast_shutdown

Considered in isolation from an inference strategy, both rules may fire in situations where $light = \mathsf{red} \wedge temp > 95$. However, whether they fire depends on the inference mechanism employed:

- If only one applicable rule fires, and rule selection is performed according to the physical order of the rules in the knowledge base, then *action* will be slow_shutdown. Rule-2 will be redundant.
- If all applicable rules are fired, then there is a conflict in the assignment to *action*.
- If the most specific rule is fired, then *action* will be fast_shutdown.

This list could easily be extended to yet other schemes of rule selection.

The knowledge base verification tools presented earlier typically suffer limitations with respect to knowledge representation mechanisms and inference strategies.

- They support only specialized and restrictive formalisms and interpreter strategies.
- Strict assumptions are made on the available data and the inference process. E.g., it is assumed all possible facts are initially available or rules are allowed to fire only once.

Knowledge base verification tools are usually add-ons to existing development environments for knowledge-based systems (expert system shells). Furthermore, because of the assumptions on availability of facts and domain knowledge, these techniques are applicable only after the knowledge base is nearly complete and not as tools supporting the development process.[3]

We claim that the development of knowledge-based systems is quite similar to the development of conventional systems. We, therefore, argue that the software engineering paradigm presented earlier as support for the development of conventional software systems also applies to the development of knowledge-based systems. In an earlier paper [368], we presented a system supporting the development of knowledge-based systems.

[3]We see below that knowledge base verification can be important to the knowledge engineer *during the development* of the knowledge base. Inconsistencies or other pathologies in the knowledge base often point to shortcomings in the understanding of the problem domain.

- A high-level specification language (similar to FRORL) allows the representation of the knowledge-based system independent of a particular expert system shell.
- The nonmonotonic logic presented in Chapter 3 serves as the semantic foundation of this specification language. The representational constructs (methods, demons, frames, etc.) of the specification language are translated into constructs of the underlying nonmonotonic logic.
- The specification, as expressed in the underlying logic, is translated into a knowledge base of a target expert system shell.

This strategy allows the development of knowledge-based systems completely independent of the proposed target run-time shell. The nonmonotonic logic in Chapter 3 was chosen as the logical foundation of the development process because the widely used constructs of modern expert system shells (frames, demons, rules, objects) can be easily expressed in this logic. The development of knowledge-based systems according to this strategy differs from the development process for conventional software systems only in that the mapping from the underlying logic to the target language is more straightforward. Developing knowledge-based systems in this way has the added advantage of allowing optimizing transformations to be applied to the knowledge base during target code generation.[4]

Another difference between the development of knowledge-based and conventional systems is that the semantics of programming techniques (i.e., rule-based programming) is cleaner and better understood than the semantics of conventional programming constructs. Therefore, more powerful methods for the verification of knowledge-based systems are available. In the remainder of this chapter, we concentrate on verification mechanisms for knowledge-based systems.

We assume the knowledge base is specified in a language similar to FRORL, as shown by the following rule schema:

Rule-⟨rule-number⟩**:** ⟨hypothesis name⟩
  Precond: ⟨activity-desc⟩ ∧ ⟨activity-desc⟩ ∧ ...
  Actions: ⟨activity-desc⟩ ∧ ⟨activity-desc⟩ ∧ ...

The rules of a knowledge base are analogous to activities in a conventional software system. We refer to the name of a rule as its hypothesis. Rules may have preconditions, actions, and alternative actions. A rule fires if all its preconditions evaluate to true. Firing a rule means executing its actions (if the preconditions cannot be satisfied, the alternative actions will be executed[5]). If a rule involves objects (see Chapter 2), these are stated in the parts slot. Actions may either assign values to variables (or objects) or cause the firing of other rules by referring to the hypothesis of a rule.

[4] A process control system for a steel mill has been developed using this strategy [309].

[5] Again, alternative actions simplify specifications, but are not strictly necessary.

Preconditions may also lead to rule-firing in the same way. We allow *demons* to describe the behavior of a knowledge base. Demons are a sequence of actions that are executed should certain events occur during evaluation of the rules of the knowledge base: An **if-fetched** demon is activated by accessing the value of a variable. Changing the value of a variable leads to execution of any **if-changed** demon defined for that variable.

Execution of a knowledge base is performed by forward-chaining, as usual. Given a set of hypotheses and input facts, applicable rules are fired until no further rule can be fired or a stopping condition is reached. Rule invocation in the precondition of a rule (either through demons or by the hypothesis of a rule being included among the preconditions) leads to backward-chaining behavior. Such rule-chaining may occur by including a hypothesis in the preconditions of a rule (LHS-hypo call) or in the actions of a rule or demon (RHS-hypo call).

For convenience in representing rules, we also allow loop constructions (such as while-loops) in the actions of a rule. However, the induction variable of the loop is not considered as potentially causing a conflict (because the induction variable typically changes from one iteration to the next). Furthermore, variables may be declared as set- or bag-valued, in which case they are not considered to be potential sources of conflicts.

Verification of a knowledge base may be accomplished through static algorithms and by dynamic means, such as symbolically evaluating the knowledge base. Properties of a knowledge base that can be checked statically include *syntax checks* (missing declarations, multiple declarations, type mismatch), *unused elements* of the specification, simple notions of *redundancies* (textual inclusion of preconditions), and *cycles* in object hierarchy or rules.

Unused objects or attributes in a specification either indicate they have been forgotten or have become unnecessary during development of the knowledge base. Redundant rules do not affect the knowledge base as long as they are redundant, but may suddenly change the behavior of the knowledge base should other rules be added or deleted resulting in loss of their redundant character. Cycles in the class hierarchy point to drastic misunderstandings of the application domain. Cycles between rules may lead to infinite loops during inference.

Important properties of knowledge bases, such as conflicts, dead-end rules, more complete notions of redundancy, and subsumption cannot be determined statically.

7.4.2 Potential-Conflict Backtracking

Conflicts are situations in which several solutions are generated where only one is intended. During the inference process, the same variable is given different values based on the same facts. *Redundancies* are similar, except the variable receives the same value more than once. *Dead-end rules* do not occur on any inference path.

When conflicts are present in knowledge-based systems, they often arise only from certain (of the potentially large number of) combinations of input facts. Systems that assume these facts are known before checking for conflicts can begin are impracticable. Furthermore, conflicts cannot be identified statically, by looking at the rules of the knowledge base. Consider

> **Rule-3:** set_switch
> **Precond:** low_pressure
> **Actions:** *switch* ← true
>
> **Rule-4:** set_switch
> **Precond:** high_energy
> **Actions:** *switch* ← false

These rules assign conflicting values to *switch*. To decide whether this is indeed a conflict, we look at the knowledge base as a whole. For example, there may be rules stating that high_energy arises only when pressure is high. If so, these rules would not be conflicting since there could be no situation where *switch* is given both values.

In addition, to decide whether a conflict occurs, it is insufficient to look at an uninterpreted knowledge base. Unlike in logic, the facts leading to the conflicting solution must hold true in the application domain and not in an arbitrary domain. Additional domain knowledge is often required to decide whether two facts can coexist.

In contrast to approaches presented in the literature which, starting from the initial facts, iteratively apply inference rules and check the resulting knowledge base for syntactic or domain-dependent contradictions, our approach proceeds in the opposite direction. We begin by locating a potential conflict in the form of rules which assign different values to the same variable. The knowledge base is then run "backwards" to a predefined depth. If the facts obtained at that level are not jointly satisfiable, no conflict can arise. If this cannot be determined from syntactic inspection and analysis of additional domain knowledge, the users are asked to make a decision. In our experience, users can often quickly decide whether a particular combination of facts is indeed possible in the application domain. If the combination of facts is possible, a conflict in the rule base is identified. If the users deem the particular combination of facts impossible, this information is remembered as an additional constraint of the application domain.

Let $c_1,\ldots,c_n$ denote preconditions of rule R, let h denote the hypothesis of R, and let $a_1, \ldots, a_m$ denote actions of R. Furthermore, let $PF(e)$ denote the potential facts for expression e as defined in Def.7.6.

Definition 7.5 *The* inference path *to e, $IP(e)$, is*

(i) $PF(c_1)$, if e is the precondition c_1 of R

(ii) $IP(c_{i\text{-}1}) \cup PF(c_i)$, if e is the precondition c_i of R, $1 \le i \le n$

(iii) $IP(c_n) \cup \{h = \textbf{true}\}$, if e is the hypothesis of R

(iv) $IP(h) \cup \bigcup_{1 \leq j \leq m} PF(a_j)$, if e is the rule R.

An *inference path* consists of all facts that become true when we reason backwards from a given rule in the knowledge base. Since a demon has no preconditions, the inference path to a demon is simply the union of the potential facts of its actions. The inference path is constructed from *potential facts*, by which we mean, facts that need to hold for a precondition of a rule to be true or for an action to fire.

Definition 7.6 *Let R be a rule. The* potential facts *for e, $PF(e)$, are*

(i) $\{c_i\}$, if e is a boolean precondition c_i of R and there are no demons associated with variables in c_i

(ii) $\{c_i\} \cup IP(D)$, if D is an if-fetched demon associated with a variable in c_i

(iii) $\{c_i = \textsf{true}\} \cup \bigcup_{1 \leq j \leq k} IP(R_j)$, if e is a hypothesis (a LHS-hypo call), $R_1 \ldots R_k$ are rules of the knowledge base with hypothesis h such that the preconditions of R_1 through R_k and $IP(c_{i\text{-}1})$ are consistent

(iv) $\{v = E'\}$, if e is an action $v \leftarrow E$, and there is no demon associated with v; if E is a function call or a run-time input, then E' is a new constant, otherwise $E' = E$

(v) $\{v = E'\} \cup IP(D)$, if e is an action $v \leftarrow E$, and D is an if-changed demon associated with v, and E' is as in (iv)

(vi) $\{a_i = \textsf{true}\} \cup \bigcup_{1 \leq j \leq k} IP(R_j)$, if e is a hypothesis (a RHS-hypo call), and the same conditions hold as in (iii).

Assignments of values to a variable that arise from inputs during run-time or from the execution of external functions (as typically possible in modern knowledge-based systems) are assumed each time to yield a new value E'. This is a worst-case assumption: If a conflict can arise (for example, due to inputs at run-time), it will arise. Note that Def.7.6(iii) and Def.7.6(vi) include facts obtained through the chaining of inference rules. Only those rules with matching hypothesis, consistent with the inference path obtained thus far, are considered. Note that Def.7.6 assumes all rules of the knowledge base applicable at any given moment will fire. If we wanted to apply conflict resolution between rules, we could do so by introducing domain knowledge to that effect.[6]

---

[6]For example, given two rules

Rule-5: h
  Precond: c
  Actions: a

Definition 7.7 *An inference path $IP(e)$ is consistent if and only if there do not exist two potential facts $e_1, e_2 \in IP(e)$ such that e_1 and e_2 are mutually exclusive.*

The notion of mutual exclusion between two potential facts includes cases where two facts cannot hold simultaneously due to algebraic and arithmetic constraints. Potential facts may also be mutually exclusive if the added domain knowledge deems them contradictory.

Alg.7.1 determines whether a conflict exists in the knowledge base. This algorithm relies on backtracking from potential conflicts to a certain depth k.

Algorithm 7.1 (Locate conflict)

/*Let $IP_k(e)$ be the inference path to e to depth k.*/
for each rules R_1 and R_2 of the knowledge base such that $a_1 \in R_1$, $a_2 \in R_2$, $PF(a_i) = \{c_i = e_i\}$, $i = 1, 2$, $c_1 = c_2$, and $e_1 \neq e_2$
  if $\nexists e_1 \in IP_k(a_1), e_2 \in IP_k(a_2) \cdot$ e_1 and e_2 are mutually exclusive $\wedge$ $IP_k(a_1)$ and $IP_k(a_2)$ are consistent
  then report R_1 and R_2 are conflicting

A similar algorithm finds redundant rules. A rule is redundant if either the same value can be assigned to a variable by several rules or if a rule can never fire due to mutual exclusion between some elements on its inference path. Alg.7.2 determines further dynamic properties indicating shortcomings of the knowledge base under consideration.

Example 7.2 We demonstrate that application of the above verification techniques can, beyond helping to ensure correctness of the knowledge base under development, also aid in the elicitation of knowledge from domain experts. We consider the simple example of a pump which directs the flow of material between two tanks (see Fig.7.1). The goal is to operate the pump in such a way that the levels of the two tanks remain within certain allowed bounds. Assume in the initial interview the knowledge engineer elicits the following four rules from the domain expert:

Rule-7: set_pump
  Precond: $\text{tank}_1.level >$ max
  Actions: $overflow_1 \leftarrow$ true
    and $pump \leftarrow$ on

Rule-6: h'
  Precond: c'
  Actions: a'

the domain rule $a \wedge a' \Rightarrow \neg h'$ would resolve these two rules in favor of the first rule.

Algorithm 7.2 (Properties of rules)

/*Let Pre(R) be the preconditions of rule R, let Act(R) be the actions or alternative actions of rule R. Let h be the hypothesis of R.*/
for each rule R of the knowledge base
  if $\exists c \in R \cdot IP(c)$ is not consistent
  then report R is inconsistent
  if $\exists R' \cdot \forall a \in \mathsf{Act}(R) \cdot a \in \mathsf{Act}(R')$ and
    $\forall c \in \mathsf{Pre}(R') \cdot c \in IP(R)$
  then report R is subsumed by R'
  if $\nexists R' \cdot\ h \in IP(R') \wedge IP(h)$ (in R') is consistent or $h \in \mathsf{Act}(R')$
  then report R is a dead-end rule

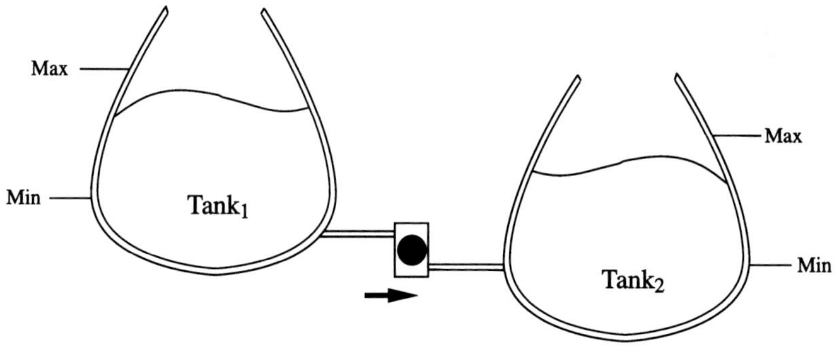

Figure 7.1. The tank problem.

Rule-8: set_pump
  Precond: tank$_2$.$level$ > max
  Actions: $overflow_2 \leftarrow$ true
    and $pump \leftarrow$ off

Rule-9: set_pump
  Precond: tank$_1$.$level$ < min
  Actions: $underflow_1 \leftarrow$ true
    and $pump \leftarrow$ off

Rule-10: set_pump
  Precond: tank$_2$.$level$ < min
  Actions: $underflow_2 \leftarrow$ true
    and $pump \leftarrow$ on

(The idea here being quite simple: In the event that the liquid level in one tank reaches a disallowed limit, the pump should be turned on or off to balance the liquid contents between the two tanks.)

When applying the dynamic knowledge base verification techniques presented above, we begin by locating potential conflicts in the knowledge base. For example, Rule-7 and Rule-8 both assign conflicting values to *pump*. Reasoning backwards from these rules, it becomes apparent that if it is possible that

$$\mathsf{tank}_1.\mathit{level} > \mathsf{max} \wedge \mathsf{tank}_2.\mathit{level} > \mathsf{max}$$

then the potential conflict identified will lead to a conflict in the knowledge base. There is no domain knowledge or other information in this minimalistic knowledge base to exclude such a possibility.

Here the knowledge engineer might recognize that several other potential conflicts concerning the various assignments of states to the *pump* are present in this knowledge base. A natural approach to solving this conflict would be to make the problematic rules mutually exclusive by adding preconditions. The knowledge engineer replaces Rule-7 and Rule-8 with the following:

Rule-7′: set_pump
  Precond: $\mathsf{tank}_1.\mathit{level} > \mathsf{max} \wedge \mathit{pump} = \mathsf{off}$
  Actions: $\mathit{overflow}_1 \leftarrow \mathsf{true}$
    and $\mathit{pump} \leftarrow \mathsf{on}$

Rule-8′: set_pump
  Precond: $\mathsf{tank}_2.\mathit{level} > \mathsf{max} \wedge \mathit{pump} = \mathsf{off}$
  Actions: $\mathit{overflow}_2 \leftarrow \mathsf{true}$
    and $\mathit{pump} \leftarrow \mathsf{on}$

However, the rule checker now detects a possible redundancy between Rule-7′ and Rule-10, if it is possible that

$$\mathsf{tank}_1.\mathit{level} > \mathsf{max} \wedge \mathsf{tank}_2.\mathit{level} < \mathsf{min}$$

both hold simultaneously.

The knowledge engineer may think that adding another precondition will alleviate the problem, again modifying the above two rules:

Rule-7″: set_pump
  Precond: not $\mathit{overflow}_2 \wedge \mathsf{tank}_1.\mathit{level} > \mathsf{max} \wedge \mathit{pump} = \mathsf{off}$
  Actions: $\mathit{overflow}_1 \leftarrow \mathsf{true}$
    and $\mathit{pump} \leftarrow \mathsf{on}$

Rule-8″: set_pump
  Precond: not $\mathit{overflow}_1 \wedge \mathsf{tank}_2.\mathit{level} > \mathsf{max} \wedge \mathit{pump} = \mathsf{off}$
  Actions: $\mathit{overflow}_2 \leftarrow \mathsf{true}$
    and $\mathit{pump} \leftarrow \mathsf{on}$

A static check of the knowledge base reveals a cycle in the inference process: $overflow_1$ (Rule-7″) leads to the attempt to infer $overflow_2$ (Rule-8″), which leads to $overflow_2$ (Rule-7″), and so on.

At this point, the knowledge engineer may realize that additional information should be sought from the domain expert.

In their meeting, the knowledge engineer may learn that it is impossible for both limits to be above maximum or below minimum simultaneously. In this case, the initial version of the rules would be correct, provided one adds said piece of domain knowledge to the knowledge base. Or, the domain expert may tell the knowledge engineer that it is more important for the liquid level to stay below the maximum allowable limit in tank_2 (e.g., an overflow in tank_2 may endanger human operators). It might also be more important that the liquid level in tank_1 not fall below its minimum allowable limit, otherwise the pump may be damaged. This added information may lead the knowledge engineer to reformulate the rules:

Rule-7‴: set_pump
  Precond: $\mathsf{tank}_1.level > \mathsf{max} \wedge \mathsf{tank}_2.level <= \mathsf{max}$
  Actions: $overflow_1 \leftarrow \mathsf{true}$
    and $pump \leftarrow \mathsf{on}$

Rule-8‴: set_pump
  Precond: $\mathsf{tank}_2.level > \mathsf{max}$
  Actions: $overflow_2 \leftarrow \mathsf{true}$
    and $pump \leftarrow \mathsf{off}$

Rule-9′: set_pump
  Precond: $\mathsf{tank}_1.level < \mathsf{min}$
  Actions: $underflow_1 \leftarrow \mathsf{true}$
    and $pump \leftarrow \mathsf{off}$

Rule-10′: set_pump
  Precond: $\mathsf{tank}_2.level < \mathsf{min} \wedge \mathsf{tank}_1.level >= \mathsf{min}$
  Actions: $underflow_2 \leftarrow \mathsf{true}$
    and $pump \leftarrow \mathsf{on}$

The knowledge-base checker determines that these rules do not exhibit any pathologies.

Note that this example demonstrates that the presence of rule pathologies (cycles, conflicts, redundancies, etc.) may point to missing knowledge instead of poorly formulated rules. A knowledge-base verification tool becomes an important aid in knowledge acquisition.

8

Knowledge-Based Implementation

In this chapter, we discuss the step-by-step transformation of FRORL specifications into programs written in a procedural programming language, such as Pascal or Ada. FRORL, like any other logic-based specifications relies on several features not usually present in conventional programming languages. The most apparent are computational multi-directionality, logical variables, and search for solutions through backtracking. Although these features are essential in satisfying the demands on requirements specification languages stated earlier, the amount of nondeterminism and inefficiency introduced by them dictates that they be elliminated from the derived implementation. Any implementation of a logic-based specification must eliminate the use of these features in favor of deterministic constructs of the target language.
This chapter focuses on several aspects of the derivation of target code from FRORL specifications: Data dependency and flow analysis provides the information necessary to elliminate logical variables and determine the execution sequence of the resultant program. The analysis of item sets from the specification yields the information required to elliminate unnecessary nondeterminism. Code generation itself proceeds by program transformation which is illustrated by a set of canonicalizing transformations which necessarily precede flow analysis.[1]

8.1 Automated Program Construction

Logic-based languages have been advocated by many researchers [43, 61, 77, 110, 116, 157, 176–182, 211, 239, 256, 263, 277, 315, 320] as tools for software development. Although logic-based languages are good candidates for prescribing the requirements of software systems, their declarative semantic interpretation is not yet suitable for sequential execution. Nondeterminism and inefficient execution mechanisms clearly demand that we be unsatisfied with an operational interpretation of a logic-based

[1] Further detail on code generation are not given. The reader is referred to the excellent text book by Partsch [246], which gives many examples of implementation through transformational programming.

specification language. We must provide a deterministic interpretation as given by conventional programming languages.

The transformation of high-level logic-based languages into lower-level conventional languages has been extensively studied [24, 28, 43, 52, 75, 101, 245–247, 263, 277, 320] from various viewpoints. Sato and Tamaki [277, 320] have investigated the transformation of a logical theory (full first-order logic) into another logical theory (Prolog). However, most effort thus far has been directed towards transforming logical theories into functional programming languages (or into the lambda-calculus) and on transforming logical theories into procedural (imperative) languages.

The transformation of a FRORL specification into procedural programming languages discussed in this chapter relies on an integration of the analytical approach for transforming the nondeterminism of logic-based specifications and the knowledge-based approach for generating target code. This helps in avoiding some complexity pitfalls that have haunted automated programming techniques. We will present a matrix-based approach to data flow analysis. The flow of computation intended by the specification is determined by a combination of algorithms and constraining rules.

The transformation of a FRORL specification into target code (Fig.8.1) begins by processing the multiple inheritance hierarchy of FRORL objects and activities. The result being a standard logic-based specification, e.g., in a Prolog-like language. (The resultant specification represents the nonmonotonically extended theory corresponding to it.) This logic-based specification is then subject to canonicalizing transformations, which include *equality-introduction*, *equality-substitution*, *decomposition*, and *simplification*. The logic-based specification is thus converted into a form suitable for the application of data flow and dependency analysis. Note that the canonicalizing operations need often be applied several times. Based on the analysis of data dependencies between the clauses of a specification and the flow of information between the clauses of the specification, mode information is inferred. Mode information is essential in determining the order of clause evaluation for a logic-based specification. Since a purely logic-based specification does not have a preferred control mechanism for choosing clauses to unify against and resolve with, an appropriate mechanism must be provided. Lastly, backtracking has to eliminated from deterministic specifications, and necessary backtracking must be made explicit. Finally, target code has to be generated.

We will not discuss all aspects of the transformation from logic-based specification to implementation in detail. Instead, we will focus on data flow analysis, execution sequence determination, and the removal of unnecessary nondeterminism.

Although the ultimate goal of applying artificial intelligence techniques to software engineering may be the development of automatic programming techniques [19, 22, 30, 135, 211, 229, 267, 361, 372], the successes accomplished thus far have been far more modest [266]. Research towards this goal has progressed along several lines.

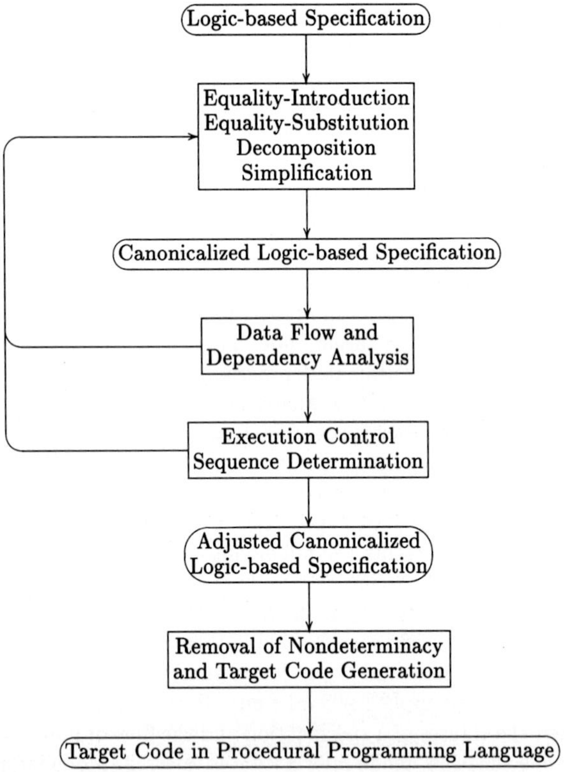

Figure 8.1. System organization of the transformation system.

8.1.1 Deductive Program Synthesis

Deductive program synthesis is based on the observation that the constructive proof of a theorem constituting the specification of a problem is at the same time also a program solving the given problem. From the constructive proof of the "specification theorem," one can extract by simple means a program that implements that theorem. In a sense, each step of a constructive proof can be interpreted as a step of the computation.

Deductive program synthesis begins with massaging the specification into the form of a theorem to be proven. A constructive proof of the theorem is generated; and finally, a program is extracted from the constructive proof. Green [134] and Waldinger [361] give examples of how programs could be synthesized as a side effect of resolution proofs. The most thorough approach to date is Constable's NUPRL system, which proves the specification theorems in Martin-Löf type theory [69–71].

Related approaches derive programs from specifications through the application of inference rules, such as splitting conjunctions or disjunctions, resolution rules for eliminating certain subexpressions, polarity strategies for restricting the resolution rules, and mathematical induction [83, 212]; by matching a specification against an "algorithm theory" [294]; or by attempting to partially duplicate the reasoning of a human program designer [165].

8.1.2 Program transformation

Given a specification or program fragment as input, transformation rules can be used to modify it successively into an output program. Program transformations normally have three steps: The pattern of a rule is matched against an input program to determine where the transformation rule is applied. Preconditions of the applicable rules are evaluated, and if successful, a new program is obtained by replacing the matched fragment of the input program with the modified, but equivalent, program fragment.

The transformational system of Burstall and Darlington consists of a complete set of transformation rules based on the substitution principle of equational reasoning. Fold/unfold transformations are guided by a set of powerful, efficiency-oriented transformations to improve the performance of input programs [52]. A detailed example of the transformation process is given in [14].

8.1.3 Knowledge-based program generation

Attempts to encode programming knowledge of human programmers into a form that could be automatically applied to a specification. For example, PECOS [22] shows how programs can be efficiently obtained by heavily relying on built-in domain expertise. This approach is concerned with identifying concepts and decisions used in human programming designs and converting them into rule form.

Most often, the knowledge-based approach is applied to the synthesis of low-level implementations for high-level abstract data-types used in a specification, since the selection of appropriate realizations for abstract data-types is a very knowledge-intensive task especially driven by domain knowledge.

8.1.4 Intelligent programmer's assistants

A less ambitious approach is to provide the human programmer with tools that alleviate some of the burden involved in formal program construction, without claiming to actually "derive" or "automatically develop" the program. Machine-based proving is emphasised in tools such as the Designer/Verifier's Assistant [228]. KBEmacs [364] focuses mainly on providing the users with knowledge-based templates for the construction of programs.

8.2 Canonicalization

A specification formulated in a language based on logic relies on semantics radically different from that of an ordinary programming language. The most obvious difference is that many predicates in a logic-based specification can be used in several directions, depending on the mode of their arguments. For example, append([1,2],[3,4],X) appends two lists and returns the result in X; append([1,2],X,[1,2,3,4]) computes lists which when appended to [1,2] yield the list [1,2,3,4]; and append([1,2],[3,4],[1,2,3,4]) tests whether appending two lists yields the list [1,2,3,4]. As a consequence, terms in a logic-based specification may have multiple meanings, when viewed from a standard, procedural point of view. Most prominently, the list notation $[H \mid T]$ can either denote the construction of a list from an element H and a list T, or it can denote the destructuring of an existing list in its head (H) and tail (T) components. Which of the two meanings is intended by the specification depends on the sequence in which clauses are evaluated. The order of clause evaluation can be determined within the semantic domain of Horn-Clause logic; it may change from input (query) to input (query). Such multi-directionality is characteristic of a logic-based specification language and constitutes the main difficulty in transforming the logic-based specification into a procedural program.

To deal more easily with these semantic issues, we first put the original specification into a canonical form. Canonicalization is accomplished via a sequence of preparatory transformation steps. The preparatory steps are equivalence preserving, in the sense that they preserve both semantics and input/output relations.

Canonicalization mainly makes explicit the constraints on variable bindings, etc., implicit in the original specification. Furthermore, it isolates the explicit mode constraints supplied by the users or imposed by built-in predicates of the specification language.

In this section, we identify four basic operations to transform a logic-based specification into an equivalent, canonical form that is suitable for the application of matrix-based flow analysis.

- *Equality-Introduction* — New variables are introduced for the arguments of a clause head and assigned a value through unification in the clause body. The purpose of this operation is to move value assignments from the clause head to the clause body allowing for further simplification of the clause body.

- *Equality-Substitution* — Nonvariable terms in the clause body partaking in unifications are replaced by variables. This operation makes further simplification of the clause possible.

- *Decomposition* — Built-in predicates and functions in a clause body are decomposed by expanding them into a sequence of simpler operations. The predicates and functions become more amenable to mode analysis.

- *Simplification* — Clauses of the specification are simplified either by manipulating the clause form (folding and unfolding of literals, clause pruning) or by partial evaluation.

It is necessary to apply the canonicalizing transformations until no further change occurs. After application of transformations, new opportunities for canonicalization may arise. Other opportunities may need to be explored due to the emergence of new mode information.

A transformation rule is represented in the following notation, adopted from [27]:

$$\textbf{Rule-}\langle\text{rule-number}\rangle\ \ (\langle\text{domain name}\rangle)$$
$$\frac{\langle\text{pattern}\rangle}{\langle\text{replacement}\rangle}\Big[\ \langle\text{condition}\rangle$$

where

- *Pattern* — Describes the parse tree to which a rule may apply. One may refer to components of the specification by variables constructed from the syntactical category which they are intended to match (possibly adding an identifier). Such variables in a rule are bound to the matching subtree in the specification. If used later in the rule, they refer to the matched subtree.

- *Condition* — States syntactic or semantic constraints on the matched pattern. Only if these constraints are met is a match of the pattern against a parse tree considered successful.

- *Replacement* — Describes how to modify the specification when the rule pattern matches successfully. The replacement may either state a substitution of parts of the matched specification or declare attributes on parts of the specification (such as mode information, etc.).

Transformation rules may be written under the assumption that matching is performed modulo equational theories, where appropriate. In particular, when writing transformation rules, one may assume the unification operator is treated as commutative and the conjuncts in a clause body as connected by an associative and commutative operator.

The canonicalizing transformation rules massage a logic-based specification into a form suitable for application of matrix-based data flow and dependency analysis. These rules are developed to handle all possible structures which may occur in a logic-based specification.

8.2.1 Equality-Introduction

The meaning of "equal" is not equality of arithmetic expressions but unification between two terms. As such, "equal" encompasses both matching and destructuring of the involved arguments. According to the procedural interpretation, "equal" could be either an assignment between the left- and right-hand-side literals, or a testing condition for any two ground terms. It is necessary to remove "noncanonical" arguments from clause heads, since we want the entries of the matrix (see Section 8.3) to be variables rather than compound terms or literals. Equality-introduction creates a new variable for each argument in the clause head. In the clause body, arguments and the corresponding newly introduced variables are unified.

Equality-introduction is accomplished by the following set of transformation rules:

Rule-1 (Equality-Introduction)

$\langle\text{pred}\rangle(\langle\text{var}\rangle_1, \ldots, \langle\text{var}\rangle_n) \leftarrow$

———————[$\langle\text{var}\rangle_1, \ldots, \langle\text{var}\rangle_n$ are mutually distinct variables

prohibit Equality-Introduction

This rule simply says if a clause has no body and its mutually distinct arguments are neither constants nor compound terms, then we can stop applying equality-introduction to it.

Rule-2 (Equality-Introduction)

$\langle\text{pred}\rangle(\ldots, \langle\text{trm}\rangle_1, \ldots) \leftarrow \langle\text{lit}\rangle_1 \wedge \ldots \wedge \langle\text{lit}\rangle_m$

———————[$\langle\text{var}\rangle_2$ is a new variable

$\langle\text{pred}\rangle(\ldots, \langle\text{var}\rangle_2, \ldots) \leftarrow$

$\quad \langle\text{var}\rangle_2 = \langle\text{trm}\rangle_1 \wedge \langle\text{lit}\rangle_1 \wedge \ldots \wedge \langle\text{lit}\rangle_m$

New variables are introduced for the arguments of the clause head (which then contains only variables as arguments). These variables are given their original value through unification in the clause body.

We illustrate the canonicalizing transformations as well as data flow and data dependency analysis by the successive refinement of the following sample specification. The example is adopted from [276] where it was used to demonstrate the item-set construction (cf. Section 8.5.1). Using our approach, we can obtain the information necessary to transform it into a program stated in a procedural programming language. The example specification describes a parser for a very simple language, as given in the following productions (in BNF-notation):

$\langle\text{factor}\rangle$ ::=

$\quad$ ($\langle\text{exp}\rangle$) $\langle\text{primary}\rangle$

$\langle\text{primary}\rangle$ ::=

* ⟨primary⟩ | ϵ

Example 8.1 Consider the following set of clauses, describing the regular expression language above. We added a clause top for further illustration.

$$\mathsf{top}(X, Y, \mathsf{print}(N)) \leftarrow \mathsf{factor}(X, Y) \wedge Y = N \tag{8.1}$$

$$\mathsf{factor}(['(' \mid X_7], Y_7) \leftarrow \mathsf{exp}(X_7, [')' \mid Z_7]) \wedge \mathsf{primary}(Z_7, Y_7) \tag{8.2}$$

$$\mathsf{primary}(['*' \mid X_{11}], Y_{11}) \leftarrow \mathsf{primary}(X_{11}, Y_{11}) \tag{8.3}$$

$$\mathsf{primary}(X_{12}, X_{12}) \leftarrow \tag{8.4}$$

We apply the equality-introduction rules to above specification to obtain the following clauses. All clauses resulted from application of Rule-2.

$$\mathsf{top}(X, Y, A_1) \leftarrow \mathsf{factor}(X, Y) \wedge Y = N \wedge A_1 = \mathsf{print}(N)$$
$$\mathsf{factor}(A_1, Y_7) \leftarrow A_1 = ['(' \mid X_7] \wedge \mathsf{exp}(X_7, [')' \mid Z_7]) \wedge \mathsf{primary}(Z_7, Y_7)$$
$$\mathsf{primary}(A_1, Y_{11}) \leftarrow A_1 = ['*' \mid X_{11}] \wedge \mathsf{primary}(X_{11}, Y_{11})$$
$$\mathsf{primary}(A_1, A_2) \leftarrow A_1 = X_{12} \wedge A_2 = X_{12}$$

8.2.2 Equality-Substitution

Equality-substitution is designed to replace those terms in the body of a rule given values through unification. The effect of equality-substitution is simplification of the literals in the clause body. After applying equality-substitution, some literals expressing unification (those carrying redundant information) can be eliminated later in the simplification step. Equality-substitution reduces groundedness of a clause as much as possible. Groundedness is measured by a partial ordering in which constants are more ground than variables, which are more ground than function or predicate symbols, which in turn are more ground than literals.

Rule-3 (Equality-Substitution)

$$\frac{\langle\text{pred}\rangle(\ldots) \leftarrow \ldots \wedge \langle\text{trm}\rangle_i = \langle\text{var}\rangle_k \wedge \ldots \wedge \langle\text{trm}\rangle_j = \langle\text{var}\rangle_k \wedge \ldots}{\langle\text{pred}\rangle(\ldots) \leftarrow \ldots \wedge \langle\text{trm}\rangle_i = \langle\text{var}\rangle_k \wedge \ldots \wedge \langle\text{trm}\rangle_j = \langle\text{var}\rangle_k \wedge \ldots \wedge \langle\text{trm}\rangle_i = \langle\text{trm}\rangle_j} \left[\ \langle\text{var}\rangle_k \text{ is a variable}\right.$$

This rule makes explicit (in the clause body) the data dependency due to transitivity of unification implicit in the clause head of the original clause.

Rule-4 (Equality-Substitution)

$$\frac{\langle\text{pred}\rangle(\ldots) \leftarrow \ldots \wedge \langle\text{trm}\rangle_i = \langle\text{trm}\rangle_j \wedge \ldots}{\textbf{prohibit}\ \text{Equality-Substitution}} \left[\ \langle\text{trm}\rangle_j \text{ is a constant}\right.$$

Because a constant is already minimal according to the partial ordering used to measure groundedness, equal substitution should not be applied in this case (lest additional complexity be introduced by later canonicalizing transformations).

Rule-5 (Equality-Substitution)

$$\frac{\langle\text{pred}\rangle(\ldots) \leftarrow \ldots \wedge \langle\text{trm}\rangle_i = \langle\text{var}\rangle_j \wedge \ldots}{\langle\text{pred}\rangle(\ldots) \leftarrow (\ldots \wedge \ldots)\{^{\langle\text{var}\rangle_j}/_{\langle\text{trm}\rangle_i}\} \wedge \langle\text{trm}\rangle_i = \langle\text{var}\rangle_j} \Big[\langle\text{var}\rangle_j \text{ is a variable}$$

Rule-6 (Equality-Substitution)

$$\frac{\langle\text{pred}\rangle(\ldots) \leftarrow \ldots \wedge \langle\text{trm}\rangle_i = \langle\text{trm}\rangle_j \wedge \ldots}{\langle\text{pred}\rangle(\ldots) \leftarrow (\ldots \wedge \ldots)\{^{\langle\text{var}\rangle_j}/_{\langle\text{trm}\rangle_i}\} \wedge \langle\text{trm}\rangle_i = \langle\text{var}\rangle_j} \Big[\langle\text{trm}\rangle_j \text{ is a compound term or predicate}$$

These rules maintain consistency by preparing for the elimination of newly introduced but unnecessary variables. The continuation of our example follows.

Example 8.2 (Continued.) Equality-introduction leaves several unifications behind, which now need to be represented consistently.

$$\mathsf{top}(X, Y, A_1) \leftarrow \mathsf{factor}(X, Y) \wedge Y = N \wedge A_1 = \mathsf{print}(N)$$

$$\mathsf{factor}(A_1, Y_7) \leftarrow A_1 = ['(' \mid X_7] \wedge A_2 = [')' \mid Z_7] \wedge \mathsf{exp}(X_7, A_2) \wedge \mathsf{primary}(Z_7, Y_7) \qquad \text{by Rule-6}$$

$$\mathsf{primary}(A_1, Y_{11}) \leftarrow A_1 = ['*' \mid X_{11}] \wedge \mathsf{primary}(X_{11}, Y_{11})$$

$$\mathsf{primary}(A_1, A_2) \leftarrow A_1 = X_{12} \wedge A_2 = Y_{12} \wedge A_1 = A_2 \qquad \text{by Rule-3}$$

8.2.3 Decomposition

A logic-based specification relies also on built-in predicates. The semantics of these components usually requires several operations to be realized using procedural programming languages. If we considered each of these predicates as a unit when performing flow analysis, we would find it very difficult to follow the execution sequence and provide "detailed" information to facilitate the transformation into a procedural programming language. Therefore, we need to decompose a built-in predicate into components that jointly provide more information for flow analysis than the built-in predicate considered as a unit. Although the rules shown below are restricted (for space limitations) to only a few of the built-in predicates provided by FRORL, the strategy is general. The essential point here is to extract the operations constituting a built-in predicate as well as the constraints that the built-in predicate may impose on its arguments. This information is then used during data flow and dependency analysis.

Our discussion of built-in predicates is mainly concerned with their operations instead of the possible side-effects these operations may have on a database.[2] We first introduce some rules used for decomposition of built-in literals. The predicate **head** is used to retrieve the first element of a list. The predicate **tail** returns the rest of a list (the list with its first element removed). Furthermore, we define a function **listcnstr** to construct a single-element list from an individual element. In the following rules, mode information is also extracted during decomposition. At this stage, the mode information can be understood as indicating the groundedness of the arguments of built-in predicates (with "ground' denoted by "+" and "unground" denoted by "−").

Rule-7 (Decomposition)

$$\frac{\langle \mathrm{trm} \rangle_2 = [\langle \mathrm{trm} \rangle_1 \mid \langle \mathrm{list} \rangle]}{\mathsf{listcnstr}(\langle \mathrm{trm} \rangle_1, \langle \mathrm{list} \rangle_2) \wedge \mathsf{append}(\langle \mathrm{list} \rangle_2, \langle \mathrm{list} \rangle_1, \langle \mathrm{trm} \rangle_2)} \left[\langle \mathrm{list} \rangle_2 \text{ is a new variable} \right.$$

mode listcnstr("+", "−"), append("+", "+", "−")

Rule-8 (Decomposition)

$$\frac{\langle \mathrm{trm} \rangle_2 = [\langle \mathrm{trm} \rangle_1 \mid \langle \mathrm{list} \rangle]}{\mathsf{head}(\langle \mathrm{trm} \rangle_2, \langle \mathrm{trm} \rangle_1) \wedge \mathsf{tail}(\langle \mathrm{trm} \rangle_2, \langle \mathrm{list} \rangle)} \left[\right.$$

mode head("+", "−"), tail("+", "−")

The above two rules describe the two different operations a list structure can represent. A list in a logic-based specification can either be constructed from an element and a shorter list (Rule-7), or the list may be input and then decomposed into an element and a shorter list (Rule-8).

Initially, we have no basis from which to choose between the two options available, and an arbitrary choice has to be made. But, with additional mode information collected during data dependency analysis (Section 8.3) it may turn out that our initial choice was wrong, and that the mode assignment obtained under the chosen decomposition for a list is inconsistent. Data dependency analysis follows a backtracking control regime.[3] The discovery of an inconsistent mode assignment later on (see p.160) returns us to this point where we have to switch the decomposition of a list to other alternatives available.

---

[2]This is in line with other approaches presented in the literature [79, 214, 263].

[3]We are not concerned here with the details of implementing the control regime for mode analysis. For definiteness sake the reader may assume that a backtracking control mechanism similar to that of Prolog is available.

Rule-9 (Decomposition)

$$\frac{\langle\mathrm{trm}\rangle_1 \textbf{ is } \langle\mathrm{trm}\rangle_2\ \langle\mathrm{op}\rangle\ \langle\mathrm{trm}\rangle_3}{\langle\mathrm{op}\rangle(\langle\mathrm{trm}\rangle_2, \langle\mathrm{trm}\rangle_3, \langle\mathrm{trm}\rangle_1)}\left[\ \langle\mathrm{op}\rangle \text{ is one of } + - * /\text{mod (arithmetic operators)}\right.$$

mode $\langle\mathrm{op}\rangle$(“+”, “+”, “−”)

Rule-10 (Decomposition)

$$\frac{\langle\mathrm{trm}\rangle_1 \textbf{ is } \langle\mathrm{trm}\rangle_2}{\text{assign}(\langle\mathrm{trm}\rangle_2, \langle\mathrm{trm}\rangle_1)}\left[\ \right.$$

mode assign(“+”, “−”)

When dealing with arithmetic operations we assume their operands are always ground and the results are always unground.

Rule-11 (Decomposition)

$$\frac{\langle\mathrm{trm}\rangle_1\ \langle\mathrm{op}\rangle\ \langle\mathrm{trm}\rangle_2}{\langle\mathrm{op}\rangle(\langle\mathrm{trm}\rangle_1, \langle\mathrm{trm}\rangle_2)}\left[\ \langle\mathrm{op}\rangle \text{ is one of } \backslash=, ==, \backslash==, <, >, >=, \text{ or } =<\right.$$

let $\langle\mathrm{op}\rangle$ be a testing condition
mode $\langle\mathrm{op}\rangle$(“+”, “+”)

Rule-12 (Decomposition)

$$\frac{\langle\mathrm{pred}\rangle(\langle\mathrm{trm}\rangle)}{\text{“}\langle\mathrm{pred}\rangle\text{”}(\langle\mathrm{trm}\rangle)}\left[\ \langle\mathrm{pred}\rangle \text{ is one of atom, integer, or atomic}\right.$$

let “$\langle\mathrm{pred}\rangle$” be a testing condition
mode $\langle\mathrm{pred}\rangle$(“+”)

The latter two rules are used in handling tests. If invocation of a literal has no lasting effect (such as binding a variable) we call that literal a testing condition. Later, when we generate code in a procedural programming language implementing the logic-based specification, these testing conditions will serve as the condition parts of conditional statements.

The built-in predicates var and nonvar test arguments for groundedness. In these cases, the mode information obtained can only be used to reduce some impossible mode combinations. It cannot provide a definite mode status as the rules discussed earlier do.

Rule-13 (Decomposition)

$$\frac{\langle\text{pred}\rangle(\langle\text{trm}\rangle)}{\text{``}\langle\text{pred}\rangle\text{''}(\langle\text{trm}\rangle)} \;\Big[\; \langle\text{pred}\rangle \textsf{ is either var or nonvar}$$

$$\textbf{not mode } \langle\text{pred}\rangle(\text{``}-\text{''})$$

Although we do know that these predicates will never generate output, we cannot be certain that these predicates will be called with ground arguments, their function being to test for groundedness in the first place.

Neither can unification provide definite mode status. Unification may test its two arguments for equality or it may unify a (partially) instantiated argument with a variable and bind the variable to it. We can only exclude the case where both arguments of the unification are unground. This mode constraint can be used at a later stage to determine the mode of the arguments of unifications by elimination of inconsistent mode assignments.

Rule-14 (Decomposition)

$$\frac{\langle\text{term}\rangle_1 = \langle\text{term}\rangle_2}{\text{``}=\text{''}(\langle\text{trm}\rangle_1, \langle\text{trm}\rangle_2)} \;\Big[$$

$$\textbf{not mode } \text{``}=\text{''}(\text{``}-\text{''}, \text{``}-\text{''})$$

If a nonvariable argument for a literal remains, that argument is a function (or structure, in Prolog terminology). It represents a data structure in the logic-based specification. We normalize such literals further by lifting functions out of the literals, and again passing the values into the literal by unification with a newly introduced variable. (Note that although this transformation logically belongs to equality-introduction, it must be performed during decomposition, since the treatment of lists may introduce further literals.) No additional mode-information is available about such functions.

Rule-15 (Decomposition)

$$\frac{\ldots \wedge \langle\text{pred}\rangle(\ldots, \langle\text{func}\rangle(\ldots), \ldots) \wedge \ldots}{\ldots \wedge \langle\text{var}\rangle = \langle\text{func}\rangle(\ldots) \wedge \langle\text{pred}\rangle(\ldots, \langle\text{var}\rangle, \ldots) \wedge \ldots} \;\Big[\; \langle\text{var}\rangle \textsf{ is a new variable}$$

If the argument to such a function (data structure) is a variable and occurs elsewhere in the clause, the value of that variable is communicated between the literals in which it occurs. We introduce an artificial literal maintaining this relationship during mode analysis. The added literal serves only to preserve information about that mode relationship and will be removed before code generation.

Rule-16 (Decomposition)

$\ldots \wedge \langle\text{pred}\rangle(\ldots, \langle\text{var}\rangle_2, \ldots) \wedge \ldots \langle\text{var}\rangle_2 = \langle\text{func}\rangle(\ldots, \langle\text{var}\rangle_1, \ldots) \wedge \ldots$

$\ldots \wedge \langle\text{pred}\rangle(\ldots, \langle\text{var}\rangle_2, \ldots) \wedge \ldots \langle\text{var}\rangle_2 = \langle\text{func}\rangle(\ldots, \langle\text{var}\rangle_1, \ldots) \wedge$
$\quad$ "$\langle\text{func}\rangle$"$(\langle\text{func}\rangle(\ldots, \langle\text{var}\rangle_1, \ldots), \langle\text{var}\rangle_2) \wedge \ldots$

not mode "$\langle\text{func}\rangle$("+", "+")"

not mode "$\langle\text{func}\rangle$("−", "−")"

Similar rules can be designed for functions more deeply nested.

If a clause is asserted and called only within another clause, we can then delete the assertion after applying the most general unifier θ between the arguments of the predicate $\langle\text{pred}\rangle_2$ within the assertion, and the arguments of the predicate $\langle\text{pred}\rangle_2$ outside the assertion.

Rule-17 (Decomposition)

$\langle\text{pred}\rangle_1(\ldots) \leftarrow$
$\quad \ldots \wedge$ assert$(\langle\text{pred}\rangle_2(\langle\text{trm}\rangle_{2_1} \wedge \ldots \wedge \langle\text{trm}\rangle_{2_n})) \wedge \ldots$
$\quad \wedge\, \langle\text{pred}\rangle_2(\langle\text{trm}\rangle_{1_1}, \ldots, \langle\text{trm}\rangle_{1_n}) \wedge \ldots$

--- [θ is a most general unifier between $\langle\text{trm}\rangle_{2_1}, \ldots, \langle\text{trm}\rangle_{2_n}$ and $\langle\text{trm}\rangle_{1_1}, \ldots, \langle\text{trm}\rangle_{1_n}$]

$(\langle\text{pred}\rangle_1(\ldots) \leftarrow \ldots)\theta$

The following rule constructs the compound goals in a query. It reflects exactly the meaning of the 'and' construct. As a result of applying this rule, we can also assume both conjuncts are ground.

Rule-18 (Decomposition)

$\langle\text{lit}\rangle_1 \wedge \langle\text{lit}\rangle_2$

$\langle\text{lit}\rangle_1, \langle\text{lit}\rangle_2$

mode "+" $\wedge$ "+"

A consequence of don't-care nondeterminism is that no binding of variables occurs before successful evaluation of the precondition. Therefore, no output can be generated from variables occurring in the precondition, and we may safely assume all variables occurring in a precondition and the clause head are ground, as expressed in the following rule.

Rule-19 (Decomposition)

$$\frac{\langle\text{pred}\rangle_1(\ldots,\langle\text{trm}\rangle,\ldots) \leftarrow \ldots \wedge \langle\text{pred}\rangle_2(\ldots,\langle\text{trm}\rangle,\ldots) \wedge \ldots \mid \ldots}{\textbf{mode}\ \langle\text{pred}\rangle_2(\ldots,\text{``+''},\ldots)}$$

Many other built-in predicates may occur in a logic-based specification. Again, mode information is implicit and can be used to eliminate redundant mode combinations during flow analysis. Built-in predicates include:

- File Handling
- Procedure Augmentation
- Clause Handling
- Term Modification
- Built-in temporal and communication predicates

The mode information carried by these is straightforward.

Whenever the predicates discussed here occur in a logic-based specification, we first restrict the possible mode combinations to a set which meets the mode requirements of these built-in predicates and then build procedures in a target language which realize the semantic meanings of these predicates.

Example 8.3 (Continued.) After decomposition we have

$$\mathsf{top}(X, Y, A_1) \leftarrow \mathsf{factor}(X, Y) \wedge =(Y, N) \wedge \text{``}\mathsf{print}\text{''}(N, A_N) \wedge =(A_N, A_1) \qquad \text{by Rule-16,Rule-14}$$

$$\mathsf{factor}(A_1, Y_7) \leftarrow \mathsf{head}(A_1, '(') \wedge \mathsf{tail}(A_1, X_7) \wedge \mathsf{head}(A_2, ')') \wedge \mathsf{tail}(A_2, Z_7) \wedge \mathsf{exp}(X_7, A_2) \wedge \mathsf{primary}(Z_7, Y_7) \qquad \text{by Rule-8}$$

$$\mathsf{primary}(A_1, Y_{11}) \leftarrow \mathsf{listcnstr}('*', A_{'*'}) \wedge \mathsf{append}(A_{'*'}, X_{11}, A_1) \wedge \mathsf{primary}(X_{11}, Y_{11}) \qquad \text{by Rule-7}$$

$$\mathsf{primary}(A_1, A_2) \leftarrow =(A_1, X_{12}) \wedge =(A_2, Y_{12}) \wedge =(A_1, A_2) \qquad \text{by Rule-14}$$

Note that in clause (2) we chose to decompose the list structure into head/tail pairs, while in clause (3) it was decomposed into listcnstr/append. The alternative mode combinations can be used to derive other possible data dependencies and as a consequence, different execution sequences.

8.2.4 Simplification

Simplification is the removal of redundancy from a specification. Redundancy in a logic-based specification derives from two sources. Either it already existed in the original specification or it may have been introduced by the canonicalizing transformations steps described above. To eliminate redundancy, we rely on

- *Folding* — Merges a clause body with another clause in the specification.
- *Clause pruning* — Eliminates clauses either unreachable or implied by some other clause in the specification.
- *Partial evaluation* — Symbolically computes the result of calls to literals in a clause body.

Definition 8.1 (Folding literals) *Let the following be clauses in a logic-based specification.*

$$\mathsf{p}(Arg_1, \ldots, Arg_i) \leftarrow \mathsf{Q}_{1_1} \wedge \ldots \wedge \mathsf{Q}_{1_n}$$
$$\mathsf{u}(Arg_1, \ldots, Arg_j) \leftarrow \mathsf{Q}_{2_1} \wedge \ldots \wedge \mathsf{Q}_{2_m}$$

If there is a substitution θ, such that $\forall s \in \{1, \ldots, m\} \cdot \mathsf{Q}_{2_s}\theta = \mathsf{B}_s$, where $\mathsf{B}_s \in \{\mathsf{Q}_{1_1}, \ldots, \mathsf{Q}_{1_n}\}$ and no other clauses the heads of which can unify with $\mathsf{u}(Arg_1, \ldots, Arg_j)$ exist in the specification, then the folding of $\mathsf{p}(\ldots)$ is

$$\mathsf{p}(Arg_1, \ldots, Arg_i) \leftarrow \mathsf{C}_{1_1} \wedge \ldots \wedge \mathsf{C}_{1_{n\text{-}m}} \wedge \mathsf{u}(Arg_1, \ldots, Arg_j)\theta$$

where for all t, such that $1 \le t \le n - m$, $\mathsf{C}_{1_t} \in (\{\mathsf{Q}_{1_1}, \ldots, \mathsf{Q}_{1_n}\} - \{\mathsf{B}_1, \ldots, \mathsf{B}_m\})$

The condition on folding, which states that the specification may not contain other clauses the heads of which can unify with the literal to be folded, preserves correctness. Ignoring this condition might lead us astray, due to the presence of other clauses defining the predicate u. We may also encounter the situation where two different clauses have unifiable (or identical) bodies but have different clause heads. This situation is legal, since it is possible that two such clauses might mean different things. In such a situation, we assume the two clauses carry different meanings and the software developers are responsible to differentiate them.

Example 8.4 Consider the following two clauses.

$$\mathsf{p}(A, B, C, L) \leftarrow \mathsf{q}(A, B, D) \wedge \mathsf{r}(B, C, F) \wedge B > F \wedge \mathsf{s}(D, C, L) \tag{8.5}$$
$$\mathsf{u}(X, Y, Z, W) \leftarrow X > T \wedge \mathsf{s}(Z, Y, W) \wedge \mathsf{r}(X, Y, T) \tag{8.6}$$

then the substitution, $\theta = \{^X/_B, {}^Y/_C, {}^Z/_D, {}^T/_F, {}^W/_L\}$ results in the body of (6) being contained in the body of (5). Thus, we can fold for (5) and obtain

$$\mathsf{p}(A, B, C, L) \leftarrow \mathsf{q}(A, B, D) \wedge \mathsf{u}(B, C, D, L)$$

Clause pruning is designed to eliminate any clause which is either implied by some other clause(s) or unreachable from any other clause. A clause is not reachable when it cannot be invoked by any other clause or by a query. During clause pruning, we again consider only the logical meanings of clauses and ignore possible side-effects they may have on input/output or the database. So, even if two clauses may have different results considering their input/output or modification on a logic database, if they meet the following criteria, one of them can be considered as redundant and be eliminated.

Determining whether a clause is not reachable from any other clause is straightforward. We can scan through clauses and check if any clause contains a literal unifiable with a clause suspected to be unreachable. To determine whether a clause is implied by some other clause(s) is arbitrarily hard.

Definition 8.2 (Clause Pruning) *Given two clauses of a specification*

$$\mathsf{p}(Arg_1, \ldots, Arg_i) \leftarrow \mathsf{Q}_{1_1} \wedge \ldots \wedge \mathsf{Q}_{1_n}$$
$$\mathsf{p}(Arg_1, \ldots, Arg_j) \leftarrow \mathsf{Q}_{2_1} \wedge \ldots \wedge \mathsf{Q}_{2_m}$$

if we can find a nonground substitution, θ, such that

$$\forall s \in \{1, \ldots, m\} \cdot \mathsf{Q}_{2_s}\theta \in \{\mathsf{Q}_{1_1}, \ldots, \mathsf{Q}_{1_n}\}$$

then we say that the former clause is implied *by the latter.*

Rule-20 (Simplification)

$$\frac{\ldots \langle \text{clause} \rangle_i \ldots \langle \text{clause} \rangle_j \ldots}{\ldots \langle \text{clause} \rangle_j \ldots} \left[\text{clause } \langle \text{clause} \rangle_i \text{ is implied by } \langle \text{clause} \rangle_j \right.$$

If a clause is implied by another clause in the specification, then the implied clause can be eliminated from the specification.

Clause pruning also occurs within a clause body and eliminates a literal involved in a unification, if one of the parameters is not used elsewhere within the same clause.

Rule-21 (Simplification)

$$\frac{\langle \text{pred} \rangle(\ldots) \leftarrow \ldots \wedge \langle \text{Var} \rangle_i = \langle \text{Var} \rangle_j \wedge \ldots}{\langle \text{pred} \rangle(\ldots) \leftarrow \ldots \wedge \ldots} \left[\text{no other literal contains } \langle \text{Var} \rangle_i \right.$$

Example 8.5 Consider the following set of clauses, to illustrate simplification within a clause body.

$$\mathsf{p}(X_1, Y_1, Z_1) \leftarrow X_1 = [\,] \wedge Y_1 = C \wedge Z_1 = [\,]$$
$$\mathsf{p}(X_2, Y_2, Z_2) \leftarrow \mathsf{q}(X_2, Y_2) \wedge \mathsf{s}(Y_2, Z_2) \wedge \mathsf{t}(Z_2, 3)$$
$$\mathsf{p}(X_3, Y_3, Z_3) \leftarrow \mathsf{q}(X_3, Y_3) \wedge \mathsf{s}(Y_3, Z_3)$$

We apply simplification and elimination to the above clauses, and obtain

$$\mathsf{p}(X_1, Y_1, Z_1) \leftarrow X_1 = [\,] \wedge Z_1 = [\,]$$
$$\mathsf{p}(X_3, Y_3, Z_3) \leftarrow \mathsf{q}(X_3, Y_3) \wedge \mathsf{s}(Y_3, Z_3)$$

after applying variable substitution $\{{}^{X_3}/_{X_2}, {}^{Y_3}/_{Y_2}, {}^{Z_3}/_{Z_2}\}$.

Partial evaluation is applied to literals in a clause to simplify the representation, especially when all arguments of these literals are ground. In this chapter, we consider only partial evaluation of literals with all arguments ground and of fact clauses.

The following example demonstrates partial evaluation of a testing literal.

Example 8.6 Given the following clauses,

$$\mathsf{p}(X, Y) \leftarrow 10 < 9 \wedge Y = 4 \tag{8.7}$$
$$\mathsf{p}(X, Y) \leftarrow 10 >= 9 \wedge Y = 16 \tag{8.8}$$

If we evaluate the first literal (a testing condition), we realize that clause (7) is always false. Therefore, we apply clause pruning to eliminate (7). For clause (8), partial evaluation of the first literal shows it to be always true, and therefore, redundant. We change (8) to

$$\mathsf{p}(X, Y) \leftarrow Y = 16$$

As far as partial evaluation of fact clauses is concerned, we do not presuppose that a data base is available to bind with rule clauses (procedures) to achieve partial evaluation of rule clauses. However, there are situations when a set of clauses contains "predefined" fact clauses which may represent a constant or known fact in the problem domain. In situations like these, we apply fact propagation to bind the facts with the literals which invoke the fact clauses.

A fact clause is a clause without a body and possessing only ground arguments. There may exist multiple fact clauses for the same predicate with different arguments. This raises the issue of when, and how, facts should be propagated. Considering that fact propagation multiplies the number of clauses invoking the fact clause, for a specification with a large number of fact clauses many partially evaluated clauses with identical clause heads will be generated. This results in loss of design information exhibited by the original clause structure. We need to restrict fact propagation to a small number of fact clauses. The choice of how many fact clauses will be used for fact propagation depends on the implementation of the rule base.

Definition 8.3 (Fact propagation) *Let a logic-based specification contain the following clauses*

$$\mathsf{p}(Arg_1, \ldots, Arg_n) \leftarrow \mathsf{Q}_{1_1} \wedge \ldots \wedge \mathsf{Q}_{1_n}$$
$$\mathsf{u}(\mathsf{c}_1, \ldots, \mathsf{c}_m) \leftarrow$$

where $\mathsf{c}_1, \ldots, \mathsf{c}_m$ *are constants. If there exists a most general unifier* θ*, such that*

$$\mathsf{Q}_{1_k}\theta = \mathsf{u}(\mathsf{c}_1, \ldots, \mathsf{c}_m)\theta$$

then the unfolding of the former clause is

$$\mathsf{p}(Arg_1, \ldots, Arg_n) \leftarrow (\mathsf{Q}_{1_1} \wedge \ldots \wedge \mathsf{Q}_{1_{k-1}} \wedge \mathsf{Q}_{1_{k+1}} \wedge \ldots \wedge \mathsf{Q}_{1_n})\theta$$

Rule-22 (Simplification)

$\langle\text{pred}\rangle_1(\ldots) \leftarrow \ldots \wedge \langle\text{pred}\rangle_2(\langle\text{trm}\rangle_{1_1} \wedge \ldots \wedge \langle\text{trm}\rangle_{1_n}) \wedge \ldots$

there is a clause $\langle\text{pred}\rangle_2(\langle\text{trm}\rangle_{2_1} \wedge \ldots \wedge \langle\text{trm}\rangle_{2_n}) \leftarrow \wedge$
there is no other clause with head $\langle\text{pred}\rangle_2 \wedge$
θ is a most general unifier between
$\langle\text{trm}\rangle_{1_1}, \ldots, \langle\text{trm}\rangle_{1_n}$ and $\langle\text{trm}\rangle_{2_1}, \ldots, \langle\text{trm}\rangle_{2_n} \wedge$
$\langle\text{trm}\rangle_{1_1}, \ldots, \langle\text{trm}\rangle_{1_n}$ are ground

$\langle\text{pred}\rangle_1(\ldots) \leftarrow (\ldots \wedge \ \ldots)\theta$

Above rule eliminates literals from a clause body which are true by fact propagation.

Example 8.7 Given the following clauses,

$$\mathsf{p}(X, Y, Z) \leftarrow \mathsf{q}(X, W) \wedge \mathsf{s}(W, Y) \wedge Z \textbf{ is } Y + 10$$
$$\mathsf{q}(U, V) \leftarrow U = 2 \wedge V = 10$$
$$\mathsf{s}(U, V) \leftarrow U = 10 \wedge V = 4$$

we apply fact propagation and get

$$\mathsf{p}(X, Y, Z) \leftarrow X = 2 \wedge Y = 4 \wedge Z \textbf{ is } Y + 10$$

We then apply partial evaluation within the clause to obtain

$$\mathsf{p}(X, Y, Z) \leftarrow X = 2 \wedge Y = 4 \wedge Z = 14$$

We continue the original example. Again, various rules can be used to simplify the program obtained at the current stage.

Example 8.8 (Continued.) The final result of applying canonicalizing transformations to the example specification is as follows (clause (12) is obtained by applying Rule-21).

$$\mathsf{top}(X, Y, A_1) \leftarrow \mathsf{factor}(X, Y) \wedge =(Y, N) \wedge \text{“print”}(N, A_N) \wedge =(A_N, A_1) \tag{8.9}$$

$$\mathsf{factor}(A_1, Y_7) \leftarrow \mathsf{head}(A_1, '(') \wedge \mathsf{tail}(A_1, X_7) \wedge \mathsf{head}(A_2, ')') \wedge \mathsf{tail}(A_2, Z_7) \wedge \mathsf{exp}(X_7, A_2) \wedge \mathsf{primary}(Z_7, Y_7) \tag{8.10}$$

$$\mathsf{primary}(A_1, Y_{11}) \leftarrow \mathsf{listcnstr}('*', A_{'*'}) \wedge \mathsf{append}(A_{'*'}, X_{11}, A_1) \wedge \mathsf{primary}(X_{11}, Y_{11}) \tag{8.11}$$

$$\mathsf{primary}(A_1, A_2) \leftarrow =(A_1, A_2) \tag{8.12}$$

8.3 Data Dependency and Control Flow Analysis

As indicated earlier, one of the main features of logic-based specification languages is that the same clause may be used to perform computations in several directions. The arguments of a clause may serve both as sources of input for the computation described by the clause, and as the location of output for the same computation. No standard procedural programming language provides such a feature. Therefore, to transform a logic-based specification into procedural form, we must first eliminate any multi-directionality present in the clauses of a logic-based specification. We need to analyze the specification to deduce information regarding the flow of data and the data dependency between the clauses of a specification. Using that information, we obtain the execution sequence for a given specification.

Traditionally, data flow and data dependency analyses have been investigated within the framework of logic programming. One approach in dealing with the multi-directionality of a logic program has been to provide mode information for each clause (e.g., in PARLOG, Concurrent Prolog, or Strand88). Bruynooghe [47] and Smolka [299] have investigated the issue of verifying the consistency of mode declarations for arguments to predicates, as supplied by programmers. Automatic mode inference has been discussed by Mellish [218] and Reddy [263], and more recently by Bruynooghe [48] and Mannila and Ukkonen [214]. The most promising approach to mode inference to date has been presented by Debray in [79, 80]. Debray uses an interpreter to reason over the four-valued lattice of modes *don't know, empty, free*, and *ground.* Its purpose is to enable a compiler to optimize a logic program. Mannila and Ukkonen [214] limit themselves to the simple modes *ground* and *unground.* Reddy relies on syntactic analysis to assign modes to predicates.

The approach presented in this section, similar to Debray and Warren's, relies on reasoning over a lattice of mode values. However, we do not rely on symbolic execution by an interpreter to obtain mode information. Instead, we present an analytical approach using a matrix of mode information built up by an interaction of algorithms and transformation rules.

8.3.1 Matrix-based Data Flow and Dependency Analysis Algorithm

In this section, we present a novel approach to mode inference relying on a matrix representation of clauses to perform data flow and dependency analysis and to generate the corresponding execution sequence. We reason over the four-valued lattice of the following mode values:

- don't know, both ("?")
- input mode ("+")
- output mode ("−")
- empty (" ")

Input mode corresponds to a predicate being ground, while an unground predicate is considered to have output mode.

For each clause in the specification, we construct a two-dimensional matrix, with the literals in the clause along one dimension, and the variables of the clause along the other. This matrix is filled in with mode values by applying algorithms and constraining rules.

Initially arguments of literals are marked as don't know ("?"), since mode information about the parameters in a predicate is not available. Arguments that do not occur in a corresponding literal are marked with " ". The next step is to collect and apply all known mode constraints of literals (user-defined predicates and built-in operators) within this clause.

The mode values of the arguments for literals in a clause body follow the normal definition of data flow: input is marked with "+" and output with "−". In other words, an argument which generates data (exports a value for the argument) is said to have output mode and an argument which consumes data (needs a value to bind to) is said to have input mode. Data is viewed as flowing into the predicate across its "boundary."

The mode convention for the arguments of a predicate in a clause head should be opposite that of the arguments of predicates in the clause body. This is because a clause head has a dual role: It unifies with the calling (invoking) literal (and thus passes data between the calling literal and the clause) and it communicates data to and from the clause body through variables sharing the same name. We can interpret the communication of data to a clause in two steps: First the calling literal is unified with the clause head of the invoked rule clause; second, data is passed between the head of the clause and the literals forming the clause body. The modes for the arguments of a clause head are normally viewed according to the former. However, when performing the analysis of a particular clause, we look at the clause as a unit, and therefore consider the modes for the arguments of the clause head from the latter point of view. Fig.8.2 gives an example of the two-staged process of data communication.

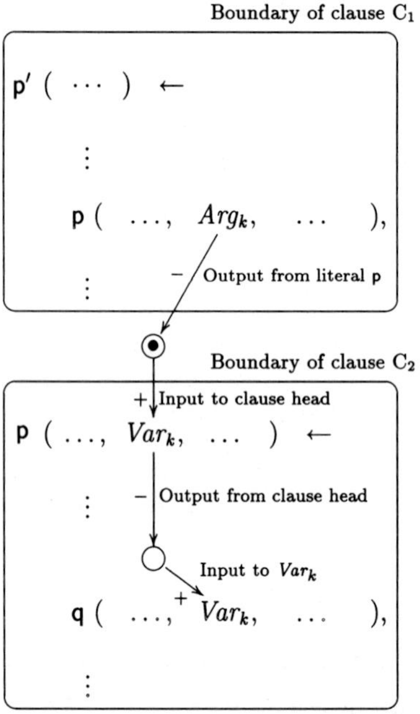

Figure 8.2. An illustration of data transformation by a clause head literal.

If a clause C_2 with clause head $\mathsf{p}(\ldots, \mathit{Var}_k, \ldots)$ is called within the body of clause C_1, the calling literal in C_1 may provide data to clause C_2 by way of unification of the argument Var_k of the head of C_2 against the parameter Arg_k of the call to p within clause C_1. In that case, the mode of Arg_k in C_1 is output, whereas Var_k in the head of C_2 has mode input, for the balance of flow to be preserved. However, aside from receiving data from Arg_k in C_1, the variable Var_k in the head of clause C_2 also provides data to the predicates in the body of C_2 that share this variable. Since mode analysis is performed within the boundaries of a clause, the mode conventions for the clause head have to match those of the clause body. Therefore, "+" ("−") in the clause head has the opposite meaning in the clause body, and vice versa. The same holds true for data flow communicated from the head of clause C_2 to the calling literal in C_1.

We then apply the data dependency and flow analysis algorithm below to the mode matrix of each clause; applications of the algorithm are interleaved with applications of the constraining rules. This gradually builds up the mode information for the clause under consideration. If we restrict our attention to argument positions in a literal, we can refer to literals as "producers" and "consumers." If a literal "consumes" the value of a variable generated by other literals, we call this literal a "consumer." If a literal "produces" (binds) the value of an ungrounded variable, we call this literal a "producer." The following algorithm is based on two assumptions:

- *Unique-Producer Assumption* — Any argument, other than a constant, with a mode of "+" demands exactly one producer for the value that it consumes.
- *Existence-of-Consumers Assumption* — A producer of a value (with the exception of dead-end values generated but not used by any other literal in the clause) has at least one consumer.

The algorithm below calculates the mode matrix for a given clause. The matrix initially contains only " " and "?" in its cells, except for built-in predicates and predicates for which information is already available from previous runs of the algorithm on other clauses. The algorithm is exhibited in two parts: initialization of the matrix (Alg.8.1) and dynamic analysis (Alg.8.2). In the following, let **Lit** be the sequence formed from the multi-set of the literals mentioned in a clause (note that a literal could occur more than once in the sequence), let **Arg** be the sequence constructed from the set of arguments occurring in the clause.

Algorithm 8.1 (Data dependency and flow analysis)

```
types MM: Lit × Arg → {"+", "−", "?", " "}
for each literal l ∈ Lit
        if ∃! v ∈ Arg · v is not a constant
        then MM_{l,v} ← "−"
for each argument v ∈ Arg
        if v is a constant
        then for each l ∈ Lit ∧ MM_{l,v} = "?"
                  MM_{l,v} ← "+"
        if v is a predicate
        then if all of v's arguments depend on constants
                then for each l ∈ Lit ∧ MM_{l,v} = "?"
                          MM_{l,v} ← "+"
```

The main section of the data dependency and flow analysis algorithm (Alg.8.2) deduces mode information based on the mode information obtained in the preparatory step.

The algorithm continues to consider literals to determine if the mode status in the cell provides additional mode information. The algorithm examines the mode matrix in two directions: In the horizontal direction the analysis is based on mode constraints on the arguments of a single literal, which may also be a built-in or user-defined

Algorithm 8.2 (Data dependency and flow analysis, continued)

for each literal $l \in$ Lit
    call rule-based flow analysis
    if $\exists v \in$ Arg $\cdot$ $\mathsf{MM}_{l,v}$ = "−"
    then for each $l' \in Lit \wedge \mathsf{MM}_{l',v}$ = "?"
        $\mathsf{MM}_{l',v} \leftarrow$ "+"
    if l is the clause head $\wedge \exists l' \cdot$
            l' is a matching recursively called literal
    then for each $v \in$ Arg
        $v' \leftarrow$ argument in l' corresponding to v
        if $\mathsf{MM}_{l,v} \neq$ opposite of $\mathsf{MM}_{l',v'}$
        then fail
        if $\mathsf{MM}_{l,v}$ = "?"
        then $\mathsf{MM}_{l,v} \leftarrow$ opposite of $\mathsf{MM}_{l',v'}$
        if $\mathsf{MM}_{l',v'}$ = "?"
        then $\mathsf{MM}_{l',v'} \leftarrow$ opposite of $\mathsf{MM}_{l,v}$
    if l = "=" $\wedge \exists v \in$ Arg $\cdot$ $\mathsf{MM}_{l,v}$ = "−"
    then for each $v' \in$ Arg $\wedge v' \neq v$
        $\mathsf{MM}_{l,v'} \leftarrow$ "+"
    if modes for literal l are ruled out by constraints
    then fail

predicate. In the vertical direction, the analysis is based on the two above-mentioned assumptions. The algorithm also handles cases where a recursive literal occurs in the clause body. In such cases, we have to adjust the mode assignments based on the opposing sign conventions for predicates in clause head and body. Lastly, the algorithm checks whether any of the mode assignments violates mode constraints such as those given by the users or derived by Rule-13 and Rule-14. By elimination of choices due to the constraints on mode assignments determinate mode information can be derived. For example, in a unification, if one of the arguments receives a value during execution, then the other argument must provide this value. The algorithm exploits the constraint that a unification cannot have both arguments unground.

Several optimizations are possible to the above algorithm. Particularly, by differentiating literals without determined mode information into those that have already been examined but their mode could not be determined and those which have yet to be analyzed, we can avoid unnecessarily reevaluating the same literal over and over.

In addition to the operations given by the algorithm, the following rules derive further mode constraints and lead to adjustment of modes within a single column or row of the mode matrix. Several rules eliminate mode status "?" from the matrix.

Rule-23 (FlowAnalysis)

$$\frac{\mathsf{MM}_{l,v} = \text{“?”}}{\mathsf{MM}_{l,v} = \text{“}-\text{”}} \left[\ \forall l' \neq l \cdot \mathsf{MM}_{l',v} = \text{“+”}\right.$$

This rule is based on the existence-of-consumers assumption. Further mode information to trim "?" could consist of mode declarations provided by the users, or modes ruled out by mode constraints given by the users, as in the following example:

Example 8.9 Consider the predicate

$\mathsf{append}(X, Y, Z) \leftarrow \ldots$

The mode combination

$\mathsf{append}(\text{“+”}, \text{“}-\text{”}, \text{“}-\text{”})$

and

$\mathsf{append}(\text{“}-\text{”}, \text{“+”}, \text{“}-\text{”})$

are impossible when considering the procedural meanings implied by these clauses. They are generating infinite sequences of lists.[4] By eliminating them from the mode analysis, we generate a more accurate mode status. This applies to append as a user predicate, rather than append as obtained from the decomposition of a list construct, since the latter has a determined mode assignment.

The users can aid the mode analysis process by explicitly describing mode constraints among the arguments of a user-defined predicate. Alternatively, when the operation of the transformed program does not meet the users' requirements, the users can force a selection among the multiple procedural interpretations generated due to several possible mode combinations.

Further rules constituting mode constraints are:

Rule-24 (Flow-Analysis)

$$\frac{\mathsf{MM}_{l,v} = \text{“}-\text{”}}{\mathsf{fail}} \left[\ \mathsf{MM}_{l',v} = \text{“}-\text{”} \wedge l \neq l'\right.$$

According to the unique-producer assumption, any mode information that includes more than one literal marked "–" for the same variable can be discarded. Thus, this rule terminates a particular search branch during flow analysis. The following rule

[4]Such generators for infinite data structures are useful for programming paradigms based on lazy evaluation, but are ruled out for FRORL specifications.

eliminates mode assignments which do not provide for at least one producer for the value of a variable, again violating the unique-producer assumption.

Rule-25 (Flow-Analysis)

$$\frac{\mathsf{MM}_{l,v} = \text{“+”}}{\mathsf{fail}} \left[\, v \text{ is not a constant} \wedge \forall l' \in \mathsf{Lit} \cdot \mathsf{MM}_{l',v} = \text{“+”} \right.$$

If all but one cell in a column of the matrix are assigned input mode or if there is only one cell in a column (in which case the condition of the rule is vacuously satisfied), the unique-producer assumption allows us to infer the mode for the remaining cell to be output mode:

Rule-26 (Flow-Analysis)

$$\frac{\mathsf{MM}_{l,v} = \text{“?”}}{\mathsf{MM}_{l,v} = \text{“−”}} \left[\, \forall l' \in \mathsf{Lit}, l' \neq l \cdot \mathsf{MM}_{l',v} = \text{“+”} \right.$$

As pointed out earlier, there several ways of decomposing the list constructs of a specification. An erroneous choice leads to inconsistent mode assignments, i.e., choices for modes which violate either mode constraints or the two above-mentioned assumptions. The algorithm and several rules check for such violations. An inconsistency in the mode assignment requires us to backtrack and find a different assignment. Backtracking will return us to the point in the canonicalization phase where we selected a decomposition for the list constructs in the clause. If no consistent mode assignment could be found, an alternative list decomposition must be chosen then.

In contrast to the data dependency and flow analysis technique presented here, Debray and Warren's approach lacks the ability to handle multiple-mode combinations. Therefore, the modes for the arguments of a predicate are found by taking the least upper bound of all possible success patterns generated by all possible calling patterns. Our approach explicitly considers the possibility of multiple modes and is flexible enough to determine all possible mode combinations. For Debray and Warren, a logic program always has a single mode assignment, whereas on our approach differing data dependencies and execution sequences are permitted (and therefore, different target programs may be generated).

Example 8.10 (Continued.) Ex. 8.8 left off after the canonicalizing transformations. We are ready to enter flow analysis.

Initially (Fig.8.3) there is hardly any information available for clause (9). Most entries contain no mode information and are therefore marked “?”. This mode status may change due to more specific mode information found at a later stage. We assume the mode for the function print(...) is known to be ground on its first, but unground on its second argument. (In the following figures exhibiting data dependency matrices,

$$
\begin{array}{ccccc}
 & X & Y & A_1 & N & A_N \\
\text{top} & \text{``?''} & \text{``?''} & \text{``?''} & & \\
\text{factor} & \text{``?''} & \text{``?''} & & & \\
\text{``}=\text{''} & & & \text{``+''} \longleftarrow & & \text{``\_''} \\
\text{``print''} & & & \text{\textcircled{``+''}} & \text{\textcircled{``\_''}} & \\
\text{``}=\text{''} & & & \text{``?''} & & \text{``+''} \\
\end{array}
$$

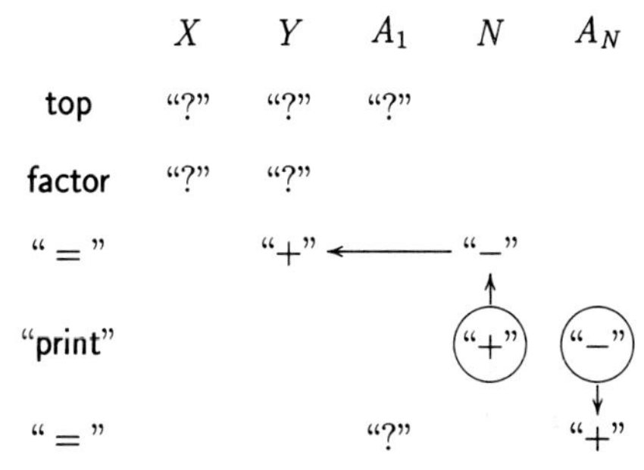

Figure 8.3. Partial matrix for clause (9).

we mark entries resulting from either the data flow analysis on other clauses or from Alg.8.1 by circling them.

Fig.8.4 shows the data dependency matrix obtained for clause (10). The chosen decomposition for the list constructs of the FRORL specification allows us to eliminate from consideration the situation in which argument A_1 of (10) has mode "+". This

$$
\begin{array}{cccccccc}
 & A_1 & Y_1 & \text{'('} & X_1 & A_2 & \text{')'} & Z_1 \\
\text{factor} & \text{``\_''} \leftarrow \text{``?''} & & & & & & \\
\text{head} & \text{\textcircled{``+''}} & & & \text{\textcircled{``\_''}} & & & \\
\text{tail} & \text{\textcircled{``+''}} & & & \text{\textcircled{``\_''}} & & & \\
\text{head} & & & & & \text{\textcircled{``+''}} & \text{\textcircled{``\_''}} & \\
\text{tail} & & & & & \text{\textcircled{``+''}} & & \text{\textcircled{``\_''}} \\
\text{exp} & & & & \text{``+''} & \text{``\_''} & & \\
\text{primary} & & \text{``?''} & & & & & \text{``+''} \\
\end{array}
$$

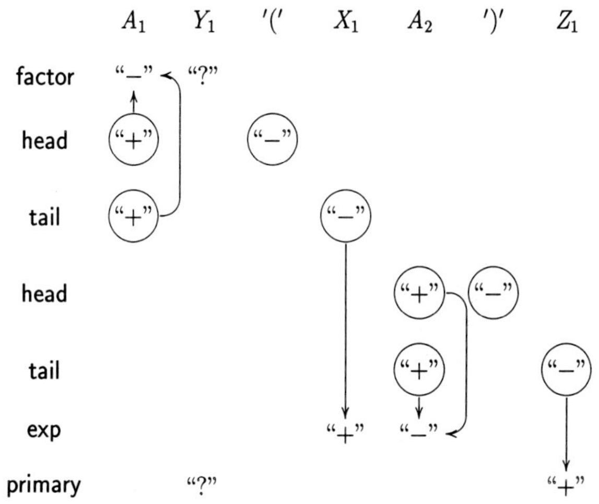

Figure 8.4. Partial matrix for clause (10).

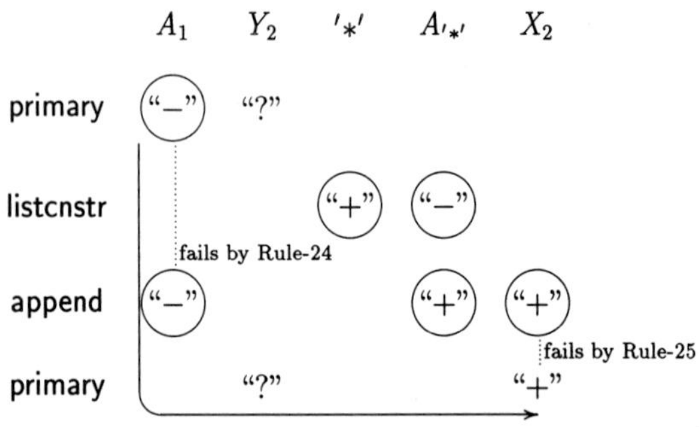

Figure 8.5. Inconsistent matrix for clause (11).

alone does not completely determine the mode information for clause (10).

We, therefore, use the partial mode information for clause (11) obtained so far and begin to build the matrix for that clause. Again, the chosen decomposition for the list constructs determines some of the entries. The bottom entry in the column for X_{11} is given by algorithm Alg.8.2. However, both Rule-24 and Rule-25 detect that the resulting partial matrix for (11) shown in Fig.8.5 is inconsistent according to the unique-producer assumption. The selection of this particular decomposition for the list construct in clause (10) does not prejudice mode analysis. Upon failing to find a consistent mode assignment, we backtrack to the decomposition phase of canonicalization and choose an alternative decomposition.[5] As a consequence, we must also change this clause to

$$\mathsf{factor}(A_1, Y_7) \leftarrow \mathsf{listcnstr}('(', A_{'('}) \wedge \mathsf{append}(A_{'('}, X_7, A_1) \wedge \mathsf{listcnstr}(')', A_{')'}) \wedge \mathsf{append}(A_{')'}, Z_7, A_2) \wedge \mathsf{exp}(X_7, A_2) \wedge \mathsf{primary}(Z_7, Y_7) \quad (8.13)$$

Fig.8.6 shows an alternative decomposition choice and the partial mode assignments obtained. The matrix for (12) determines the calling modes for predicate primary (Fig.8.7). Note that the meaning of the equality predicate in this matrix is that of assignment. We use the obtained modes to build the matrix for clause (11) and finally, for clause (13).

[5] The decomposition of lists may also need to be changed if the users request other possible mode combinations, in which case we may have to explore all alternatives that can be generated by decomposing lists in different ways.

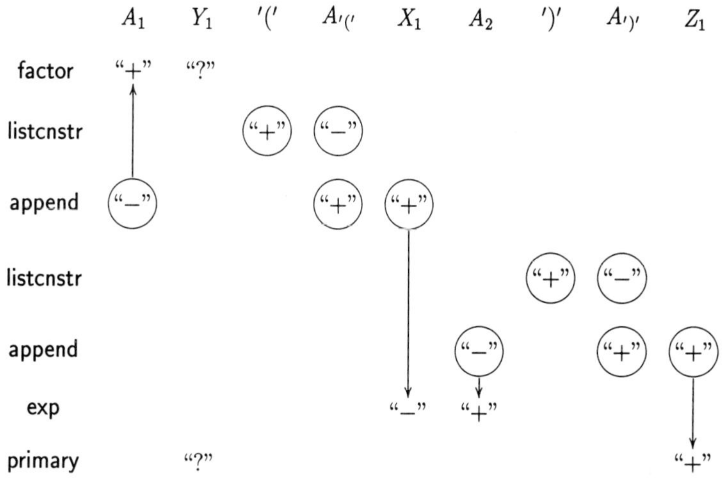

Figure 8.6. Partial matrix for clause (13).

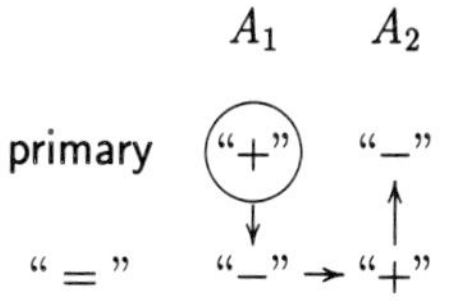

Figure 8.7. Final matrix for clause (12).

8.4 Determination of Execution Sequence

The operational semantics for logic-based specifications allows for variables to occur unbound in computations. These unbound (logical) variables will receive a value at some point during the computation. The value will be passed through unification to all occurrences of the logical variable.

The results of data flow and dependency analysis can be used in determining the execution sequence for the literals of a clause in the specification. In an allowable execution sequence for a procedural program, variables are not used unless they are ground. Execution sequence determination reorders the literal in the clauses of the specification so that each literal is called only after all its input arguments have been

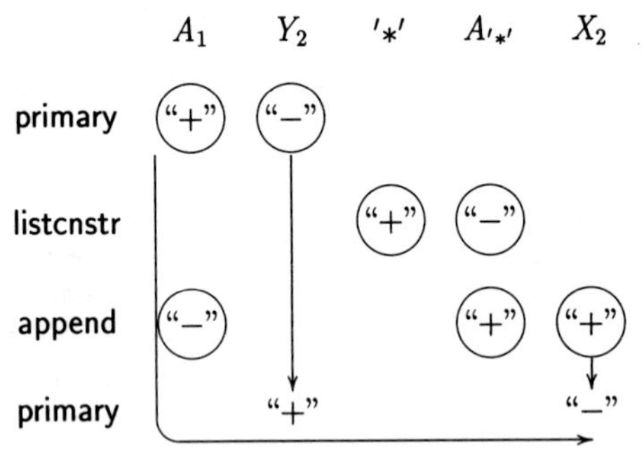

Figure 8.8. Final matrix for clause (11).

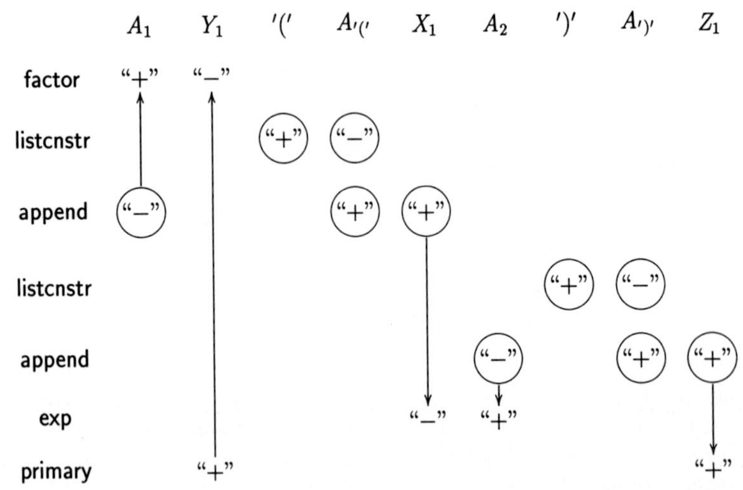

Figure 8.9. Final matrix for clause (13).

given a value. In the following, we present the algorithm for determining an execution sequence from the obtained mode matrix. The algorithm yields the execution sequence of the clause, adjusted from the procedural viewpoint (i.e., the algorithm generates an allowable execution sequence for the rule clause).

If the data flow and dependency matrix for a clause are completely determined, the algorithm selects the correct execution sequence. If there are still literals with mode "?" remaining in the matrix, several execution sequences may be possible. The algorithm will then select one such sequence, and provide for selection of alternative choices through backtracking, should the users disagree with the selected sequence. The literals with mode "?" remaining in the matrix are completely independent (with the exception of certain mode combinations being ruled out for a literal by mode constraints). Any interdependency of modes would have been discovered by the data flow and dependency analysis algorithm. We can, therefore, arbitrarily assign modes to these literals keeping in mind the constraints imposed by the unique-producer and existence-of-consumers assumptions. Because of the close relationship between the modes in the columns (due the two assumptions) and rows (due the constraints on arguments within a predicate), it is unlikely that many entries in the matrix remain undetermined.

Algorithm 8.3 (Execution Sequence)

types $args$: **list**
  $lits$: **sequence**
$l \leftarrow$ clause head
$lits \leftarrow \{l\}$
$v \leftarrow \iota\, v' \in \text{Arg} \cdot \text{MM}_{l,v'} = \text{"?"}$
$\text{MM}_{l,v} \leftarrow \text{"}-\text{"}$
for each $l' \in \text{Lit}$
  if $\text{MM}_{l',v} = \text{"?"}$
  then $\text{MM}_{l',v} \leftarrow \text{"+"}$
  for each $v' \in \text{Arg}$
    if $\text{MM}_{l,v} = \text{"}-\text{"}$
    then $args \leftarrow args \cup \{v'\}$

The main part of the algorithm examines each literal in a clause whether all its arguments with input modes are ground. If so, then the literal is "legal" for the next execution sequence. If the selected literal has arguments with undetermined modes, an arbitrary choice of mode assignments is made. (In the algorithm, the nondeterministic, arbitrary choice of an element from a domain is indicated by the function ι.) These mode assignments again constitute choice points for backtracking, should an alternative execution sequence be requested. Backtracking will also be initiated if a selection is made that violates known mode constraints.

Algorithm 8.4 (Execution Sequence, continued)

while there is a cell with mode "?" remaining
  for each $l \in \mathsf{Lit}$
    if modes for literal l are ruled out by constraints
    then fail
  $l \leftarrow \iota\, l' \in \mathsf{Lit} \cdot$
    l' is a constant $\vee\ \forall v \in \mathsf{Arg} \cdot \mathsf{MM}_{l',v} = \text{“+”} \ \Rightarrow\ v \in args$
  $lits \leftarrow lits + l$
  $v \leftarrow \iota\, v' \in \mathsf{Arg} \cdot \mathsf{MM}_{l,v'} = \text{“?”}$
  $\mathsf{MM}_{l,v} \leftarrow \text{“−”}$
  $args \leftarrow args \cup \{v\}$
  for each $l' \in \mathsf{Lit}$
    if $\mathsf{MM}_{l',v} = \text{“?”}$
    then $\mathsf{MM}_{l',v} \leftarrow \text{“+”}$
return *lits* /**lits* contains the correct execution sequence*/

Example 8.11 (Continued.) After applying the execution sequence determination algorithm to the running example and removing the literals introduced by Rule-16 we obtain the adjusted program as follows:

$$\mathsf{top}(X, Y, A_1) \leftarrow \mathsf{factor}(X, Y) \wedge {=}(Y, N) \wedge \text{“}\mathsf{print}\text{”}(N, A_N) \wedge {=}(A_N, A_1)$$

$$\mathsf{factor}(A_1, Y_7) \leftarrow \mathsf{listcnstr}('(', A_{'('}) \wedge \mathsf{listcnstr}(')', A_{')'}) \wedge \mathsf{primary}(Z_7, Y_7) \wedge \mathsf{append}(A_{')'}, Z_7, A_2) \wedge \mathsf{exp}(X_7, A_2) \wedge \mathsf{append}(A_{'('}, X_7, A_1)$$

$$\mathsf{primary}(A_1, Y_{11}) \leftarrow \mathsf{listcnstr}('*', A_{'*'}) \wedge \mathsf{primary}(X_{11}, Y_{11}) \wedge \mathsf{append}(A_{'*'}, X_{11}, A_1)$$

$$\mathsf{primary}(A_1, A_2) \leftarrow {=}(A_1, A_2) \qquad \text{by Rule-21}$$

After the final execution sequence is selected, several opportunities for optimization remain. For example, the meta-predicates var and nonvar are used to test for groundedness of literals. At this point, we completely determined the calling mode for every literal. We can, therefore, decide the truth-value of these predicates. If the predicate var is called with mode "+", this literal will fail, as will the clause that invoked it. If it is called with mode "−", var will evaluate to true and can be eliminated from the clause.

Rule-27 (Control-Analysis)

$$\frac{\ldots \wedge \mathsf{var}(\langle\text{lit}\rangle) \wedge \ldots}{\ldots \wedge \ldots} \left[\ \mathsf{mode}(\langle\text{lit}\rangle) = \text{“−”}\right.$$

Rule-28 (Control-Analysis)

$$\frac{\ldots \wedge \mathsf{var}(\langle \mathrm{lit} \rangle) \wedge \ldots}{\ldots \wedge \mathsf{fail} \wedge \ldots} \Big[\ \mathsf{mode}(\langle \mathrm{lit} \rangle) = \text{“+”}$$

The situation for **nonvar** is opposite. Furthermore, we can recognize a unification with both arguments having mode "+" as a testing condition, as expressed in the following rule:

Rule-29 (Control-Analysis)

$$\frac{\text{“=”}(\langle \mathrm{trm} \rangle_1, \langle \mathrm{trm} \rangle_2)}{\textbf{let}\ \text{“=”}(\langle \mathrm{trm} \rangle_1, \langle \mathrm{trm} \rangle_2)\ \mathsf{be\ a\ testing\ condition}} \Big[\ \mathsf{mode}(\langle \mathrm{trm} \rangle_1) = \text{“+”} \wedge \mathsf{mode}(\langle \mathrm{trm} \rangle_2) = \text{“+”}$$

8.5 Removal of Unnecessary Nondeterminacy

The meaning of a logic-based requirements specification is given in terms of the intersection of all models of the requirements specification (the declarative view). In Chapter 3, we showed how one can obtain this model by a fix-point construction. We have also shown that the declarative semantics corresponds to a procedural view: the procedural meaning of the requirements specification is the set of ground clauses that are instances of queries solved by an abstract interpreter.

The procedural view gives us a mechanism by which we can operationally interpret the requirements specification and subject it to verification. The abstract interpreter executing the specification is nondeterministic. At times more than one clause may be able to be chosen (the procedural semantics merely requires that the selection procedure be fair). The interpreter will simply choose one of the alternatives and attempt to construct a refutation. The interpreter selects a different clause should this alternative fail and tries again (we say that the interpreter has to *backtrack* to the previous subgoal in the refutation).

At each clause invocation (which corresponds to a procedure call in a standard programming language), the abstract interpreter has to prepare for backtracking and save the computation state of the goal literal. The Warren Abstract Machine [362, 363] became the standard mechanism to implement such abstract interpreters (although the WAM is geared towards the compilation of Prolog programs). The WAM maintains several stacks to control backtracking: The local stack stores the environments of procedures; the choice stack stores backtracking locations; data structures created by unification are held in the heap; and the trail maintains the addresses of variables that need to be unbound during backtracking. Maintenance of these stacks is a time-

and memory-consuming task resulting in slow computation.

However, for deterministic programs no backtracking is necessary. The key to generating efficient procedural programs from logic-based requirements specifications is to detect such determinacy in programs. [153] and [171] discuss the use of mode information of clause head arguments and head indexing to detect head determinism and primitive determinism. Taylor [327] tries to cause failure to happen earlier through reordering of built-in predicates and thus, reduce the information that must be stored in shallow choice-points. Bruynooghe [49] relies on static search of a trace tree generated by a meta-interpreter to detect determinism. Similar work for proving termination conditions for logic programs can be found in [359].

8.5.1 Item-set construction

In [276], Sato introduces a method to analyze programs written in the Prolog programming language to determine necessary conditions for successful computation of a clause. This method is easily adapted to the analysis of requirements specifications given in FRORL. Sato's analysis is based on term-depth abstraction. Term-depth abstraction reduces a possibly infinite set of terms to a finite set. We can, therefore, actually carry out the fix-point constructions which give meaning to our specification and determine whether a given abstracted term is a logical consequence of the specification. Because we did not consider the terms of the specification directly, but only their abstractions, this analysis yields necessary conditions for logical consequence only.

Knowing necessary conditions for the success of computations from the specification helps to avoid backtracking. If an invoked clause does not meet the necessary condition, the clause must fail, and backtracking inevitably occurs during the following computation. However, if we know that such a computation will fail, we can eliminate its invocation and thus, avoid backtracking upon its failure.

Given a term t, term-depth abstraction yields a term t' such that t is an instance of t'. If a term has depth k, its immediate subterms have depth $k+1$. Term-depth abstraction generalizes a term from a given depth on:

Definition 8.4 *Given a term t, the term-depth abstraction $t[k]$ of t is obtained by replacing every subterm of t of depth k by a new variable.*

Note that for some substitution θ, $t[k]\theta = t$.

An item is a clause the body of which is decorated with a mark ($\bullet$). In a sense, the mark in the body of the clause shows the current state of the "computation" (the fix-point construction one performs to see if a given term is satisfiable). We call an item with a terminal mark a *closed* item.

Definition 8.5 *For a theory Θ and a goal $G = \{\leftarrow A\}$ the item set*

$$\mathsf{Init}(\theta, G) = \{\leftarrow \bullet A\} \cup \{A \leftarrow \bullet \mid A \leftarrow \ \in \Theta\}$$

is called the initial item set for Θ and G.

Next we define two operators D and U on item sets.

Definition 8.6 *Let Θ be a theory, Γ an item set, θ a substitution, and k an integer, then*

$$D_{\Theta,k}(\Gamma) = \Gamma \cup \left\{ \begin{array}{l} (B \leftarrow \bullet B_1 \wedge \ldots \wedge B_m)\theta[k] \mid A \leftarrow A_1 \wedge \ldots \bullet A_j \wedge \ldots \wedge A_n \\ \in \Gamma, B \leftarrow B_1 \wedge \ldots \wedge B_n \in \Theta, \textit{ such that } A_j\theta = B\theta \end{array} \right\}$$

and

$$U_k(\Gamma) = \Gamma \cup \left\{ \begin{array}{l} (A \leftarrow A_1 \wedge \ldots \wedge A_j \bullet \ldots \wedge A_n)\theta[k] \mid A \leftarrow A_1 \wedge \ldots \bullet A_j \wedge \ldots \\ \wedge A_n \in \Gamma, B \leftarrow B_1 \wedge \ldots \wedge B_m \bullet \in \Gamma, \textit{ such that } A_j\theta = B\theta \end{array} \right\}$$

We can obtain the fix-points of the operators D and U by the construction used to find approximations to the fix-points of operators in Chapter 3. Because the depth-abstractions of terms occurring in the item sets used to construct these fix-points are finite, the fix-points of the operators D and U are finite also. Sato describes a process of alternately applying D and U to an initial item set obtained from a given theory and a goal. Only finitely many items can be constructed given some depth k, and therefore, at some finite step in this construction, we will again reach a fix-point. Call this fix-point the closure of a theory Θ and a goal (with depth k).

Definition 8.7 *Given a theory Θ, a goal $\{\leftarrow G\}$, and an integer k, define a series of item sets $\mathcal{C}_{\Theta,G,0}$, $\mathcal{C}_{\Theta,G,1}$, ..., as follows:*

$$\begin{array}{rcl} \mathcal{C}_{\Theta,G,0} & = & \mathsf{Init}(\Theta, G) \\ \mathcal{C}_{\Theta,G,i} & = & U_k(D_{\Theta,k}(\mathcal{C}_{\Theta,G,i\text{-}1})) \\ \mathcal{C}_{\Theta,G} & = & \bigcup_{i \geq 0} \mathcal{C}_{\Theta,G,i} \end{array}$$

We call $\mathcal{C}_{\Theta,G}$ the closure *of the item set for theory Θ and goal $\{\leftarrow G\}$.*

Note that $\mathcal{C}_{\Theta,G}$ is finite. Since both D and U are monotonic and continuous functions over item sets

$$\mathcal{C}_{\Theta,G} \leq D_{\Theta,k}(\mathcal{C}_{\Theta,G}) \leq U_k(D_{\Theta,k}(\mathcal{C}_{\Theta,G})) = \mathcal{C}_{\Theta,G}.$$

Therefore, the closure $\mathcal{C}_{\Theta,G} = D_{\Theta,k}(\mathcal{C}_{\Theta,G})$, as well as $\mathcal{C}_{\Theta,G} = U_k(\mathcal{C}_{\Theta,G})$.

8.5.2 Relationship between Item Set Construction and Refutation

A derivation of $\Theta \cup G$ is a sequence of goals $G_1, G_2, \ldots$, where each G_i is derived from an earlier goal in the sequence and Θ, as described in Def.3.12: Let the current goal be $G_i = \{\leftarrow A_1 \wedge \ldots \wedge A_n\}$, then the next goal in the sequence, G_{i+1} will be either

(i) $\{\leftarrow (A_1 \wedge \ldots \wedge A_{m-1} \wedge B_1 \wedge \ldots \wedge B_k \wedge A_{m+1} \wedge \ldots \wedge A_n)\theta\}$, if there is a clause $B \leftarrow B_1 \wedge \ldots \wedge B_k \in \Theta$ such that $A_m\theta = B\theta$ (θ is a most general unifier), and A_m is not of the form $\P C$, or

(ii) $\{\leftarrow A_1 \wedge \ldots \wedge A_{m-1} \wedge A_{m+1} \wedge \ldots \wedge A_n\}$, if $A_m = \P C$, for some ground literal C, and the attempt to construct a derivation of $\Theta \cup \{\leftarrow \overline{C}\}$ fails finitely.

A refutation is a derivation of finite length n, such that the final goal G_n is the empty clause $\Box$.

The following theorem describes the relation between the closure of the item set for theory Θ and goal G and derivations from $\Theta \cup G$.

Theorem 8.1 (Sato [276]) *Assume that during the refutation of $\Theta \cup G$ for some theory Θ and goal G the clause $B \leftarrow B_1 \wedge \ldots \wedge B_n$ is invoked, and some subgoal in a derivation from $\Theta \cup G$ is $(B_j \wedge \ldots \wedge B_n)\theta$, then*

(i) there is an item $B' \leftarrow B'_1 \wedge \ldots \wedge B'_{j\text{-}1} \wedge \bullet B'_j \wedge \ldots \wedge B'_n$ in the closure $\mathcal{C}_{\Theta,G}$ generated from $B \leftarrow B_1 \wedge \ldots \wedge B_n$, and

(ii) there is a substitution θ' for the variables in $B' \leftarrow B'_1 \wedge \ldots \wedge B'_{j\text{-}1} \wedge \bullet B'_j \wedge \ldots \wedge B'_n$ such that $B\theta = B'\theta'$ and $(B_j \wedge \ldots \wedge B_n)\theta = (B'_j \wedge \ldots \wedge B'_n)\theta'$.

The proof procedes by induction on the number of conjuncts in the current subgoal and is ommitted.

Theorem 8.2 *For a theory Θ, a goal G, and an integer k, construct the closure $\mathcal{C}_{\Theta,G}$ of the item set for Θ and G. If a clause $B \leftarrow B_1 \wedge \ldots \wedge B_n$ is called in the derivation, then if the subgoal $B_1 \wedge \ldots \wedge B_n$ is successfully solved, there exists an item $B' \leftarrow B'_1 \wedge \ldots \wedge B'_n\bullet$ in $\mathcal{C}_{\Theta,G}$ and for some substitution θ, $B'\theta = B$.*

Therefore, the set of items $B' \leftarrow B'_1 \wedge \ldots \wedge B'_n\bullet$ obtained from $B \leftarrow B_1 \wedge \ldots \wedge B_n$ yields the instantiation patterns of this clause at the time its subgoal has been successfully solved. But, as Sato points out, this "local" success may become invalidated by later failure. To enumerate only those closed items which might have taken part in a refutation of $\Theta \cup G$ for top-level goal $G = \{\leftarrow B_0\}$ begin with the item $\{\leftarrow B_0\bullet\}$ generated from G and include all descendant items:

Definition 8.8 *If item $C = (A \leftarrow A_1 \wedge \ldots \wedge A_j \bullet \ldots \wedge A_n)\theta[k]$ was obtained from a closed item $B \leftarrow B_1 \wedge \ldots \wedge B_m\bullet$ according to* Def.8.6, *then the latter is called a* descendant *of C. Any closed item which is a descendant of $A \leftarrow A_1 \wedge \ldots \wedge A_n$ is also a descendant of C.*

Nonenumerated items correspond to failed refutations. Enumerated items are called success items:

Definition 8.9 *Let Θ be a theory, G a goal, Γ an item set, θ a substitution, and k an integer, then the success item $Isucc_{\Theta,G,k}$ is given by*

$$Isucc_{\Theta,G,k,0} = \{\leftarrow G\bullet\}$$

$$Isucc_{\Theta,G,k,i} = \left\{ (B \leftarrow B_1 \wedge \ldots \wedge B_n \bullet)\theta \;\middle|\; \begin{array}{l} A \leftarrow A_1 \wedge \ldots \wedge A_m \in Isucc_{\Theta,G,k,i\text{-}1}, \\ B \leftarrow B_1 \wedge \ldots \wedge B_n \bullet \textit{ is its descend-} \\ \textit{ant, and } A_j = B\theta, 1 \leq j \leq k \end{array} \right\}$$

$$Isucc_{\Theta,G,k} = \bigcup_{i \geq 0} Isucc_{\Theta,G,k,i}.$$

Theorem 8.3 *Let Θ be a theory, G a goal, and k an integer. If a clause $B \leftarrow B_1 \wedge \ldots \wedge B_n$ is used in the refutation of $\Theta \cup G$ with computed answer substitution θ, then there is a closed item $B' \leftarrow B'_1 \wedge \ldots \wedge B'_n$ generated from $B \leftarrow B_1 \wedge \ldots \wedge B_n$ in $Isucc_{\Theta,G,k}$ such that for some substitution θ', $(B \leftarrow B_1 \wedge \ldots \wedge B_n)\theta = (B' \leftarrow B'_1 \wedge \ldots \wedge B'_n)\theta'$.*

Thm.8.3 gives us a necessary condition for a successful refutation: If a clause $B \leftarrow B_1 \wedge \ldots \wedge B_n$ is invoked during the derivation of $\Theta \cup G$, and instantiated by some substitution θ, then there must be an item $B' \leftarrow B'_1 \wedge \ldots \wedge B'_n$ in the success item set $\mathrm{Isucc}_{\Theta,G,k}$ such that $(B \leftarrow B_1 \wedge \ldots \wedge B_n)\theta$ is an instance of that item. If the substitution θ violates the condition given in Thm.8.3 the refutation cannot succeed.

8.5.3 Backtracking Removal

We can use the necessary condition for global success given in Thm.8.3 to eliminate unnecessary backtracking. Looking at the instantiation patterns of variables in the clause heads we call a term t a *success value* of the variable V in a clause $B \leftarrow B_1 \wedge \ldots \wedge B_n$ if V takes t as its value in some success item $B' \leftarrow B'_1 \wedge \ldots \wedge B'_n$ generated from this clause.

If the value of a variable V in an invoked clause is not an instance of a success value of V in the refutation of the top-level goal, the invoked clause will succeed globally. By checking success values, we can eliminate backtracking that would occur here.

We illustrate the use of the item-set construction to discover determinism within a specification by continuing the example from Section 8.2 (this example is due to Sato [276]). The full specification of the small regular expression language in [276, p.235] is

⟨exp⟩ ::=
  ⟨term⟩ ⟨exp1⟩

⟨exp1⟩ ::=
  + ⟨term⟩ ⟨exp1⟩ | ϵ

⟨term⟩ ::=
  ⟨factor⟩ ⟨term1⟩

⟨term1⟩ ::=
  ⟨factor⟩ ⟨term1⟩ | ϵ

⟨factor⟩ ::=
  (⟨exp⟩) ⟨primary⟩ | a ⟨primary⟩ | b ⟨primary⟩ | emp ⟨primary⟩

⟨primary⟩ ::=
    * ⟨primary⟩ | ϵ

Example 8.12 Above grammar is expressed by the following specification (note how each predicate corresponds to a nonterminal symbol in the grammar).

$$\mathsf{exp}(X_1, Y_1) \leftarrow \mathsf{term}(X_1, Y_1) \wedge \mathsf{exp1}(Y_1, Z_1) \tag{8.14}$$

$$\mathsf{exp1}(['+' \mid X_2], Y_2) \leftarrow \mathsf{term}(X_2, Z_2) \wedge \mathsf{exp1}(Z_2, Y_2) \tag{8.15}$$

$$\mathsf{exp1}(X_3, X_3) \leftarrow \tag{8.16}$$

$$\mathsf{term}(X_4, Y_4) \leftarrow \mathsf{factor}(X_4, Z_4) \wedge \mathsf{term1}(Z_4, Y_4) \tag{8.17}$$

$$\mathsf{term1}(X_5, Y_5) \leftarrow \mathsf{factor}(X_5, Z_5) \wedge \mathsf{term1}(Z_5, Y_5) \tag{8.18}$$

$$\mathsf{term1}(X_6, X_6) \leftarrow \tag{8.19}$$

$$\mathsf{factor}(['(' \mid X_7], Y_7) \leftarrow \mathsf{exp}(X_7, [')' \mid Z_7]) \wedge \mathsf{primary}(Z_7, Y_7) \tag{8.20}$$

$$\mathsf{factor}(['\mathsf{a}' \mid X_8], Y_8) \leftarrow \mathsf{primary}(X_8, Y_8) \tag{8.21}$$

$$\mathsf{factor}(['\mathsf{b}' \mid X_9], Y_9) \leftarrow \mathsf{primary}(X_9, Y_9) \tag{8.22}$$

$$\mathsf{factor}(['\mathsf{emp}' \mid X_{10}], Y_{10}) \leftarrow \mathsf{primary}(X_{10}, Y_{10}) \tag{8.23}$$

$$\mathsf{primary}(['*' \mid X_{11}], Y_{11}) \leftarrow \mathsf{primary}(X_{11}, Y_{11}) \tag{8.24}$$

$$\mathsf{primary}(X_{12}, X_{12}) \leftarrow \tag{8.25}$$

As Sato pointed out, an execution of this specification which simply follows the procedural semantics of FRORL often backtracks: For example, the ungrammatical input $['*', '\mathsf{a}']$ invokes clauses (14) through (17), then clauses (20) through (23), where backtracking occurs. Grammatical input may cause backtracking as well. In the parsing of $['\mathsf{a}', '+', '\mathsf{a}']$ (18) is called for the subterm $['+', '\mathsf{a}']$ which is backtracked as well.

To apply the item-set construction we select an appropriate general goal which covers all inputs; in this example $\{\leftarrow \mathsf{exp}(X, [])\}$ will do. We choose 2 as the depth of term abstraction, since we are interested in considering the first element of an argument list. The constructed item-set for above specification, goal $\{\leftarrow \mathsf{exp}(X, [])\}$, and depth 2 consists of 201 items. We then form the success item-set, which consists of 133 items. Finally, we extract the success values for the variables in the heads of each clause. As described above, we unify the head of each clause with the success items generated from that clause. The resultant success values are listed in Fig.8.10 (cf. [276]).

Consider again the ungrammatical sentence $['*', '\mathsf{a}']$. The first call to the parser is $\leftarrow \mathsf{exp}(['*', '\mathsf{a}'], [])$. However, $'*'$ is not a success value for variable X_1 (cf. Fig.8.10). We therefore know that the computation cannot succeed, and there is no point continuing. The parsing can be aborted immediately, thus saving all computation which would occur until backtracking. As for the sentence $['\mathsf{a}', '+', '\mathsf{a}']$, when we reach the subterm $['+', '\mathsf{a}']$ both clauses (18) and (19) apply. However, inspecting the success values we

Variable	Success values
X_1	'a', 'b', 'emp', '('
X_3	')', []
X_4	'a', 'b', 'emp', '('
X_5	'a', 'b', 'emp', '('
X_6	'+', ')', []
X_{12}	'a', 'b', 'emp', '(', ')', '+', []

Figure 8.10. Success values for head variables in specification.

find that '+' is a success value for X_6 but not for X_5. We should therefore choose clause (19) to avoid backtracking.

Together with the mode analysis in Section 8.3 the parser above can be shown to be completely deterministic.

9

Specification Debugging

The debugging process is indispensable to producing a good program. As pointed out over and over again, mistakes in the earlier phases of the software life cycle cost more to be fixed in the later phases (Boehm cites cost increases of up to 100 times for errors deriving from the requirements phase, but discovered and fixed in the maintenance phase). Validation and verification of the specification are crucial. Validating a specification by executing it (as discussed earlier) will also involve debugging, albeit at a more abstract level.

This chapter introduces techniques for debugging specifications. We have introduced extensions to algorithmic debugging that support the nondeterministic and nonmonotonic nature of FRORL specifications including inheritance. These debugging techniques will aid the users in pinpointing bugs they encountered when validating the specification.

9.1 Knowledge-Based Debugging

The debugging and testing process is indispensable to producing a good program. It becomes more difficult as the complexity of the program increases and yet more difficult when programs are written in concurrent languages where several tasks may be executing in parallel. Traditionally, debugging is performed in the implementation phase of the software life cycle. The executability of a specification makes it possible to apply debugging techniques earlier, during validation of the requirements specification. Validation of the requirements specification will exhibit errors in the specification. Debugging techniques aid in locating the errors and correcting them.

In traditional debugging, the programmer inserts trace statements into the program. Observing the trace during program execution, the programmer attempts to locate the error in the program, should incorrect behavior result. Algorithmic debugging [287] attempts to locate errors by relying on declarative knowledge about the program, such as its expected input-output behavior, rather than by inspecting the execution trace. Originally intended for debugging logic programs, algorithmic debugging involves localizing inconsistent program statements by systematically comparing the actual to the intended behavior (or model [248]) of a program. The cause of incorrect behavior is traced to a single incorrect clause or procedure. A program is considered as a theory, and its input-output behavior is taken to be its model.

FRORL provides additional expressive power over logic programming languages, e.g., through multiple inheritance and nondeterminism. These features can also be exploited during the debugging process and may actually reduce the complexity of the debugging process. For example, information regarding multiple inheritance could be used to derive compound queries which can pinpoint many bugs faster.

Debugging systems comprise diagnosis algorithms, which identify bugs in a program and correction algorithms, which eliminate bugs. A debugging system typically takes a specification and a set of input/output samples and executes the input. When it uncovers incorrect output, the diagnosis algorithm identifies the bug and the correction algorithm corrects it. In [287], Shapiro presented a theoretical frame work for program debugging. He described a computational model abstracting various programming languages based on a compositional semantics. Compositional semantics is based on the following simple principle: if a computation of a procedure gives an incorrect result, while all the subcomponents it invokes compute correct results, then the code of this procedure is erroneous [287]. In this model he presented three types of bugs:

- termination with incorrect output
- termination with missing output
- nontermination.

For each of the above types of errors Shapiro defines a property of an erroneous procedure.

9.1.1 Algorithmic Debugging

Algorithmic debugging originated from [287], and numerous extensions have been proposed.

Abstract algorithmic debugging [196] tries to minimize user interaction, by relying on an abstraction function to consider only the relevant data and ignore the irrelevant. The algorithm searches for a faulty procedure in the abstract domain. If one is found, it checks whether the procedure covers the process also in the concrete domain. If so, then the procedure is incorrect. Several useful abstractions have been identified: abstractions which preserve only the declarative aspect of the computation, the temporal aspect, or the modes of arguments.

Deductive Debugging [84] attempts to rely on minimal user involvement. Test cases are generated from executable specifications in the form of Horn-clauses. The test data helps to reveal bugs when the program fails to complete its execution successfully. Bug localization algorithms simulate the execution of a Prolog program and verify the computational result of each procedure call. Once the bug is located, bug fixing strategies are used to generate a correction.

Rational Debugging [248] uses dynamic information regarding term dependencies to track down wrong solutions and to limit the search to find goals with missing solutions. The ability to go back to sub-derivations irrelevant to failures prevents unnecessary querying.

9.1.2 Code checking

The Aspect code checking method [156] attempts to find code-level bugs. To check a procedure, the programmer writes a formal Aspect specification for the procedures called, and a specification for the procedure itself, and then runs the checker on the annotated code. Each program object is divided into a finite number of components (called aspects). The checker constructs the control flow for the code and reports an error if it does not meet the minimum flow specification. When a procedure is called that has no specification or one that is incomplete, the checker generates the most conservative specification, in which, roughly, every aspect of the post-invocation state depends on every aspect of the pre-invocation state. This ensures the absence of bogus errors.

9.1.3 Debugging of Concurrent Programs

Concurrent Algorithm Debugging [197] extends abstract debugging to concurrent programs. Query complexity is generally high, since one needs to check the correctness of computational histories of goals occurring in the computation. Temporal debugging [102] attempts to reduce query complexity and the number of queries in concurrent algorithmic debugging. Temporal debugging works for incomplete or nonterminating computations because the state of the computation history at the time of the first error manifestation is sufficient for temporal debugging to isolate a bug.

The declarative debugger for guarded Horn-clause programs [353] operates on the computation history of a given goal. This technique can be applied to other parallel logic programming languages such as PARLOG and Concurrent Prolog. The computation history represents a proof tree of the goal; all substitutions obtained during computation are applied to this tree. Consideration of the proof tree allows to consider computations in disjoint subtrees as independent computations. Debugging for concurrent logic programs addresses additional bugs

- incorrect answers without termination, and
- incorrect suspension.

Two more types of bugs are difficult to handle in these types of systems: bugs without re-appearance due to indeterminacy and bugs due to concurrency pathologies (such as starvation and deadlock).

9.2 Debugging of FRORL Specifications

We have adapted the algorithmic debugging approach developed by Shapiro for logic programming [287] to the debugging of FRORL specifications. We assume that the basic computational mechanism is a call to an activity, which is insensitive to the inner workings of the activity. The debugging algorithm abstracts away all details of the computation. It considers only the activity calls performed and their externally observable behavior: input-output relations, interaction with the environment, and termination status. We will refer to an activity call plus this relevant information as a *process*. A process will be represented by a triple $\langle A, \vec{x}, \vec{y} \rangle$, where A is an activity, $\vec{x}$ is its input and $\vec{y}$ its behavior (output and termination status).

The intended meaning of an activity is a set of processes. The activity is "buggy" if it computes a process that is not in that set. Algorithmic debugging examines the computation of an activity and compares it to the intended meaning of that activity. We will not be concerned here about how we can obtain the computation history of the program but assume that it is given to us in the form of a computation tree.[1]

The nodes in a computation tree are processes. If $\langle A, \vec{x}, \vec{y} \rangle$ is a leaf node it represents an activity call that yields behavior $\vec{y}$ on input $\vec{x}$ without any further subcomputation. If a node $\langle A, \vec{x}, \vec{y} \rangle$ has a set of children $\{\langle A_1, \vec{x_1}, \vec{y_1} \rangle, \ldots, \langle A_k, \vec{x_k}, \vec{y_k} \rangle\}$ we assume that computing A can be accomplished by computing in parallel $A_1 \ldots A_k$ and composing the results. We will refer to the sequence $\{\langle A_1, \vec{x_1}, \vec{y_1} \rangle, \ldots, \langle A_k, \vec{x_k}, \vec{y_k} \rangle\}$ as the *top level trace* of A. Note that the processes in a top level trace may be concurrent and may interact by communicating messages. The operational semantics of the computational mechanism presupposed maps activities onto top level traces.

In the following, we will refer to the intended meaning of an activity as a model $\mathcal{M}$. A model is simply a set of processes.

Definition 9.1 *An activity A covers a process $\langle A, \vec{x}, \vec{y} \rangle$ with respect to $\mathcal{M}$ if $\langle A, \vec{x}, \vec{y} \rangle$ has a top-level trace which is a subset of $\mathcal{M}$.*

Algorithmic debugging compares the computation tree for an activity to the intended meaning (the model) of that activity. It does this by making use of an *oracle* to determine the correctness of computations. Given a process $\langle A, \vec{x}, \vec{y} \rangle$, the oracle for the model $\mathcal{M}$ answers *yes* if the process $\langle A, \vec{x}, \vec{y} \rangle$ is in $\mathcal{M}$ and answers *no* otherwise. Typically the users function as the oracle, although previous answers may be remembered by the system to avoid repeating the same questions to the users. It is also possible to use an alternative and executable specification, or some other known correct but inefficient version of the specification to debug a more efficient but possibly faulty specification.

---

[1]For sequential programs the computation tree can simply be obtained by expanding the definitions of activities. However, in computing FRORL specifications nondeterministic choices may be made (either implicitly by the relative speed of independent sub-computations, or explicitly at choice points within activities). [195] and [197] discuss approaches to reconstructing the computation tree from the initial state of the computation and its trace.

We describe several simple algorithmic debugging algorithms which are due to Shapiro [287]. These algorithms ask the oracle at every ground computation. Shapiro has improved the query complexity by suggesting divide-and-query diagnosis algorithms. The number of queries necessary can be further decreased by paying attention to the syntactic restrictions afforded by FRORL (e.g., the computation can be traced back along preconditions or message sends and receives. Furthermore, the verification mechanisms of FRORL (see Chapter 6) can provide a measure of synchronic distance between the clauses of the specification as well as other dynamic properties of the specification. By knowing the mutual dependence among the clauses of a specification the number of queries for debugging can be reduced further.

9.2.1 Diagnosing Termination With Incorrect Output

Definition 9.2 *An activity A is correct in $\mathcal{M}$ if every process $\langle A, \vec{x}, \vec{y}\rangle$ covered by A with respect to $\mathcal{M}$ is in $\mathcal{M}$. Otherwise A is incorrect in $\mathcal{M}$.*

If an activity A is incorrect in $\mathcal{M}$, then there is a top-level trace in $\mathcal{M}$ for some process $\langle A, \vec{x}, \vec{y}\rangle$ not in $\mathcal{M}$. The following theorem shows that if an activity has a finite computation that yields incorrect behavior, then it contains an incorrect activity.

Theorem 9.1 (Shapiro) *Let A be an activity, and $\mathcal{M}$ a model. If A is not correct in $\mathcal{M}$ then A contains an activity incorrect in $\mathcal{M}$.*

Proof: Let A be an activity that on input $\vec{x}$ yields the incorrect behavior $\vec{y}$. We show the result by induction on the height of the computation tree for the corresponding process $\langle A, \vec{x}, \vec{y}\rangle$. If the computation tree consists of a single node, then A has an empty top level trace and is therefore covered by A, and thus incorrect. Now suppose the computation tree has height $n+1$. If all the sons of its root node are in $\mathcal{M}$, then this node is covered and, therefore, incorrect. Otherwise, one of the sons is not in $\mathcal{M}$. This subtree has height $\leq n$, and by the induction hypothesis is incorrect. ∎

Alg.9.1 is obtained from the proof of above theorem. It simply executes a query and asks the oracle at every ground computation. Since the users typically have to function as the oracle, reducing the number of queries is highly desirable. Shapiro has suggested the following improvement over the single-stepping querying strategy described above: query that node in the computation tree which will divide the tree into two roughly equal parts. If its process $\langle B, \vec{u}, \vec{v}\rangle$ is in $\mathcal{M}$, then omit the subtree rooted at that node and iterate; otherwise apply the algorithm recursively to that subtree [287].

Example 9.1 (This and the following examples are taken from Section A.2 where a subscriber-line controller of a telephone exchange is specified.) After the dialed number has been entered and has been passed on to the controller via the activities first_digit and next_digit, next_digit attempts to connect to the called party's line; the activity connecting establishes the call once both ends of the phone line are on line. Let us consider a scenario, in which a correct sequence of digits fails and consequently

Algorithm 9.1 (Trace incorrect activity)

> **input** computation tree T with root $p = \langle A, \vec{x}, \vec{y} \rangle \notin \mathcal{M}$
> **output** process $\notin \mathcal{M}$
> $t \leftarrow$ top level trace of p
> **if** p is a leaf or $\forall t' \in t \cdot t' \in \mathcal{M}$
> **then return** p
> **else** $q \leftarrow t'$ such that $t' \in t$ and $t' \notin \mathcal{M}$
>   **return** Trace incorrect activity(computation tree rooted at q)

attempts to connect to an incorrect number. Assume that first_digit has been incorrectly specified in the following way (at the marked place, the entered digit is passed on, rather than stop_tone, which will lead to a spurious duplication of an entered digit).

MAXActivity: first_digit(*contr*)
  Parts: *contr*: subscriber_line_controller
  Time_constraint: 45 sec
  To: receive(*contr.terminal_line*, *digit*)
  Actions: | **send**(contr.terminal_line,digit), | ⟸
    send(*contr.resource_alloc_out*, *digit*), next_digit(*contr*)
  Alt_Actions: send(*contr.terminal_line*, timeout_tone),
    send(*contr.resource_alloc_out*, release), terminate(*contr*)

To help locating the bug, the declarative debugger begins by (conceptually) constructing the computation tree for the executed specification which is shown in Fig.9.1.

Below we show the trace of the debugging sequence for the input phone number 123, which resulted in the buggy output 1213 (using the divide-and-query strategy). The debugger shows input and behavior[2] prior to each question, and the oracle (in other words, the users) is simply to respond with yes or no. For example, the last query listed checks whether the process send(controller, res_alloc_out, 1) is correct; the oracle can see that the output correctly adds the result of the message send to the resource allocator.

```
input:  controller(res_alloc_out,1111), controller(terminal_line,1),
        controller(res_alloc_out,1), controller(terminal_line,3), controller(res_alloc_out,2)
ouput:  controller(res_alloc_out,1111), controller(res_alloc_out,1),
        controller(res_alloc_out,2), controller(res_alloc_out,1), controller(res_alloc_out,3),
        controller(terminal_line,timeout_tone), controller(resource_alloc_out,release),
        controller(res_alloc_out,free)
```

[2]Note that we have restricted input and behavior descriptions displayed to the state of the subscriber line controller which is all that is of interest in this and the following examples.

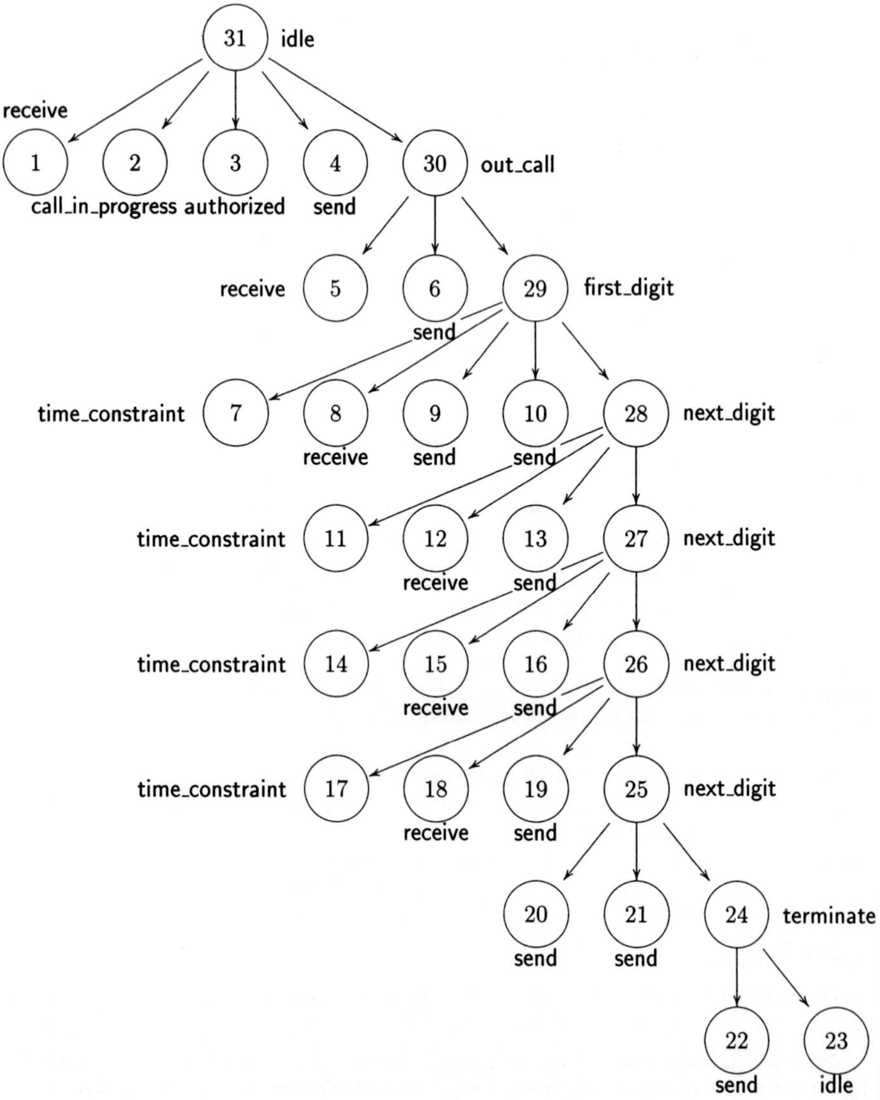

Figure 9.1. Computation tree for Ex. 9.1 (nodes labelled according to order encountered).

```
Checking: next_digit(controller) --- Correct ? (y/n): y
input:  controller(res_alloc_in,decoder_ok), controller(terminal_line,1),
        controller(res_alloc_out,1111)
ouput:  controller(res_alloc_out,1111), controller(res_alloc_out,1),
        controller(res_alloc_out,2), controller(res_alloc_out,1), controller(res_alloc_out,3),
        controller(terminal_line,timeout_tone), controller(resource_alloc_out,release),
        controller(res_alloc_out,free)
Checking: out_call(controller) --- Correct ? (y/n): n
input:  controller(res_alloc_out,1111), controller(terminal_line,2),
        controller(terminal_line,1), controller(res_alloc_out,1)
ouput:  controller(res_alloc_out,1111), controller(res_alloc_out,1),
        controller(res_alloc_out,2), controller(res_alloc_out,1), controller(res_alloc_out,3),
        controller(terminal_line,timeout_tone), controller(resource_alloc_out,release),
        controller(res_alloc_out,free)
Checking: next_digit(controller) --- Correct ? (y/n): y
input:  controller(terminal_line,1), controller(res_alloc_out,1111)
ouput:  controller(terminal_line,1), controller(res_alloc_out,1111)
Checking: time_constraint(max,45) --- Correct ? (y/n): y
input:  controller(terminal_line,1), controller(res_alloc_out,1111)
 CONTROLLER sending ...controller(terminal_line,2)
ouput:  controller(res_alloc_out,1111), controller(terminal_line,2)
Checking: receive(controller,terminal_line,1) --- Correct ? (y/n): y
input:  controller(terminal_line,1), controller(res_alloc_out,1111)
ouput:  controller(res_alloc_out,1111), controller(res_alloc_out,1),
        controller(res_alloc_out,2), controller(res_alloc_out,1), controller(res_alloc_out,3),
        controller(terminal_line,timeout_tone), controller(resource_alloc_out,release),
        controller(res_alloc_out,free)
Checking: first_digit(controller) --- Correct ? (y/n): n
input:  controller(res_alloc_out,1111), controller(terminal_line,2)
ouput:  controller(res_alloc_out,1111), controller(terminal_line,2),
        controller(terminal_line,1)
Checking: send(controller,terminal_line,1) --- Correct ? (y/n): y
input:  controller(res_alloc_out,1111), controller(terminal_line,2),
        controller(terminal_line,1)
ouput:  controller(res_alloc_out,1111), controller(terminal_line,2),
        controller(terminal_line,1), controller(res_alloc_out,1)
Checking: send(controller,res_alloc_out,1) --- Correct ? (y/n): y
 Suspicious node: first_digit(controller)
```

The first incorrect input/output relation is encountered at the second query (the node queried is numbered 30 in Fig.9.1) which shows that the digits 1, 2, 1, 3 are sent to the terminal line, where only the sequence 1, 2, 3 is expected. Incorrect output is again encountered at node 29, which seeks in the spurious digit 1. Since the descendent nodes 9 and 10 are determined to be correct, the algorithm returns node 29 as the suspicious activity.

9.2.2 *Diagnosing Finite Failures*

An activity A is said to be *finitely failed* on process $\langle A, \vec{x}, \vec{y}\rangle$, if every computation of A on input $\vec{x}$ terminates with a behavior correct in $\mathcal{M}$, but the behavior $\vec{y}$ is not among those. If an activity A finitely fails on a process $\langle A, \vec{x}, \vec{y}\rangle \in \mathcal{M}$, then A is not complete, since calling A with input $\vec{x}$ should have resulted in behavior $\vec{y}$.

Definition 9.3 *An activity A is complete with respect to a model $\mathcal{M}$ if for every process $\langle A, \vec{x}, \vec{y}\rangle \in \mathcal{M}$, there is a computation of A on input $\vec{x}$ that yields behavior $\vec{y}$.*

Theorem 9.2 (Shapiro) *Let A be an activity, $\mathcal{M}$ be a model. If A finitely fails on a process $\langle A, \vec{x}, \vec{y}\rangle$, then A contains an incomplete activity.*

Proof: Show the result by induction on d, the maximal depth of any computation tree of A rooted at $\langle A, \vec{x}, \vec{y}\rangle$. If $d = 1$, then A has no top level trace for $\langle A, \vec{x}, \vec{y}\rangle$, hence it does not cover $\langle A, \vec{x}, \vec{y}\rangle$. Since the process $\langle A, \vec{x}, \vec{y}\rangle \in \mathcal{M}$, A is incomplete. Now assume the claim holds for d-1. If no top level trace of $\langle A, \vec{x}, \vec{y}\rangle$ is in $\mathcal{M}$, then A does not cover $\langle A, \vec{x}, \vec{y}\rangle$, and the result holds. Otherwise, consider the processes in the top level trace. For at least one process $\langle B, \vec{u}, \vec{v}\rangle$, there is no computation tree (otherwise there would be a computation tree for $\langle A, \vec{x}, \vec{y}\rangle$ contradictory to the assumption). Therefore, by the inductive hypothesis, A contains an incomplete activity. ■

The following algorithm immediately follows from above proof. Alg.9.2 uses existential queries to detect incomplete activities. An existential query in a model $\mathcal{M}$ returns the set of all processes in the model with given activity A and input $\vec{x}$.

Algorithm 9.2 (Trace incomplete activity)

input $\langle A, \vec{x}, \vec{y}\rangle \in \mathcal{M}, A$ fails finitely
output process not covered
$p \leftarrow$ result of existential query on $A, \vec{x}$
$t \leftarrow$ top level trace of p
if $\nexists t' \in t \cdot t' \in \mathcal{M}$
then return p
else find a process $t' \in t$ that finitely fails in $\mathcal{M}$
  return Trace incomplete activity(t')

9.2.3 *Diagnosing Nontermination*

A well-founded ordering on a nonempty set is binary relation $\succ$ over that set which is transitive, asymmetric, and irreflexive, such that for no infinite sequence $x_1, x_2, \ldots$ of elements of that set we have that $x_1 \succ x_2 \succ \ldots$.

Theorem 9.3 *An activity A is everywhere terminating iff there is a well-founded ordering $\succ$ on its processes such that for every computation of A in which $\langle A, \vec{x}, \vec{y}\rangle$ calls $\langle B, \vec{u}, \vec{v}\rangle$, $\langle A, \vec{x}, \vec{y}\rangle \succ \langle B, \vec{u}, \vec{v}\rangle$.*

Proof: Assume that every computation of A terminates. Let $d(\langle A, \vec{x}, \vec{y}\rangle)$ be the depth of this computation. Define the ordering $\succ$ as $\langle A, \vec{x}, \vec{y}\rangle \succ \langle B, \vec{u}, \vec{v}\rangle$ iff $d(\langle A, \vec{x}, \vec{y}\rangle) > d(\langle B, \vec{u}, \vec{v}\rangle)$. This ordering is well-founded. Thus the depth of any computation of A is finite, and hence terminates. ∎

Definition 9.4 *Let $\mathcal{M}$ be a model and $\succ$ a well-founded ordering on activity calls. An activity A is said to* diverge *if there exists a process $\langle A, \vec{x}, \vec{y}\rangle$ with a top level trace t such that there is a process $\langle B, \vec{u}, \vec{v}\rangle \in t$ for which $\langle A, \vec{x}, \vec{y}\rangle \not\succ \langle B, \vec{u}, \vec{v}\rangle$ and all processes that precede $\langle B, \vec{u}, \vec{v}\rangle$ are in $\mathcal{M}$.*

Theorem 9.4 (Shapiro) *Let A be an activity, $\mathcal{M}$ a model, and $\succ$ a well-founded ordering over activity calls. If A is diverging then it contains an activity incorrect in $\mathcal{M}$ or an activity that diverges.*

Proof: Assume that some computation of A on input $\vec{x}$ does not terminate. Therefore, there is an infinite computation tree which must contain two processes $\langle A, \vec{x}, \vec{y}\rangle$ and $\langle B, \vec{u}, \vec{v}\rangle$ such that $\langle A, \vec{x}, \vec{y}\rangle \not\succ \langle B, \vec{u}, \vec{v}\rangle$, since $\succ$ is well-founded. Consider all activity calls that A performed before calling B with input u. If any of them returned with incorrect output then A is not correct. Otherwise, there is a top level trace of A on input $\vec{x}$ that contains the process $\langle B, \vec{u}, \vec{v}\rangle$, such that every process preceding it is in $\mathcal{M}$, and by definition, A diverges. ∎

Alg.9.3 requires an oracle that can answer queries of the form "is $\langle A, \vec{x}, \vec{y}\rangle \succ \langle B, \vec{u}, \vec{v}\rangle$?". The search for violations of $\succ$ first attempts to locate a loop of the form $\langle A, \vec{x}, \vec{y}\rangle \ldots \langle A, \vec{x}, \vec{y}\rangle$. If such a loop is found, it must contain two consecutive activity calls that violate $\succ$. This pair can be detected by the oracle.

Algorithm 9.3 (Trace diverging activity)

> **input** computation tree T with root $\langle A, \vec{x}, \vec{y}\rangle$
> **output** process $\notin \mathcal{M}$ or two activity calls violating $\succ$
> **if** consecutive processes $\langle A, \vec{x}, \vec{y}\rangle$ and $\langle B, \vec{u}, \vec{v}\rangle$ such that $\langle A, \vec{x}, \vec{y}\rangle \succ \langle B, \vec{u}, \vec{v}\rangle$
>   can be found in T
> **then if** a process in the top level trace of $A \notin \mathcal{M}$
>   **then return** Trace incorrect activity($\langle B, \vec{u}, \vec{v}\rangle$)
>   **else return** $\langle A, \vec{x}, \vec{y}\rangle, \langle B, \vec{u}, \vec{v}\rangle$

9.2.4 More Detailed Error Diagnosis

Application of above algorithms locates errors in faulty activities, but does not give any indication as to what precisely the error is. We can rely on the syntactic features of FRORL to give additional information as to the source of errors. Although errors may show up in a particular activity, the true source of the error may be, for example, a faulty precondition in an earlier call, or a faulty message send.

The following algorithms traverse the computation tree from the location of the error (as determined by the previous algorithms) in search for more specific failure conditions. Once the earlier algorithms have located an error, we attempt to find those nodes in the computation tree that are (in a yet to be determined sense) *relevant* to the problem at hand. We trace the computation backward along these "relevancy" relationships. An oracle will again be used to determine whether located processes are correct.

Algorithm 9.4 (Trace relevancy)

> **input** computation tree T, process $p = \langle A, \vec{x}, \vec{y} \rangle$ faulty by earlier algorithms
> $L \leftarrow$ **reverse** pre-order list of nodes in T
> **for each** $l \in L$
>   **if** l is relevant to p
>   **then if** oracle reports problem with l, p
>   **then report** l
>   **return** Trace relevancy(l)
>   **else** $p \leftarrow l$

Various "relevancy" relationships and corresponding oracle queries yield additional information.

For example, activities contain a precondition slot which determines whether the action slot or the alternative action slot will be executed. The arguments of the "called" activity can be checked against the precondition of the "calling" activity: The "relevancy" relationship becomes "does l contain a precondition ϕ and call p?" with the oracle query "was it correct that l called p given that precondition ϕ was satisfied?" In the distributed and real-time domain the built-in functions **send** and **receive** turn out to be good "leads" to the next activity which will be executed. Using message sends and corresponding receives as "relevancy" relationship we obtain "does l contain a **send** statement that was received by p?" and "was p the correct receiver for this message, and was the message correct?" Other important information may come from the relationships **an_instance_of**, **a_kind_of**, and **a_part_of** between objects and their parent objects. Incorrect activities invoked due to mistakes in the inheritance relationship will not become apparent until execution time. Timing constraints may also give us additional insight into the true sources of an error found by above algorithms.

Example 9.2 (We continue with above example.) The activity first_digit has been identified as suspicious. We can now use the trace through the precondition slot to determine which other activities may have led to the bug:

```
input: controller(terminal_line,1), controller(res_alloc_out,1111)
```

```
ouput:  controller(res_alloc_out,1111), controller(res_alloc_out,1),
        controller(res_alloc_out,2), controller(res_alloc_out,1), controller(res_alloc_out,3),
        controller(terminal_line,timeout_tone), controller(resource_alloc_out,release),
        controller(res_alloc_out,free)
Checking: first_digit(controller) --- Correct precondition? (y/n): n
input:  controller(res_alloc_in,decoder_ok), controller(terminal_line,1),
        controller(res_alloc_out,1111)
ouput:  controller(res_alloc_out,1111), controller(res_alloc_out,1),
        controller(res_alloc_out,2), controller(res_alloc_out,1), controller(res_alloc_out,3),
        controller(terminal_line,timeout_tone), controller(resource_alloc_out,release),
        controller(res_alloc_out,free)
Checking: out_call(controller) --- Correct precondition? (y/n): n
input:  controller(terminal_line,offhook), controller(res_alloc_in,decoder_ok),
        controller(terminal_line,1)
ouput:  controller(res_alloc_out,1111), controller(res_alloc_out,1),
        controller(res_alloc_out,2), controller(res_alloc_out,1), controller(res_alloc_out,3),
        controller(terminal_line,timeout_tone), controller(resource_alloc_out,release),
        controller(res_alloc_out,free)
Checking: idle(controller) --- Correct precondition? (y/n): n
```

We notice that there is no change among the output parts of the nodes. From this we can conclude that no other activity has affected the activity first_digit between the calls to the activities idle and the call to first_digit itself. Therefore, the bug must be in the definition of first_digit.

We now trace the message sends and receives of the suspicious activity. Tracing stops at this node itself, since although it contains a receive statement, the corresponding send is issued by the controller without any further message receives:

```
input:  controller(terminal_line,1),controller(res_alloc_out,1111)
 CONTROLLER sending ...controller(terminal_line,2)
ouput:  controller(res_alloc_out,1111),controller(terminal_line,2)
Checking: receive(controller,terminal_line,1) --- Correct ? (y/n): y
```

The only suspicious statements in the definition of first_digit left are the two message sends. The second message send yields correct output. Therefore, the first message send must be the source of the bug (its output is consumed somewhere during the computation).

Appendix A

Example Specifications

In this section, we present additional example specifications of real-time distributed systems using the requirements specification language FRORL.

A.1 Alternate Bit Protocol

The Alternate Bit Protocol was originally proposed in [25] to ensure error-free transmission of data over unreliable communication links. In the following, we use FRORL to describe a simple specification of this protocol.

The protocol allows a sender and a receiver to exchange information. The messages from the sender are data messages; the receiver replies with acknowledgments:

Activity: ABP()
  Actions: sender() || receiver()

Errors can be introduced into the transmission for different reasons. Despite errors, the Alternate Bit Protocol attempts to ensure that the message be correctly transmitted. For example, the protocol must account for lost messages. Acknowledgments may also be lost, in which case the sender, operating on the assumption that the message was lost, resends it. In such a case, the receiver must realize that the resent message is merely a duplicate of the original message and should discard it. [25] introduces the concept of an *alternation bit* to work around this and similar problems.

Activity: sender()
  Actions: gen_msg$(0, msg)$, **send**$(chnl, msg)$, receive_ack(am0, msg),
    gen_msg$(1, msg')$, **send**$(chnl, msg')$, receive_ack(am1, msg'),
    sender()

The sender generates a message (either bit 0 or bit 1), and adds to it a control bit. This message is sent to the receiver and the sender waits for an acknowledgment. The Alternate Bit Protocol is based on the sender alternating the control bit attached to the message. When the sender is in a state in which it sent a message encoded with the control bit 0, it only responds to acknowledgments of having received a message with control bit 0:

Activity: receive_ack(ack, msg)
  Precond: **receive**$(chnl, ack)$

Activity: receive_ack(ack, msg)
  Precond: opposite(ack, ack'), **receive**($chnl$, ack')
  Actions: **send**($chnl$, msg), receive_ack(ack, msg)

Activity: receive_ack(ack, msg)
  Precond: **receive**($chnl$, err)
  Actions: **send**($chnl$, msg), receive_ack(ack, msg)

As shown above, any acknowledgment other than the expected one (including receiving an error message) forces the sender to resend its message and once more wait for the acknowledgment. We also include timeouts as an error conditions that cause the sender to resend its data. The timeout condition is modelled by a minimum-time activity:

MINActivity: receive_ack(ack, msg)
  Time_constraint: timeout_period
  Alt_Actions: **send**($chnl$, msg), receive_ack(ack, msg)

The receiver's functions are opposite those of the sender. It alternates between expecting a message encoded with a 0 control bit and expecting one encoded with a 1 control bit. If it receives an appropriate message, it sends the corresponding acknowledgment. Again, receipt of an incorrect message, error messages, or time outs cause it to resend its original acknowledgment.

Activity: receiver()
  Actions: receive_msg(am1, msg), **send**($chnl$, am0),
    receive_msg(am0, msg'), **send**($chnl$, am1)

Activity: receive_msg(ack, msg)
  Precond: expect_msg(ack, 0, rec), **receive**($chnl$, rec)
  Actions: $msg = 0$

Activity: receive_msg(ack, msg)
  Precond: expect_msg(ack, 1, rec), **receive**($chnl$, rec)
  Actions: $msg = 1$

Activity: receive_msg(ack, msg)
  Precond: expect_msg(ack, 1, rec), opposite(rec, rec'), **receive**($chnl$, rec')
  Actions: **send**($chnl$, ack), receive_msg(ack, msg)

Activity: receive_msg(ack, msg)
  Precond: expect_msg(ack, 0, rec), opposite(rec, rec'), **receive**($chnl$, rec')
  Actions: **send**($chnl$, ack), receive_msg(ack, msg)

Activity: receive_msg(ack, msg)
  Precond: **receive**($chnl$, err)
  Actions: **send**($chnl, ack$), receive_msg(ack, msg)

MINActivity: receive_msg(ack, msg)
  Time_constraint: timeout_period
  Alt_Actions: **send**($chnl, ack$), receive_msg(ack, msg)

Clarke [63] presents a verification of the Alternate Bit Protocol using the EMC (Extended Model Checking) system. Similarly, we can verify this protocol by applying Alg.5.1 to determine whether the structure, constructed from the above specification, is indeed a model for sentences expressing important properties of the protocol. Properties of interest are, for example (we show their representation in RTμ, where ℓ_s indicates the state of sending a message, and ℓ_r indicates the state of receiving a message),

- Sending of a message strictly alternates with receiving a message:

$$\Box(\ell_s \ \Rightarrow \ (\ell_r \, \mathcal{U} \, (\neg \ell_s \wedge (\neg \ell_r \, \mathcal{U} \, \ell_s))))$$

- If a 0 bit is sent, then a 0 bit is received

$$\Box(\ell_s \wedge \mathsf{gen\_msg}(b, 0) \ \Rightarrow \\ (\ell_s \, \mathcal{U} \, (\neg \ell_s \wedge (\neg \ell_s \, \mathcal{U} \, (\ell_r \wedge msg = 0)))))$$

- If a 1 bit is sent, then a 1 bit is received

$$\Box(\ell_s \wedge \mathsf{gen\_msg}(b, 1) \ \Rightarrow \\ (\ell_s \, \mathcal{U} \, (\neg \ell_s \wedge (\neg \ell_s \, \mathcal{U} \, (\ell_r \wedge msg = 1)))))$$

Note that these properties can be shown to hold only if we add the fairness assumption to our specification, as shown on p.108. We can show that the same properties hold even if we introduce an artificial error source into our system, such as by adding a process which might corrupt the information communicated on the channel.

Activity: ABP()
  Actions: sender() || receiver() || error_source()

To explain the lower-level activities relied upon above, gen_msg generates an arbitrary data message and attaches the proper control bit. expect_msg matches an incoming data message and decodes it.

Activity: gen_msg(bit, msg)
  matches(x, msg, bit)

Activity: expect_msg(*ack*, *bit*, *msg*)
matches(*ack*, *msg*, *bit*)

Lastly, we define **opposite** and **matches** for binary messages and acknowledgments by the following lookup table.

Activity: opposite(am1, am0)

Activity: opposite(am0, am1)

Activity: opposite(dm01, dm11)

Activity: opposite(dm11, dm01)

Activity: opposite(dm00, dm10)

Activity: opposite(dm10, dm00)

Activity: matches(am1, 0, dm01)

Activity: matches(am1, 1, dm11)

Activity: matches(am0, 0, dm00)

Activity: matches(am0, 1, dm01)

A.2 Subscriber-Line Controller of a Telephone Exchange

In this section, we present the example of a component of a telephone exchange.[1] The basic functionality of a telephone exchange is to provide a subscriber with the ability to call any other subscriber reachable on the network. The exchange connects the subscriber line (the wire leading to the subscriber terminal) to either another subscriber line connected to the same exchange or to a trunk line.

Each subscriber line is connected to a subscriber-line controller. This device is responsible for arranging the appropriate connections between its subscriber line and the other (called or calling) party's line. as well as providing feedback to the subscriber terminal:

Object: exchange

Object: subscriber_line_controller
a_part_of: exchange
id:
terminal_id:
terminal_line:
resource_alloc_in:
resource_alloc_out:
call_line:

[1]This example is adopted and slightly expanded from [88].

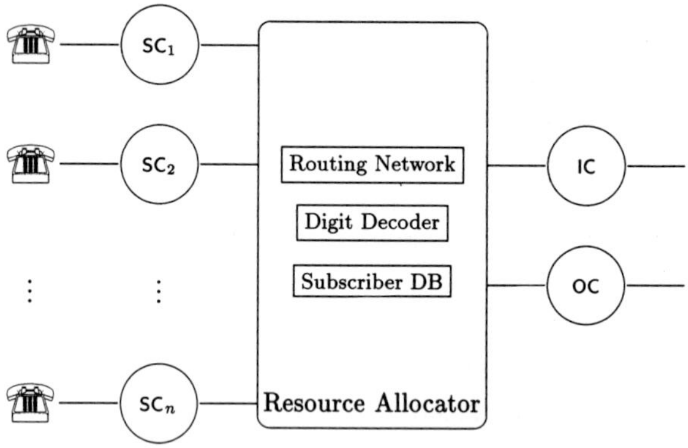

Figure A.1. Simplified Diagram of a Telephone Exchange (adapted from [88]).

As shown in Fig.A.1 there are many other components in a telephone exchange besides the subscriber controllers ($\mathsf{sc}_1 \ldots \mathsf{sc}_n$). Sparse resources (such as digit decoders or line connections, and access to the subscriber data base) are mediated by a resource allocator. Trunk lines are also provided with incoming (ic) and outgoing (oc) controllers. We are only concerned here with the behavior of the subscriber-line controller.

The subscriber-line controller is best understood as an automaton, as shown in Fig.A.2. For a call originating from the subscriber terminal connected to the subscriber-line controller, the controller moves through the states of attempting the call (**out_call**), decoding the dialed digit (**first_digit**, **next_digit**), and connecting to the appropriate line (**connecting**) into a state where speech is communicated on the line (**out_speech**). After completing the call, the controller returns to the idle state. A call may be terminated for a variety of reasons also bringing the controller back into idle. For incoming calls, state transitions are somewhat simpler.

A transition from the idle state occurs when a call is originated at the subscriber terminal by going off-hook, or by an incoming call seizing the line. Priority is given to completing a call in progress (i.e., a call will only be initiated if no incoming call is pending). Checking for a call in progress is described through a time activity:

Activity: idle(*contr*)
  Parts: *contr*: subscriber_line_controller
  Precond: **receive**(*contr.terminal_line*, offhook),
    not call_in_progress(*contr*),
    authorized(*contr.terminal_id*),
    send(*contr.resource_alloc_out*, *contr.terminal_id*)

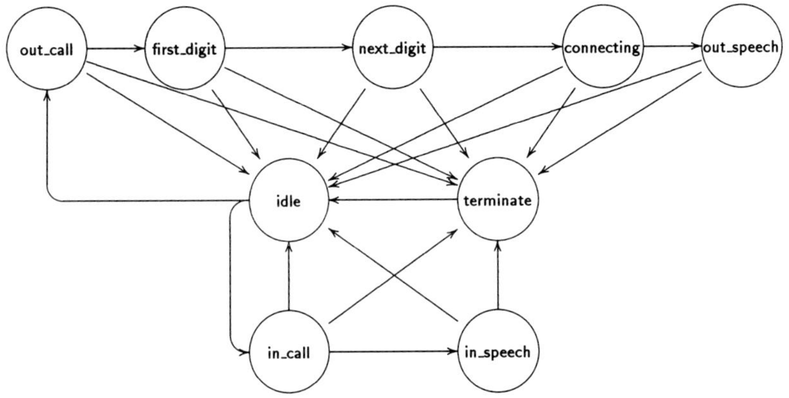

Figure A.2. State diagram for the subscriber-line controller.

Actions: out_call(*contr*)
Alt_Actions: idle(*contr*)

Activity: idle(*contr*)
Parts: *contr*: subscriber_line_controller
Precond: **receive**(*contr.call_line*, seize)
Actions: **send**(*contr.terminal_line*, ringing), in_call(*contr*)

MAXActivity: call_in_progress(*contr*)
Parts: *contr*: subscriber_line_controller
Time_constraint: 0.1 sec
To: **receive**(*contr.call_line*, seize)
Actions: **fail**

We first discuss the outgoing call. If the resource allocator provides the necessary resources (e.g., the digit decoder) a dial-tone is sent to the subscriber terminal. Should the needed resources not be available a special "congestion tone" is sent to the subscriber. The subscriber may also prematurely abort the call by going on-hook. (This condition is always possible and will not be mentioned again.)

Activity: out_call(*contr*)
Parts: *contr*: subscriber_line_controller
Precond: **receive**(*contr.resource_alloc_in*, decoder_ok)
Actions: **send**(*contr.terminal_line*, dialtone), first_digit(*contr*)

Activity: out_call(*contr*)
  Parts: *contr*: subscriber_line_controller
  Precond: **receive**(*contr.resource_alloc_in*, unable)
  Actions: **send**(*contr.terminal_line*, congestion_tone), terminate(*contr*)

Activity: out_call(*contr*)
  Parts: *contr*: subscriber_line_controller
  Precond: **receive**(*contr.terminal_line*, onhook)
  Actions: **send**(*contr.resource_alloc_out*, free), idle(*contr*)

Upon receiving the dial-tone, the subscriber is expected to dial the telephone number of the called party. We associate a maximum timing constraint with dialing of the number. The resources allocated to this call are shared and cannot be indefinitely held. If no digit is received within the timeout period (here 45 seconds), the call is terminated and the resources are released.

MAXActivity: first_digit(*contr*)
  Parts: *contr*: subscriber_line_controller
  Time_constraint: 45 sec
  To: **receive**(*contr.terminal_line*, *digit*)
  Actions: **send**(*contr.terminal_line*, stop_tone),
    send(*contr.resource_alloc_out*, *digit*), next_digit(*contr*)
  Alt_Actions: **send**(*contr.terminal_line*, timeout_tone),
    send(*contr.resource_alloc_out*, release), terminate(*contr*)

Activity: first_digit(*contr*)
  Parts: *contr*: subscriber_line_controller
  Precond: **receive**(*contr.terminal_line*, onhook)
  Actions: **send**(*contr.resource_alloc_out*, free), idle(*contr*)

The digits dialed are sent successively to the resource allocator who stores them in a register and detects a completed phone number. Again, a timeout constraint is put on the delay between dialing successive digits. There is also a minimum timing constraint given to ensure that the resource allocator has sufficient time to decode and analyze the dialed digits.

Activity: next_digit(*contr*)
  Parts: *contr*: subscriber_line_controller
  Precond: **receive**(*contr.resource_alloc_in*, more)
  Actions: next_digit(*contr*)

MAXActivity: next_digit(*contr*)
  Parts: *contr*: subscriber_line_controller
  Time_constraint: 20 sec

To: **receive**(*contr.terminal_line*, *digit*)
Actions: **send**(*contr.resource_alloc_out*, *digit*), next_digit(*contr*)
Alt_Actions: **send**(*contr.terminal_line*, timeout_tone),
send(*contr.resource_alloc_out*, release), terminate(*contr*)

MINActivity: next_digit(*contr*)
Parts: *contr*: subscriber_line_controller
Time_constraint: 0.5 sec
To: **receive**(*contr.terminal_line*, *digit*)
Actions: **send**(*contr.resource_alloc_out*, *digit*), next_digit(*contr*)
Alt_Actions: **send**(*contr.terminal_line*, timeout_tone),
send(*contr.resource_alloc_out*, release), terminate(*contr*)

Activity: next_digit(*contr*)
Parts: *contr*: subscriber_line_controller
Precond: **receive**(*contr.terminal_line*, onhook)
Actions: **send**(*contr.resource_alloc_out*, free), idle(*contr*)

After the subscriber dials enough digits to enable identification of the called party, it is determined whether an attempt should be made to connect the lines. Obviously, incorrect numbers, a called line already engaged, and overly busy telephone networks all lead to termination of the call.

Activity: next_digit(*contr*)
Parts: *contr*: subscriber_line_controller
Precond: **receive**(*contr.resource_alloc_in*, unused)
Actions: **send**(*contr.terminal_line*, unused_number),
send(*contr.resource_alloc_out*, release), terminate(*contr*)

Activity: next_digit(*contr*)
Parts: *contr*: subscriber_line_controller
Precond: **receive**(*contr.resource_alloc_in*, engaged)
Actions: **send**(*contr.terminal_line*, busy_tone),
send(*contr.resource_alloc_out*, release), terminate(*contr*)

Activity: next_digit(*contr*)
Parts: *contr*: subscriber_line_controller
Precond: **receive**(*contr.resource_alloc_in*, unable)
Actions: **send**(*contr.terminal_line*, congestion_tone),
send(*contr.resource_alloc_out*, release), terminate(*contr*)

Activity: next_digit(*contr*)
Parts: *contr*: subscriber_line_controller
Precond: **receive**(*contr.resource_alloc_in*, available)
Actions: **send**(*contr.terminal_line*, ring_tone), connecting(*contr*)

In attempting to connect a call, the called party's terminal is rung (there is a maximum time constraint on the time the called party delays to go off-hook). If the called party answers the call, speech will be transmitted until either party goes on-hook and terminates the call.

MAXActivity: connecting(*contr*)
 Parts: *contr*: subscriber_line_controller
 Time_constraint: 5 min
 To: **receive**(*contr.resource_alloc_in*, online)
 Actions: **send**(*contr.terminal_line*, speech_condition), out_speech(*contr*)
 Alt_Actions: **send**(*contr.terminal_line*, timeout_tone),
  send(*contr.resource_alloc_out*, release), terminate(*contr*)

Activity: connecting(*contr*)
 Parts: *contr*: subscriber_line_controller
 Precond: **receive**(*contr.terminal_line*, onhook)
 Actions: **send**(*contr.resource_alloc_out*, free), idle(*contr*)

Activity: out_speech(*contr*)
 Parts: *contr*: subscriber_line_controller
 Precond: **receive**(*contr.terminal_line*, onhook)
 Actions: **send**(*contr.resource_alloc_out*, free), idle(*contr*)

The situation for incoming calls is somewhat simpler. The controller need only monitor the subscriber-line for going off-hook, in which case, the ringing should be stopped. Transmitting speech is terminated by the calling party going on-hook.

Activity: in_call(*contr*)
 Parts: *contr*: subscriber_line_controller
 Precond: **receive**(*contr.terminal_line*, offhook)
 Actions: **send**(*contr.terminal_line*, stopring),
  send(*contr.resource_alloc_out*, answered), in_speech(*contr*)

Activity: in_call(*contr*)
 Parts: *contr*: subscriber_line_controller
 Precond: **receive**(*contr.call_line*, disconnect)
 Actions: **send**(*contr.terminal_line*, stopring), idle(*contr*)

Activity: in_speech(*contr*)
 Parts: *contr*: subscriber_line_controller
 Precond: **receive**(*contr.call_line*, disconnect)
 Actions: terminate(*contr*)

Termination of the call causes the resources to be freed at the resource allocator and the controller to go back into idle.

Activity: terminate(*contr*)
  Parts: *contr*: subscriber_line_controller
  Actions: **send**(*contr.resource_alloc_out*, free), idle(*contr*)

We now show two extensions of the standard subscriber-line controller presented above by introducing subclasses of the subscriber-line controller.

Object: watching_controller
  a_kind_of: subscriber_line_controller

Object: hot_line_controller
  a_kind_of: subscriber_line_controller

A hot-line controller monitors the subscriber-line after the subscriber terminal goes off-hook. If no digit is dialed within a certain time (here 5 seconds), then some predetermined number is automatically called.[2]

MAXActivity: first_digit(*contr*)
  Parts: *contr*: hot_line_controller
  Time_constraint: 5 sec
  Alt_Actions: **send**(*contr.terminal_line*, stop_tone), hot_line_id(*digit*),
    send(*contr.resource_alloc_out*, *digit*), next_digit(*contr*)

A subscriber-line controller might also allow "call-watching." This refers to the ability of either party to go on-hook without disconnecting the call.[3] The call is disconnected if the party remains on-hook for an excessive time (which is taken as an indication that the party has terminated the call).

Activity: out_speech(*contr*)
  Parts: *contr*: watching_controller
  Precond: **receive**(*contr.call_line*, offline)
  Actions: watch_out(*contr*)

MAXActivity: watch_out(*contr*)
  Parts: *contr*: watching_controller
  Time_constraint: 90 sec
  To: **receive**(*contr.call_line*, online)
  Actions: out_speech(*contr*)
  Alt_Actions: **send**(*contr.terminal_line*, timeout_tone),
    send(*contr.resource_alloc_out*, release), terminate(*contr*)

---

[2]This is a feature often found in hospitals or senior citizens homes which allows emergency calls to be automatically made, should the subscriber be unable to dial the number.

[3]Typically, this feature is present in multi-party lines, phones equipped with three-way calling, etc.

Activity: watch_out(*contr*)
Parts: *contr*: watching_controller
Precond: **receive**(*contr.terminal_line*, onhook)
Actions: **send**(*contr.resource_alloc_out*, free), idle(*contr*)

Activity: out_speech(*contr*)
Parts: *contr*: watching_controller
Precond: **receive**(*contr.terminal_line*, onhook)
Actions: **send**(*contr.resource_alloc_out*, interrupt), watch_in(*contr*)

MAXActivity: watch_in(*contr*)
Parts: *contr*: watching_controller
Time_constraint: 90 sec
To: **receive**(*contr.terminal_line*, offhook)
Actions: **send**(*contr.terminal_line*, answered), in_speech(*contr*)

Activity: watch_in(*contr*)
Parts: *contr*: watching_controller
Precond: **receive**(*contr.call_line*, disconnect)
Actions: **send**(*contr.resource_alloc_out*, free), idle(*contr*)

Appendix B

Formal Grammar of FRORL

The Backus-Naur Form (BNF) is probably the most common meta-language for specifying the context-free syntax of programming languages. In this appendix, we give a BNF definition of the syntax of object and activity frames of FRORL:[1]

⟨FRORL⟩ ::=
  ⟨Object frame⟩ ⟨s-FRORL⟩ |
  ⟨Activity frame⟩ ⟨s-FRORL⟩ |
  ⟨Built-in function⟩ ⟨s-FRORL⟩

⟨s-FRORL⟩ ::=
  ⟨FRORL⟩ | ϵ

⟨Object frame⟩ ::=
  Object : ⟨object name⟩ ⟨object body⟩

⟨object name⟩ ::=
  ⟨identifier⟩

⟨object body⟩ ::=
  ⟨inheritance⟩ ⟨attribute list⟩

⟨inheritance⟩ ::=
  ⟨abstract relation⟩ : ⟨object name⟩ | ϵ

⟨abstract relation⟩ ::=
  an_instance_of | a_part_of | a_kind_of

⟨attribute list⟩ ::=
  ⟨attribute name⟩ : ⟨attribute value⟩ ⟨attribute list⟩ | ϵ

⟨attribute name⟩ ::=
  ⟨identifier⟩

⟨attribute value⟩ ::=
  ⟨value⟩

⟨value⟩ ::=
  ⟨identifier⟩ | ⟨predicate⟩ | ⟨identifier⟩ . ⟨value⟩ | **not** ⟨predicate⟩

⟨predicate⟩ ::=
  ⟨identifier⟩ (⟨argument list⟩)

---

[1]We omit the details for the non-terminals ⟨identifier⟩ and ⟨integer⟩.

⟨argument list⟩ ::=
  ⟨argument⟩ | ⟨argument⟩ , ⟨argument list⟩ | ϵ

⟨argument⟩ ::=
  ⟨value⟩

⟨Activity frame⟩ ::=
  ⟨regular activity⟩ | ⟨time activity⟩

⟨regular activity⟩ ::=
  Activity : ⟨activity name⟩ ⟨activity body⟩

⟨time activity⟩ ::=
  ⟨TimeActivity⟩ | ⟨MAXActivity⟩ | ⟨MINActivity⟩ |
  ⟨DURMAXActivity⟩ | ⟨DURMINActivity⟩

⟨TimeActivity⟩ ::=
  TimeActivity : ⟨activity name⟩ ⟨time period⟩ ⟨activity body⟩

⟨MAXActivity⟩ ::=
  MAXActivity : ⟨activity name⟩ ⟨activity body⟩

⟨MINActivity⟩ ::=
  MINActivity : ⟨activity name⟩ ⟨activity body⟩

⟨DURMAXActivity⟩ ::=
  DURMAXActivity : ⟨activity name⟩ ⟨activity body⟩

⟨DURMINActivity⟩ ::=
  DURMINActivity : ⟨activity name⟩ ⟨activity body⟩

⟨activity name⟩ ::=
  ⟨predicate⟩

⟨time period⟩ ::=
  Period : ⟨cyclic value⟩

⟨activity body⟩ ::=
  ⟨inheritance⟩ ⟨part⟩ ⟨precond⟩ ⟨actions⟩ ⟨alt-actions⟩

⟨cyclic value⟩ ::=
  ⟨integer⟩

⟨part⟩ ::=
  Part : ⟨participating list⟩ | ϵ

⟨precond⟩ ::=
  Precond : ⟨precond body⟩ | ϵ

⟨actions⟩ ::=
  Actions : ⟨action body⟩ | ϵ

⟨alt-actions⟩ ::=
  Alt_actions : ⟨action body⟩ | ϵ

⟨participating list⟩ ::=
    ⟨attribute name⟩ : ⟨attribute value⟩ , ⟨participating list⟩ | ϵ

⟨precond body⟩ ::=
    ⟨statement block⟩ , ⟨precond body⟩ | ϵ

⟨action body⟩ ::=
    ⟨statement⟩ | ⟨statement block⟩

⟨action statement block⟩ ::=
    ⟨statement⟩ | ⟨statement⟩ , ⟨statement block⟩

⟨statement⟩ ::=
    ⟨predicate⟩ | **not** ⟨predicate⟩ | ϵ

Appendix C

Some Results about Fix-Points

We present some standard results about fix-points of functions used throughout this book. Let Π be a complete lattice under the partial order $\leq$.[1] Note that for a complete lattice we know that a greatest lower bound and a least upper bound exist. Let $\mathcal{T}$ be a mapping from Π to Π. We are interested in the fix-points of $\mathcal{T}$. First some definitions (we denote sets with Greek letters, elements of a set are denoted by lower case Greek letters):

Definition C.1 *Let Γ be a subset of Π. Γ is directed if and only if every finite subset of Γ has an upper bound in Γ.*

Definition C.2 *$\mathcal{T}$ is continuous if and only if for any directed subset Γ of Π, $\mathcal{T}(lub(\Gamma)) = lub(\mathcal{T}(\Gamma))$.*

Definition C.3 *$\mathcal{T}$ is monotonic if and only if for any two members γ_1, γ_2 of Π, if $\gamma_1 \leq \gamma_2$, then $\mathcal{T}(\gamma_1) \leq \mathcal{T}(\gamma_2)$.*

Lemma C.1 *If $\mathcal{T}$ is continuous, then $\mathcal{T}$ is monotonic.*

Proof: Suppose $\mathcal{T}$ is continuous. Consider two members γ_1, γ_2 of Π, such that $\gamma_1 \leq \gamma_2$. Then $\{\gamma_1, \gamma_2\}$ is directed. $\mathcal{T}(\text{lub}(\{\gamma_1, \gamma_2\})) = \text{lub}(\mathcal{T}(\gamma_1)) = \text{lub}\{\mathcal{T}(\gamma_1), \mathcal{T}(\gamma_2)\}$, by the continuity of $\mathcal{T}$. Then $\mathcal{T}(\gamma_1) \leq \mathcal{T}(\gamma_2)$. ■

Theorem C.2 (Knaster-Tarski) *$\mathcal{T}$ has a least fix-point (lfp) and a greatest fix-point (gfp). Furthermore,*

$$\begin{aligned} lfp(\mathcal{T}) &= glb\{\xi \mid \xi = \mathcal{T}(\xi)\} &= glb\{\xi \mid \mathcal{T}(\xi) \leq \xi\} \\ gfp(\mathcal{T}) &= lub\{\xi \mid \xi = \mathcal{T}(\xi)\} &= lub\{\xi \mid \xi \leq \mathcal{T}(\xi)\} \end{aligned}$$

Proof: We show the existence of the least fix-point. Let $\Gamma = \{\xi \mid \mathcal{T}(\xi) \leq \xi\}$, and put $\gamma = \text{lub}(\Gamma)$.

(i) First, show that $\gamma \in \Gamma$. $\forall \xi \cdot \in \Gamma, \gamma \leq \xi$. By monotonicity of $\mathcal{T}$, $\mathcal{T}(\gamma) \leq \mathcal{T}(\xi)$, and by definition of glb, $\mathcal{T}(\gamma) \leq \gamma$. But then

$$\gamma \in \Gamma$$

[1] These results hold for arbitrary lattices and partial orders. In this book, we are interested in lattices of sets and the partial order of set-inclusion $\subseteq$.

(ii) Next show that γ is a fix-point of $\mathcal{T}$. We already showed that $\mathcal{T}(\gamma) \in \gamma$, by monotonicity $\mathcal{T}(\mathcal{T}(\gamma)) \in \mathcal{T}(\gamma)$, and by definition of Γ, $\mathcal{T}(\gamma) \in \Gamma$. Then, since γ is the greatest lower bound of Γ, $\gamma \leq \mathcal{T}(\gamma)$, and therefore,

$$\gamma = \mathcal{T}(\gamma).$$

(iii) Lastly, show that γ is the least fix-point. Let $\gamma' = \text{glb}\{\xi \mid \xi = \mathcal{T}(\xi)\}$. Since γ is a fix-point, $\gamma' \leq \gamma$. Note that $\{\xi \mid \xi = \mathcal{T}(\xi)\} \leq \{\xi \mid \mathcal{T}(\xi) \leq \xi\}$, and therefore, $\gamma \leq \gamma'$. But, then $\gamma = \gamma'$. ∎

The existence of the greatest fix-point is shown in a similar way.

Definition C.4 *The ordinal powers of $\mathcal{T}$ are defined by*

$$\begin{aligned} \mathcal{T}\uparrow_0 &= \emptyset \\ \mathcal{T}\uparrow_{i+1} &= \mathcal{T}(\mathcal{T}\uparrow_i) \\ \mathcal{T}\uparrow_\omega &= lub\{\mathcal{T}\uparrow_n \mid n < \omega\} \end{aligned}$$

Theorem C.3 (Kleene) $lfp(\mathcal{T}) = \mathcal{T}\uparrow_\omega$

Proof:

(i) By Thm.C.2 we know there exists a least fix-point of $\mathcal{T}$ such that $\text{lfp}(\mathcal{T}) = \text{glb}\{\xi \mid \xi = \mathcal{T}(\xi)\}$.

(ii) Show that $\mathcal{T}\uparrow_\omega$ is a fix-point of $\mathcal{T}$, i.e., that $\mathcal{T}\uparrow_\omega = \mathcal{T}(\mathcal{T}\uparrow_\omega)$.

Note that $\mathcal{T}\uparrow_1 \leq \mathcal{T}\uparrow_2 \leq \ldots \leq \mathcal{T}\uparrow_n$, $n < \omega$, thus $\{\mathcal{T}\uparrow_n \mid n < \omega\}$ is a directed subset of Π. Since $\mathcal{T}$ is continuous, $\mathcal{T}(\text{lub}\{\mathcal{T}\uparrow_n \mid n < \omega\}) = \text{lub}(\mathcal{T}(\{\mathcal{T}\uparrow_n \mid n < \omega\})) = \mathcal{T}\uparrow_\omega$, by the definition of the ordinal powers of $\mathcal{T}$. Applying the definition of the ordinal powers of $\mathcal{T}$ to the right-hand side, we obtain

$$\mathcal{T}(\mathcal{T}\uparrow_\omega) = \mathcal{T}\uparrow_\omega .$$

(iii) Now show that $\mathcal{T}\uparrow_\omega$ is the least fix-point of $\mathcal{T}$. Consider an arbitrary fix-point ξ of $\mathcal{T}$. It suffices to show that $\mathcal{T}\uparrow_\omega \leq \xi$, by induction on the ordinal power of $\mathcal{T}$.

For the base case, let $n = 0$. Since $\emptyset \leq \xi$, $\mathcal{T}\uparrow_0 \leq \xi$. Assume the result holds for any $k \leq n$, and let $\mathcal{T}\uparrow_n \leq \xi$. By monotonicity, $\mathcal{T}(\mathcal{T}\uparrow_n) \leq \mathcal{T}(\xi)$. $\mathcal{T}(\xi) = \xi$, since ξ is a fix-point of $\mathcal{T}$, so $\mathcal{T}(\mathcal{T}\uparrow_n) \leq \xi$, and $\mathcal{T}\uparrow_{n+1} \leq \xi$. ∎

The following lemma is used in establishing Lem.3.1. It holds only for lattices which are powersets under the partial order of set inclusion $\subseteq$.

Lemma C.4 *Let Γ be a directed subset of Π, let $\{\alpha_1, \ldots \alpha_n\} \in \Pi$. Then for some $\gamma \in \Gamma$,*

$$\{\alpha_1, \ldots \alpha_n\} \subseteq lub(\Gamma) \text{ if and only if } \{\alpha_1, \ldots \alpha_n\} \subseteq \gamma.$$

Proof:
$\Leftarrow$) Let $\{\alpha_1, \ldots \alpha_n\} \subseteq \gamma$, where $\gamma \in \Gamma$, then by definition of lub, $\{\alpha_1, \ldots \alpha_n\} \subseteq \mathrm{lub}(\Gamma)$.
$\Rightarrow$) Since Γ is directed, $\exists \gamma \cdot \in \Gamma$, for any $\xi_i \in \Xi$, $\xi_i \subseteq \gamma$, where Ξ is a finite subset of Γ. If $\{\alpha_1, \ldots \alpha_n\} \subseteq \mathrm{lub}(\gamma)$, then $\exists \Xi \cdot$ such that Ξ is a finite subset of Γ, $\alpha_i \in \xi_j \in \Xi$. Since Ξ is finite, $\xi_j \subseteq \gamma$, for any $\xi_j \in \Xi$, for some γ. But, then $\{\alpha_1, \ldots \alpha_n\} \subseteq \gamma$. ∎

Appendix D

References

[1] M. Abadi. *Temporal-Logic Theorem Proving.* PhD thesis, Standard University, 1987.

[2] L. Abraido-Fandino. An overview of REFINE^{TM} 2.0. In *Proc. of the 2nd Intl. Symp. on Knowledge Eng.*, pp. 8–10, Madrid, 1987.

[3] A. Adam and J. Laurent. Laura, a system to debug student programs. *Artificial Intelligence*, pp. 75–122, 1980.

[4] W. Agresti. *New Paradigms for Software Engineering.* IEEE Computer Society Pr., Washington, 1986.

[5] M. Alavi. An assessment of the prototyping approach to information systems development. *Commun. ACM*, 9(6):556–563, 1984.

[6] M. Alford. SREM at the age of eight. *IEEE Computer*, pp. 36–46, 1985.

[7] B. Alpern. Verifying temporal properties without temporal logic. *ACM Trans. Prog. Lang. Syst.*, pp. 147–167, 1989.

[8] R. Alur and T. Henzinger. Logics and models of real time: A survey. In *Real-Time: Theory in Practice*, nr. 600 in Lect. Notes in Comp. Sci., pp. 74–106. Springer Verlag, Berlin, 1991.

[9] J. Ambras and V. O'Day. MicroScope: A knowledge-based programming environment. *IEEE Software*, pp. 50–58, 1988.

[10] K. Apt and M. van Emden. Contributions to the theory of logic programming. *J. ACM*, 29(3):841–862, 1982.

[11] B. Auernheimer and R. Kemmerer. RT-ASLAN: a specification language for real-time systems. *IEEE Trans. Softw. Eng.*, 12(9):879–889, 1986.

[12] N. Aussenac, J. Frontin, and J.-L. Soubie. Macao: A knowledge acquisition tool for expertise transfer. In *Proc. European Knowledge Acquisition Wksp.*, nr. 143 in GMD Studien, pp. 8.1–8.12. 1988.

[13] J. Baeten and W. Weijland. *Process Algebra.* Cambridge Univ. Pr., Cambridge, 1990.

[14] R. Balzer. Transformational implementation: An example. *IEEE Trans. Softw. Eng.*, 7(1):3–13, 1981.

[15] R. Balzer, T. Cheatham, and C. Green. Software technologies in the 1990's using a new paradigm. *IEEE Computer*, pp. 3–16, 1983.

[16] R. Balzer and N. Goldman. Principles of good software specification and their implementations for specification languages. In *Proc. Specification of Reliable Software Conf.*, pp. 58–67, 1979.

[17] R. Balzer, N. Goldman, and D. Wile. Operational specification as the basis for rapid prototyping. *ACM Software Eng. Notes*, 7(5), 1982.

[18] N. Barghouti and G. Kaiser. Scaling up rule-based software development environments. *Intl. J. Software Eng. and Knowledge Eng.*, 2:59–78, 1992.

[19] A. Barr and E. Feigenbaum. *The Handbook of Artificial Intelligence.* Morgan-Kaufmann, Los Altos, 1982.

[20] H. Barringer, R. Kuiper, and A. Pnueli. Now you may compose temporal logic specifications. In *Proc. 16th Ann. ACM Symp. Theory of Computing*, pp. 51–63, Washington, 1984.

[21] H. Barringer, R. Kuiper, and A. Pnueli. A really abstract concurrent model and its temporal logic. In *Proc. 13th Ann. ACM Symp. Principles of Programming Languages*, pp. 173–183, 1986.

[22] D. Barstow. An experiment in knowledge-based automatic programming. *Artificial Intelligence*, 12:73–119, 1979.

[23] D. Barstow. A perspective on automatic programming. *AI Magazine*, 5(1):5–27, 1984.

[24] D. Barstow. Automatic programming for streams II: Transformation implementation. In *Proc. 10th Intl. Conf. on Software Eng.*, pp. 439–447, Singapore, 1988.

[25] K. Bartlett, R. Scantlebury, and P. Wilkinson. A note on reliable full-duplex transmission over half-duplex links. *Commun. ACM*, 12(5):260–261, 1969.

[26] F. Bauer. From specification to machine code: Program construction through formal reasoning. In *Proc. 6th Intl. Conf. on Software Eng.*, pp. 84–91, 1982.

[27] F. Bauer et al. *The Munich Project CIP: The Wide Spectrum Language Systems CIP-L.* Nr. 183 in Lect. Notes in Comp. Sci. Springer Verlag, Berlin, 1985.

[28] F. Bauer et al. *The Munich Project CIP: The Program Transformation Systems CIP-S.* Nr. 292 in Lect. Notes in Comp. Sci. Springer Verlag, Berlin, 1987.

[29] B. Berthomieu and M. Diaz. Modeling and verification of time dependent systems using time petri nets. *IEEE Software*, 17(3):259–274, 1991.

[30] A. Biermann, G. Guiho, and Y. Kordratoff. *Automatic Program Construction Techniques.* Macmillan, 1984.

[31] R. Binder and J.-P. Tsai. KB/RMS: An intelligent assistant for requirement definition. In *Proc. IEEE Conf. on Tools for Artificial Intelligence*, pp. 13–19, Washington, 1990.

[32] D. Bobrow and T. Winograd. An overview of KRL, a knowledge representation language. *Cognitive Sci.*, 1(1):3–46, 1977.

[33] B. Boehm. Software engineering. *IEEE Trans. Comput.*, C-25(12):1226–1241, 1976.

[34] B. Boehm. *Software Engineering Economics.* Prentice-Hall, Englewood Cliffs, 1981.

[35] B. Boehm. A spiral model of software development and enhancement. *ACM SIGSOFT*, 11(2):22–42, 1986.

[36] S. Bologna, E. Ness, and T. Siverieeesen. Dependable knowledge-based systems development and verification: What we can learn from software engineering and what we need. In *Proc. IEEE Conf. on Tools for Artificial Intelligence*, pp. 86–95, 1990.

[37] G. Booch. *Object Oriented Design with Applications.* Benjamin/Cummings, Redwood City, 1991.

[38] J. Boose. A research framework for knowledge acquisition techniques and tools. In *Proc. European Knowledge Acquisition Wksp.*, nr. 143 in GMD Studien, pp. 10.1–10.13. 1988.

[39] J. Boose, D. Shema, and J. Bradshaw. Recent progress in AQUINAS: A knowledge acquisition workbench. In *Proc. European Knowledge Acquisition Wksp.*, nr. 143 in GMD Studien, pp. 2.1–2.15. 1988.

[40] A. Borgida, S. Greenspan, and J. Mylopoulos. Knowledge representation as the basis for requirements specifications. *IEEE Computer*, pp. 82–90, 1985.

[41] A. Borgida and M. Janke (eds.). Special issue on knowledge representation and reasoning in software development. *IEEE Trans. Softw. Eng.*, 18(6), 1992.

[42] A. Borgida, J. Mylopoulos, and H. Wong. Generalization/specification as a basis for software specification. In M. Brodie, J. Mylopoulos, and J. Schmidt, eds., *On Conceptual Modeling*. Springer Verlag, New York, 1984.

[43] A. Bossi, N. Cocco, and S. Dulli. A method for specializing logic programs. *ACM Trans. Prog. Lang. Syst.*, 12(2):253–302, 1990.

[44] R. Brachman and H. Levesque. *Readings in Knowledge Representation*. Morgan-Kaufmann, Los Altos, 1985.

[45] M. Brodie. Future intelligent information systems: AI and database technologies working together. In J. Mylopoulos and M. Brodie, eds., *Reading in Artificial Intelligence and Databases*. Morgan-Kaufmann, Los Altos, 1998.

[46] L. Brownston, R. Farrel, E. Kant, and N. Martin. *Programming Expert Systems in OPS5: An Introduction to Rule-Based Programming*. Addison-Wesley, Reading, 1985.

[47] M. Bruynooghe. Adding redundancy to obtain more reliable and more readable Prolog programs. In *Proc. 1st Intl. Logic Programming Conference*, Marseille, 1982.

[48] M. Bruynooghe, B. Demoen, A. Callebaut, and G. Janssens. Abstract interpretation: Towards the global optimization of Prolog programs. In *Proc. 4th IEEE Symposium on Logic Programming*, San Francisco, 1987.

[49] M. Bruynooghe, D. DeSchreye, and B. Krekels. Compiling control. *J. Logic Programming*, 6(1):135–162, 1989.

[50] J. Bubenko. On concepts and strategies for requirements and information analysis. Tech.Rep. 4, Dept. of Comp. Sci., Chalmers Univ. of Tech., 1981.

[51] B. Buchanan and E. Shortliffe. *Rule-Based Expert Systems, The MYCIN Expertiments of the Stanford Heuristic Programming Project*. Addison-Wesley, Reading, 1985.

[52] R. Burstall and J. Darlington. A transformation system for developing recursive programs. *J. ACM*, 24(1):44–67, 1977.

[53] J. Cameron. An overview of JSD. *IEEE Trans. Softw. Eng.*, 12(2):222–240, 1986.

[54] T. Carey and R. Mason. Information system prototyping: Techniques, tools, methodologies. In *Proc. INFOR*, pp. 177–191, 1983.

[55] S. Ceri, G. Gottlob, and L. Tanca. *Logic Programming and Databases*. Springer Verlag, New York, 1990.

[56] C. Chang, J. Combs, and R. Stachowitz. A report on the Expert systems Validation Associate (EVA). Tech.rep., Lockheed Missiles & Space Company, 1990.

[57] C. Chang and R. Lee. *Symbolic Logic and Mechanical Theorem Proving.* Academic Pr., New York, 1973.

[58] T. Cheatham, G. Holloway, and J. Townley. Program refinement by transformation. In *Proc. 5th Intl. Conf. on Software Eng.*, 1981.

[59] T. Christaller. Die KI-Werkbank BABYLON. Preprint, 1989.

[60] K. Clark. Negation as failure. In H. Gallaire and J. Minker, eds., *Logic and Databases*, pp. 293–322. Plenum Pr., New York, 1978.

[61] K. Clark and S. Gregory. PARLOG: Parallel programming in logic. *ACM Trans. Prog. Lang. Syst.*, 8(1):1–49, 1986.

[62] K. Clark and S. Sickel. Predicate logic: A calculus for deriving programs. In *Proc. 5th Intl. Joint Conf. on Artificial Intelligence*, pp. 419–420, Cambridge, 1977.

[63] E. Clarke, E. Emerson, and A. Sistla. Automatic verification of finite state concurrent systems using temporal logic specifications. *ACM Trans. Prog. Lang. Syst.*, 8(2):244–264, 1986.

[64] E. Clarke, O. Grumberg, and M. Browne. Reasoning about networks with many identical finite state processes. In *Proc. 5th Ann. ACM Symp. Principles of Distributed Computing*, pp. 240–248, 1986.

[65] W. Clocksin and C. Mellish. *Programming in Prolog.* Springer Verlag, New York, 1984.

[66] P. Coad and E. Yourdon. *Object-Oriented Analysis.* Prentice-Hall, Englewood Cliffs, 1989.

[67] D. Cohen, W. Swartout, and R. Balzer. Using symbolic execution to characterize behavior. In *Proc. ACM SIGSOFT '82*, pp. 25–32, 1982.

[68] J. Cohen. Describing Prolog by its interpretation and compilation. *Commun. ACM*, 28(12):1311–1324, 1985.

[69] R. Constable. On the theory of programming logics. In *Proc. 9th Ann. ACM Symp. Theory of Computing*, pp. 269–285, Boulder, 1977.

[70] R. Constable. Programs as proofs. *Inf. Process. Lett.*, 16(3):105–112, 1983.

[71] R. Constable, S. Allen, H. Bromley, W. Cleaveland, J. Cremer, R. Harper, D. Howe, T. Knoblock, N. Mendler, P. Panangaden, J. Sasaki, and S. Smith. *Implementing Mathematics with the Nuprl Proof Development System.* Prentice-Hall, Englewood Cliffs, 1986.

[72] E. Coolhan, Jr. and N. Roussopoulos. Timing requirements for time-driven systems using augmented petri nets. *IEEE Trans. Softw. Eng.*, 9:603–616, 1983.

[73] B. Cragun. A decision-table-based processor for checking completeness and consistency in rule-based expert systems. *Intl. J. Man-Machine Studies*, 26:633–648, 1987.

[74] A. Czuchry and D. Harris. KBRA: A new paradigm for requirements engineering. *IEEE Expert*, (winter):21–35, 1988.

[75] J. Darlington. An experimental program transformation and synthesis system. *Artificial Intelligence*, 16:1–46, 1981.

[76] B. Dasarathy. Timing constraints of real-time systems: Constructs for expressing them, methods of validating them. *IEEE Trans. Softw. Eng.*, 11(1):80–86, 1985.

[77] R. Davis. *Generating Correct Programs From Logic Specifications.* PhD thesis, University of California, Santa Cruz, 1977.

[78] R. Davis. Interactive transfer of expertise. In B. Buchanan and E. Shortliffe, eds., *Rule-Based Expert Systems*, pp. 171–208. 1982.

[79] S. Debray. Flow analysis of dynamic logic programs. *J. Logic Programming*, 7:149–176, 1989.

[80] S. Debray and D. Warren. Automatic mode inference for logic programs. *J. Logic Programming*, 5:207–229, 1988.

[81] M. Degl'innocenti et al. RSF: A formalism for executable requirement specifications. *IEEE Trans. Softw. Eng.*, pp. 1235–1246, 1990.

[82] N. Deo. *Graph Theory with Applications to Engineering and Computer Science.* Prentice-Hall, Englewood Cliffs, 1974.

[83] N. Dershowitz. Program abstraction and instantiation. *ACM Trans. Prog. Lang. Syst.*, 7(3):446–477, 1985.

[84] N. Dershowitz and Y.-J. Lee. Deductive debugging. In *Proc. 4th IEEE Symposium on Logic Programming*, pp. 298–306, San Francisco, 1987.

[85] R. Dewar, A. Grand, S. Liu, and J. Schwartz. Programming by refinement, as examplified by the SETL representation sublanguage. *ACM Trans. Prog. Lang. Syst.*, 1(1), 1979.

[86] J. di Piazza. Cases to models to complete expert systems. Tech.rep., General Dynamics Corp., Electronic Boat Div., 1990.

[87] E. Dubois, J. Hagelstein, E. Lahou, F. Ponsaert, and A. Rifaut. A knowledge representation language for requirements engineering. *Proc. of the IEEE*, 74(10):1431–1444, 1986.

[88] N. Elshiewy. Logic programming for real-time control of telecommunication switching systems. *J. Logic Programming*, 8(1):121–145, 1990.

[89] E. Emerson. Temporal and modal logic. In J. van Leeuwen, ed., *Handbook of Theoretical Computer Science*, vol. B, pp. 995–1072. Elsevier Science Publ., Amsterdam, 1990.

[90] E. Emerson and J. Halpern. Decision procedures and expressiveness in the temporal logic of branching time. *J. Comput. Syst. Sci.*, (30):1–24, 1985.

[91] E. Emerson and J. Halpern. 'Sometimes' and 'not never' revisited, on branching versus linear time temporal logics. *J. ACM*, 33(1):151–178, 1986.

[92] E. Emerson and C.-L. Lei. Efficient model checking in fragments of the propositional mu-calculus. In *Proc. Symp. Logic in Comp. Sci.*, pp. 267–278, Cambridge, 1986.

[93] E. Emerson, A. Mok, A. Sistla, and J. Srinivasan. Quantitative temporal reasoning. In R. K. E.M. Clarke, ed., *Computer Aided Verification*, nr. 531 in Lect. Notes in Comp. Sci., pp. 136–242. Springer Verlag, Berlin, 1990.

[94] J. Escamilla and P. Jean. Relationships in an object knowledge representation model. In *Proc. IEEE Conf. on Tools for Artificial Intelligence*, pp. 632–638, 1990.

[95] L. Esfahani and F. Teskey. A self modifying rule-eliciter. In *Proc. European Knowledge Acquisition Wksp.*, nr. 143 in GMD Studien, pp. 16.1–16.16. 1988.

[96] L. Eshelman and J. McDermott. Mole: a knowledge acquisition tool that uses its head. *Proc. AAAI*, pp. 950–955, 1986.

[97] M. Ester. Konsistenzwerkzeuge für Prolog-wissensbasen. Tech.Rep. 14, ETH, Zürich, 1989.

[98] A. Faustini and E. Lewis. Toward a real-time dataflow language. *IEEE Software*, 3(1):29–35, 1986.

[99] M. Feather. A system for assisting program transformation. *ACM Trans. Prog. Lang. Syst.*, 4(1):1–20, 1982.

[100] M. Feather. Constructing specifications by parallel elaboration. *IEEE Trans. Softw. Eng.*, 15(2):198–208, 1989.

[101] M. Feather and P. London. Implementing specification freedoms. *Sci. Comp. Progr.*, 2:91–131, 1982.

[102] Y. Feldman and E. Shapiro. Temporal debugging and its visual animation. In V. Saraswat and K. Ueda, eds., *Proc. 1991 IEEE Symposium on Logic Programming*, pp. 3–17, Cambridge, 1991. MIT Pr.

[103] S. Fickas. Automatic goal-directed program transformation. In *Proc. 1st Nat. Conf. Artificial Intelligence*, 1980.

[104] S. Fickas. Automating the transformational development of software. *IEEE Trans. Softw. Eng.*, 11(11), 1985.

[105] S. Fickas. Automating the analysis process: An example. In *Proc. 4th Intl. Wksp. on Software Specification and Design*, pp. 58–67, Los Alamitos, 1987.

[106] S. Fickas and A. Finkelstein, eds. *Proc. 1993 IEEE Requirement Engineering Symp.* 1993.

[107] R. Fikes and T. Kehler. The role of frame-based representation in reasoning. *Commun. ACM*, 28(9):904–920, 1985.

[108] P. Freeman. *Tutorial on Software Design Technique.* IEEE Computer Society Pr., Washington, 1976.

[109] S. Freudenberger, J. Schwartz, and M. Sharir. Experience with the SETL optimizer. *ACM Trans. Prog. Lang. Syst.*, 1(1):26–45, 1983.

[110] J. Gallagher. Transforming logic programs by specializing interpreters. In *Proc. 7th European Conf. on Artificial Intelligence*, pp. 109–122, Brighton Center, 1986.

[111] M. Gams. A new breed of knowledge acquisition systems uses redundant knowledge?! In *Proc. European Knowledge Acquisition Wksp.*, nr. 143 in GMD Studien, pp. 18.1–18.7. 1988.

[112] U. Gappa. CLASSIKA: A knowledge acquisition system facilitating the formalization of advanced aspects in heuristic classification. In *Proc. European Knowledge Acquisition Wksp.*, nr. 143 in GMD Studien, pp. 19.1–19.16. 1988.

[113] S. J. Garland, J. V. Guttag, and J. J. Horning. Debugging Larch shared language specifications. *IEEE Trans. Softw. Eng.*, 16:1044–1057, 1990.

[114] L. Gasser, C. Braganza, and N. Herman. Implementing distributed AI systems using MACE. In *Proc. IEEE Applications of AI*, pp. 315–320, 1987.

[115] B. Geissman and R. Schultz. Verification and validation of expert systems. *AI Expert*, pp. 26–33, 1988.

[116] M. Genesereth and M. Ginsberg. Logic programming. *Commun. ACM*, 28(9):933–941, 1985.

[117] M. Genesereth and N. Nilsson. *Logical Foundations of Artificial Intelligence.* Morgan Kaufmann, Los Altos, 1988.

[118] C. Ghezzi, D. Mandrioli, and A. Morzenti. Trio: A logic language for executable specifications of real-time systems. *J. of Systems Software*, (12):107–123, 1990.

[119] R. Giddings. Accommodating uncertainty in software design. *Commun. ACM*, 27(3):428–434, 1984.

[120] A. Ginsberg. *Automatic Refinement of Expert System Knowledge Bases.* Research Notes in Artificial Intelligence. Pitman, London, 1988.

[121] A. Ginsberg. Knowledge-base reduction: A new approach to checking knowledge bases for inconsistency & redundancy. In *Proc. 7th Nat. Conf. Artificial Intelligence*, 1988.

[122] A. Ginsberg. Theory revision via prior operationalization. Tech.rep., Knowledge Systems Research Dept., AT&T Bell Laboratories, 1988.

[123] A. Ginsberg. Checking quasi-first-order-logic rule-based systems for inconsistency and redundancy. Tech.rep., Knowledge Systems Research Dept., AT&T Bell Labs, 1990.

[124] A. Ginsberg, S. Weiss, and P. Politakis. SEEK2: a generalized approach to automatic knowledge base refinement. In *Proc. 9th Intl. Joint Conf. on Artificial Intelligence*, pp. 367–374, 1985.

[125] M. Ginsberg. *Readings in Nonmonotonic Reasoning.* Morgan-Kaufmann, Los Altos, 1987.

[126] J. Goguen. Rapid prototyping in the OBJ executable specification language. In *Proc. ACM SIGSOFT '82*, pp. 75–84, 1982.

[127] J. Goguen and J. Meseguer. EQLOG—equality, types and generic modules for logic programming. *J. Logic Programming*, 1(2):179–209, 1984.

[128] J. Goguen and J. Meseguer. Unifying functional, object-oriented and relational programming with logical semantics. In B. Shriver and P. Wegner, eds., *Research Directions in Object-Oriented Programming*, pp. 417–477. MIT Pr., Cambridge, 1987.

[129] J. Goguen and J. Tardo. An introduction to OBJ: A language for writing and testing formal algebraic program specification. In *Proc. Specification of Reliable Software Conf.*, pp. 170–189, 1979.

[130] A. Goldberg. Knowledge-based programming: A survey of program design and construction techniques. *IEEE Trans. Softw. Eng.*, 12(7), 1986.

[131] A. Goldberg and D. Robson. *Smalltalk-80: The Language and Its Implementation.* Addison-Wesley, Reading, 1983.

[132] N. Goldman and D. Wile. A relational data base foundation for process specification. In P. Chen, ed., *Entity-Relationship Approach to Systems Analysis and Design.* North-Holland, New York, 1980.

[133] H. Gomaa and D. Scott. Prototyping as a tool in the specification of user requirements. In *Proc. 5th Intl. Conf. on Software Eng.*, pp. 333–342, 1981.

[134] C. Green. Application of theorem proving to problem solving. In *Proc. 1st Intl. Joint Conf. on Artificial Intelligence*, Washington, 1969.

[135] C. Green. What is program synthesis? *J. of Automated Reasoning*, 1(1):37–40, 1985.

[136] C. Green and M. Keys. Verification and validation of expert systems. In *Proc. Western Conference on Expert Systems*, pp. 38–43, 1987.

[137] C. Green, J. Phillips, S. Westfold, T. Pressburger, S. Angebranndt, B. Kedzierski, B. Mont-Reynand, and D. Chapiro. Towards a knowledge-based programming system. Tech.Rep. KES.U.81.1, Kestrel Institute, 1981.

[138] S. Greenspan. Requirements modelling: A knowledge representation approach to software requirements definition. Tech.rep., Dept. of Comp. Sci., University of Toronto, 1984.

[139] S. Greenspan, A. Borgida, and J. Mylopoulos. A requirements modelling language and its logic. *Information Systems*, 11(1):9–23, 1986.

[140] A. Gupta. *The Logic of Common Nouns.* Yale Univ. Pr., New Haven, 1980.

[141] N. Gupta and R. Seviora. An expert system approach to real-time system debugging. In *Proc. 1st Conf. Artificial Intelligence Applications*, pp. 336–343, 1984.

[142] J. Guttag, J. Horning, and J. Wing. The Larch family of specification languages. *IEEE Software*, 2(5):24–36, 1985.

[143] J. V. Guttag, J. J. Horning, and J. M. Wing. The Larch family of specification languages. *IEEE Software*, 2:24–36, 1985.

[144] D. Harel. Statecharts: A visual formalism for complex systems. *Sci. Comp. Progr.*, (8):231–274, 1987.

[145] D. Harel et al. STATEMATE: A working environment for the development of complex reactive systems. *IEEE Software*, pp. 403–414, 1990.

[146] P. Hayes. The logic of frames. In B. Webber and N. Nilsson, eds., *Readings in Artificial Intelligence*, pp. 451–458. Tigoa Publishing Co., Palo Alto, 1979.

[147] F. Hayes-Roth. Rule-based systems. *Commun. ACM*, 28(9):921–932, 1985.

[148] E. Hehner. Predicative programming part I. *Commun. ACM*, 27(2):134–143, 1984.

[149] E. Hehner. Predicative programming part II. *Commun. ACM*, 27(2):144–151, 1984.

[150] E. Hehner, L. Gupta, and A. Malton. Predicative methodology. *Acta Inf.*, 23:487–505, 1986.

[151] M. Hennessy. *Algebraic Theory of Processes.* MIT Pr., Cambridge, 1988.

[152] T. Henzinger. Half-order modal logic. In *Proc. 9th Ann. ACM Symp. Principles of Distributed Computing*, pp. 281–296, 1990.

[153] T. Hickey and S. Mudambi. Global compilation of Prolog. *J. Logic Programming*, (7):193–230, 1989.

[154] C. Hoare. *Communicating Sequential Processes.* Prentice-Hall, Englewood Cliffs, 1985.

[155] M. M. Huntbach. Algorithmic Parlog debugging. In *Proc. 4th IEEE Symposium on Logic Programming*, pp. 288–297, San Francisco, 1987.

[156] D. Jackson. Aspect: An economical bug-detector. In *Proc. 13th Intl. Conf. on Software Eng.*, pp. 13–22, Austin, 1991.

[157] J. Jaffar and J. Lassez. Constraint logic programming. In *Proc. 15th Ann. ACM Symp. Principles of Programming Languages*, Munich, 1987.

[158] F. Jahanian and A. Mok. Safety analysis of timing properties in real-time systems. *IEEE Trans. Softw. Eng.*, 12(9):890–904, 1986.

[159] F. Jahanian and D. Stuart. A method for verifying properties of modechart specifications. In *Proc. 9th IEEE Real-Time System Symposium*, pp. 12–21, 1988.

[160] R. Jensen and C. Tonies. *Software Engineering.* Prentice-Hall, Englewood Cliffs, 1979.

[161] W. Johnson. *Intention-Based Diagnosis of Errors in Novice Programs.* Morgan-Kaufmann, Los Altos, 1986.

[162] W. Johnson and E. Soloway. Proust: Knowledge-based program understanding. *IEEE Trans. Softw. Eng.*, pp. 267–275, 1985.

[163] G. Kahn, S. Nowlan, and J. McDermott. Strategies for knowledge acquisition. *IEEE Transactions on Pattern Analysis and Machine Intelligence*, 5(7), 1988.

[164] G. Kaiser, P. Feiler, and S. Popovich. Intelligent assistance for software development and maintenance. *IEEE Software*, 5(3):40–49, 1988.

[165] E. Kant. Understanding and automating algorithm design. *IEEE Trans. Softw. Eng.*, 11(11):1361–1374, 1985.

[166] E. Kant and D. Barstow. The refinement paradigm: The interaction of coding and efficiency knowledge in program synthesis. *IEEE Trans. Softw. Eng.*, 7(5):485–471, 1981.

[167] R. Karp and R. Miller. Parallel program schemata. *J. Comp. System Sci.*, 3, 1969.

[168] V. Kelly and U. Nonnenmann. Reducing the complexity of formal specification acquisition. *Proc. AAAI*, pp. 66–72, 1988.

[169] N. Kerth. The use of multiple specification methodologies on a single system. In *Proc. 4th Intl. Wksp. on Software Specification and Design*, pp. 183–189, Los Alamitos, 1987.

[170] W. Kim and F. Lochovsky. *Object-Oriented Concepts, Databases and Applications.* Addison-Wesley, 1989.

[171] M. Kishimoto, T. Shinogi, Y. Kimura, and A. Hattori. Design and evaluation of a Prolog compiler. In *Lect. Notes in Comp. Sci.*, nr. 221, pp. 192–203. Springer Verlag, 1986.

[172] H. Kleine Büning, U. Löwen, and S. Schmitgen. Inconsistency of production systems. *J. Data and Knowledge Engineering*, (3):245–260, 1988.

[173] E. Kligerman and A. Stoyenko. Real-time Euclid: A language for reliable real-time systems. *IEEE Trans. Softw. Eng.*, 12(9):941–949, 1986.

[174] D. Knuth and P. Bendix. Simple word problems in universal algebra. In J. Leech, ed., *Computational Problems in Abstract Algebra*, pp. 263–297. Pergamon Pr., 1970.

[175] Y. Kodratoff and G. Tecuci. Learning at different levels of knowledge. In *Proc. European Knowledge Acquisition Wksp.*, nr. 143 in GMD Studien, pp. 3.1–3.17. 1988.

[176] R. Kowalski. Predicate logic as a programming language. In *Proc. of IFIP '74*, pp. 569–574, Amsterdam, 1974. North-Holland.

[177] R. Kowalski. The semantics of predicate logic as a programming language. *J. ACM*, 23(4):733–742, 1976.

[178] R. Kowalski. Algorithm = logic + control. *Commun. ACM*, 22(7):424–436, 1979.

[179] R. Kowalski. *Logic for Problem Solving*. North-Holland, New York, 1979.

[180] R. Kowalski. Software engineering and knowledge engineering in new generation computing. *Future Generation Computer Systems*, pp. 39–50, 1984.

[181] R. Kowalski. The limit of logic and its role in artificial intelligence. In *Proc. Wksp. on Knowledge Base Managements*, pp. 477–489, Crete, 1985.

[182] R. Kowalski. The relation between logic programming and logic specification. In C. Hoare and J.C.Shepherdson, eds., *Mathematical Logic and Programming Languages*, pp. 1–24. Prentice-Hall, Englewood Cliffs, 1985.

[183] R. Kowalski and M. Sergot. A logic based calculus of events. *New Generation Computing*, 4(1):67–95, 1986.

[184] R. Koymans. Specifying message buffers requires extending temporal logic. In *Proc. 6th Ann. ACM Symp. Principles of Distributed Computing*, pp. 191–204, 1987.

[185] R. Koymans. Specifying real-time properties with metric temporal logic. *Real-Time Systems*, (2):255–299, 1990.

[186] R. Koymans, R. Kuiper, and E. Zijlstra. Specifying message passing and real-time systems with real-time temporal logic. In *ESPRIT '87 Achievement and Impact*, Amsterdam, 1987. North-Holland.

[187] D. Kozen. Results on the propositional μ-calculus. *Theoretical Comput. Sci.*, (27):333–354, 1983.

[188] D. Kozen and J. Tiuryn. Logics of programs. In J. van Leeuwen, ed., *Handbook of Theoretical Computer Science*, vol. B, pp. 789–840. Elsevier Science Publ., Amsterdam, 1990.

[189] F. Kröger. *Temporal Logic of Programs.* Nr. 8 in EATCS Monographs on Theoret. Comp. Sci. Springer Verlag, Berlin, 1987.

[190] J. Lassez and M. Maher. Closure and fairness in the semantics of programming logic. *Theoretical Comput. Sci.*, (29):167–184, 1984.

[191] S. LeClair. A multiexpert paradigm for acquiring new knowledge. *SIGART Newsletter, Knowledge Aquisition Special Issue*, (108):34–44, 1988.

[192] I. Lee. Language constructs for distributed real-time programming. In *Proc. '85 IEEE Real-Time System Symposium*, pp. 57–66, 1985.

[193] S. Lee and S. Sluizer. An executable language for modeling simple behavior. *IEEE Trans. Softw. Eng.*, 17(6):527–543, 1991.

[194] N. Levy, A. Piganiol, and J. Souquieres. Specifying with SACSO. In *Proc. 4th Intl. Wksp. on Software Specification and Design*, pp. 236–241, Los Alamitos, 1987.

[195] Y. Lichtenstein, M. Codish, and E. Shapiro. Representation and enumeration of FCP computations. In E. Shapiro, ed., *Concurrent Prolog: Collected Papers.* MIT Pr., 1987.

[196] Y. Lichtenstein and E. Shapiro. Abstract algorithmic debugging. In R. A. Kowalski and K. A. Bowen, eds., *Proc. 5th Intl. Conf. Logic Programming*, pp. 512–531. MIT Pr., 1988.

[197] Y. Lichtenstein and E. Shapiro. Concurrent algorithmic debugging. *SIGPLAN Notices*, 24(1):248–260, 1989.

[198] E. Lim, J. McCallum, and K. Chan. P-graph—a graph model for anomaly checking of knowledge bases. In *Proc. IEEE Conf. on Tools for Artificial Intelligence*, pp. 871–877, 1990.

[199] J. Lloyd. *Foundations of Logic Programming.* Springer Verlag, New York, 1987.

[200] B. London and W. Clancy. Plan recognition strategies in student modelling: Prediction and description. Tech.Rep. STAN-CS-82-909, Standford University, 1982.

[201] B. Lopez, P. Meseguer, and E. Plaza. Knowledge based systems validation: A state of the art. *Artificial Intelligence Commmunications*, 3(2):58–72, 1989.

[202] M. Lubars. Schematic techniques for high level support of software specification and design. In *Proc. 4th Intl. Wksp. on Software Specification and Design*, pp. 68–75, Los Alamitos, 1987.

[203] M. Lubars. The IDeA design environment. In *Proc. 11th Intl. Conf. on Software Eng.*, pp. 23–32, 1989.

[204] M. Lubars and M. Harandi. Knowledge-based software design using design schemas. In *Proc. 9th Intl. Conf. on Software Eng.*, pp. 253–262, 1987.

[205] D. Luckham, S. Sankar, and S. Takahashi. Two-dimensional pinpointing: Debugging with formal specifications. *IEEE Software*, 8:74–84, 1991.

[206] D. C. Luckham et al. Task sequencing language for specifying distributed Ada systems. In A. N. Habermann and U. Montanari, eds., *System Development and Ada*, nr. 275 in Lect. Notes in Comp. Sci., pp. 249–305. Springer Verlag, Berlin, 1987.

[207] W. Lukaszewicz. *Non-Monotonic Reasoning: Formalization of Commonsense Reasoning.* Ellis Horwood Ltd., New York, 1990.

[208] F. Lukey. Understanding and debugging programs. *Intl. J. Man-Machine Studies*, pp. 189–202, 1980.

[209] G. MacEwen and D. Skillicorn. Using higher-order logic for modular specification of real-time distributed systems. In *Symp. Formal Techniques in Real-Time and Fault-Tolerant Systems*, nr. 331 in Lect. Notes in Comp. Sci., pp. 36–66. Springer Verlag, Berlin, 1988.

[210] Z. Manna and A. Pnueli. Verification of concurrent programs: the temporal framework. In R. Boyer and J. Moore, eds., *The Correctness Problem in Computer Science*, Intl. Lecture Series in Comp. Sci., pp. 215–273. Academic Pr., New York, 1981.

[211] Z. Manna and R. Waldinger. *Studies in Automatic Programming Logic.* North-Holland, New York, 1977.

[212] Z. Manna and R. Waldinger. A deductive approach to program synthesis. *ACM Trans. Prog. Lang. Syst.*, 2(1):90–121, 1980.

[213] Z. Manna and P. Wolper. Synthesis of communication processes from temporal logic specifications. *ACM Trans. Prog. Lang. Syst.*, 6:68–93, 1984.

[214] H. Mannila and E. Ukkonen. Flow analysis of Prolog programs. In *Proc. 4th IEEE Symposium on Logic Programming*, San Francisco, 1987.

[215] M. Marsan, G. Conte, and G. Balbo. A class of generalized stochastic Petri nets for the performance evaluation of multiprocessor systems. *ACM Trans. Comput. Syst.*, 2(2):93–122, 1984.

[216] K. Matsumoto, T. Takano, and T. Sakaguchi. A dynamic verification method for knowledge-base systems. In G. Schildt and J. Retti, eds., *Dependability of Artificial Intelligence Systems.* North-Holland, Amsterdam, 1991.

[217] P. Melliar-Smith. Extending interval logic to real-time systems. In *Temporal Logic in Specification*, nr. 398 in Lect. Notes in Comp. Sci., pp. 224–242, Berlin, 1987. Springer Verlag.

[218] C. Mellish. Some global optimizations for a Prolog compiler. *J. Logic Programming*, 2(1):43–66, 1986.

[219] J. Merlin. *A Study of the Recoverability of Computer System.* PhD thesis, Univ. California, Irving, 1974.

[220] J. Merlin and D. Farber. Recoverability of communication protocols—implications of a theoretical study. *IEEE Trans. Communication*, 24:1036–1043, 1976.

[221] P. Meseguer. A new method for checking rule bases for inconsistency: A Petri net approach. Tech.Rep. GRIAL 90/6, Grup de Recerca en Intelligencia Artificial i Logica, Blanes, 1990.

[222] P. Metzer. *Managing a Programming Project.* Prentice-Hall, Englewood Cliffs, 1973.

[223] R. Michalski, J. Carbonell, and T. Mitchell. *Machine Learning, An Artificial Intelligence Approach.* Morgan-Kaufmann, Los Altos, 1983.

[224] R. Milner. *A Calculus of Communicating Systems.* Nr. 92 in Lect. Notes in Comp. Sci. Springer Verlag, Berlin, 1980.

[225] R. Milner. *Communication and Concurrency.* Prentice-Hall, Englewood Cliffs, 1989.

[226] M. Minsky. A framework for representing knowledge. In P. Winston, ed., *The Psychology of Computer Vision.* McGraw-Hill, New York, 1975.

[227] F. Moller. Edinburgh concurrency workbench. Tech.rep., Dept. of Comp. Sci., Univ. of Edinburgh, 1992.

[228] M. Moriconi. A designer/verifier's assistant. *IEEE Trans. Softw. Eng.*, 5(4):387–401, 1979.

[229] J. Mostow. Automating program speedup by deciding what to cache. In *Proc. 9th Intl. Joint Conf. on Artificial Intelligence*, pp. 165–172, Los Angeles, 1985.

[230] T. Murata. Petri nets: Properties, analysis and applications. *Proc. of the IEEE*, 77(4):541–580, 1989.

[231] T. Murata and D. Zhang. A predicate-transition net model for parallel interpretation of logic programs. *IEEE Trans. Softw. Eng.*, 14(4):481–497, 1988.

[232] J. Mylopoulos, A. Borgida, M. Jarke, and M. Koubarakis. Telos: A language for representing knowledge about information systems. Tech.Rep. KRR-TR-89-1, University of Toronto, 1990.

[233] L. Naish, P. W. Dart, and J. Zobel. The NU-Prolog debugging environment. In A. Porto, ed., *Proc. 6th Intl. Conf. Logic Programming*, pp. 521–536, Lisboa, 1989. MIT Pr.

[234] Neuron Data Inc., Palo Alto. *Nexpert Object Fundamentals*, 1987.

[235] T. Nguyen, W. Perkins, T. Laffey, and D. Pecora. Checking an expert system's knowledge base for consistency and completeness. Tech.rep., Lockheed Missiles & Space Company, Palo Alto, 1985.

[236] T. Nguyen, W. Perkins, T. Laffey, and D. Pecora. Knowledge base verification. *AI Magazine*, 8(2):69–75, 1987.

[237] X. Nicollin and J. Sifakis. An overview and synthesis of timed process algebras. In *Real-Time: Theory in Practice*, nr. 600 in Lect. Notes in Comp. Sci. Springer Verlag, Berlin, 1991.

[238] G. Nota and G. Pacini. Querying of executable software specifications. *IEEE Trans. Softw. Eng.*, 18:705–716, 1992.

[239] J. Ostroff. *Temporal Logic for Real-Time Systems.* Research Studies Pr., Taunton, 1989.

[240] J. Ostroff. Deciding properties of timed transition models. *IEEE Trans. Parallel Dist. Syst.*, (1):170–183, 1990.

[241] J. Ostroff. A verifier for real-time properties. *Real-Time J.*, (4):5–35, 1992.

[242] J. Ostroff and W. Wonham. A temporal logic approach to real time control. In *Proc. 24th IEEE Conf. Decision and Control*, pp. 656–657, 1985.

[243] S. Owicki and L. Lamport. Proving liveness properties of concurrent programs. *ACM Trans. Prog. Lang. Syst.*, 4:455–495, 1982.

[244] M. Papazoglou. Knowledge-driven distributed information systems. In *Proc. 14th IEEE Intl. Computer Software and Applications Conf.*, pp. 671–679, 1990.

[245] H. Partsch. The CIP transformation system. In P. Pepper, ed., *Program Transformation and Programming Environments*, pp. 305–322. Springer Verlag, New York, 1983.

[246] H. Partsch. *Specification and Transformation of Programs: A Formal Approach to Software Development.* Springer Verlag, New York, 1990.

[247] H. Partsch and R. Steinbruggen. Program transformation systems. *ACM Comput. Surv.*, 15(3):199–236, 1983.

[248] L. M. Perira. Rational debugging in logic programming. Nr. 225 in Lect. Notes in Comp. Sci., pp. 203–210, Berlin, 1986. Springer Verlag.

[249] G. Peterson. Myths about the mutual exclusion problem. *Inf. Process. Lett.*, 12:115–116, 1981.

[250] J. Peterson. *Petri Net Theory and the Modelling of Systems.* Prentice-Hall, Englewood Cliffs, 1981.

[251] J. Phillips. *Self-Described Programming Environments: An Application of a Theory of Design to Programming Systems.* PhD thesis, Standford University, 1982.

[252] E. Pipard. Detection d'incoherences et d'incompletitudes dans les bases de regles: le systeme INDE. In *Proc. AVIGNON '88*, pp. 15–33, 1988.

[253] A. Pnueli. The temporal logic of programs. In *Proc. 18th Ann. IEEE Symp. Foundations of Comp. Sci.*, pp. 46–57, Province, 1977.

[254] A. Pnueli. The temporal logic of programs. In *Proc. 18th Ann. IEEE Symp. Foundations of Comp. Sci.*, pp. 46–57, 1977.

[255] A. Pnueli. Temporal semantics of concurrent programs. *Theoretical Comput. Sci.*, (27):333–354, 1983.

[256] A. Pnueli. Applications of temporal logic to the specification and verification of reactive systems: A survey of current trends. In J. de Bakker, W. de Roever, and G. Rozenberg, eds., *Current Trends in Concurrency, Overviews and Tutorials*, nr. 224 in Lect. Notes in Comp. Sci., pp. 510–584. Springer Verlag, New York, 1986.

[257] A. Preece and R. Shinghal. DARC: A procedure for verifying rule-based systems. In *Proc. World Congress on Expert Systems*, pp. 971–979, 1991.

[258] P. Puncello et al. ASPIS: A knowledge-based CASE environment. *IEEE Software*, pp. 58–65, 1988.

[259] J. Quinlan. Consistency and plausible reasoning. In *Proc. 8th Intl. Joint Conf. on Artificial Intelligence*, pp. 137–144, 1983.

[260] C. Ramamoorthy et al. Software engineering: Problems and perspectives. *IEEE Computer*, pp. 191–209, 1984.

[261] C. Ramchandani. Analysis of asynchronous concurrent systems by timed Petri nets. Tech.Rep. 120, MIT, 1974.

[262] U. Rauth and T. Gmbh. Consistency of production rules in expert systems. In G. Schildt and J. Retti, eds., *Dependability of Artificial Intelligence Systems.* North Holland, Amsterdam, 1991.

[263] U. Reddy. Transformation of logic programs into functional programs. In *Proc. IEEE Symposium on Logic Programming*, pp. 187–196, Atlantic City, 1984.

[264] M. Reinfrank, J. de Kleer, M. Ginsberg, and E. Sandewall. *Non-Monotonic Reasoning.* Lect. Notes in Artif. Intel. Springer Verlag, Berlin, 1989.

[265] H. Reubenstein and R. Waters. The Requirements Apprentice: Automated assistance for requirements acquisition. *IEEE Trans. Softw. Eng.*, 17(3):226–240, 1991.

[266] C. Rich and R. Waters. *Readings in Artificial Intelligence and Software Engineering.* Morgan-Kaufmann, Los Altos, 1986.

[267] C. Rich and R. Waters. Automatic programming myths and prospect. *IEEE Computer*, 21(8):40–51, 1988.

[268] J. Riedesel. Consistency and completeness: An exercise in knowledge base validation. Tech.rep., Graduate College of the University of Illinois, Urbana-Champain, 1985.

[269] D. S. Rosenblum. Specifying concurrent systems with TSL. *IEEE Software*, 8:52–61, 1991.

[270] M.-C. Rousset. The COVADIS-system. In *Proc. European Conf. on Artificial Intelligence*, 1988.

[271] N. Roussopoulos. CSDL: A conceptual scheme definition language for the design of data base applications. *IEEE Trans. Softw. Eng.*, 5(5), 1979.

[272] N. Roussopoulos, L. Mark, T. Sellis, and C. Faloutsos. An architecture for high performance engineering information systems. *IEEE Trans. Softw. Eng.*, 17(1):22–33, 1991.

[273] W. Royce. Managing the development of large software systems: Concepts and techniques. In *Proc. WESCON*, 1970.

[274] P. Rudnicki. What should be proved and tested symbolically in formal specifications? In *Proc. 4th Intl. Wksp. on Software Specification and Design*, pp. 190–195, Los Alamitos, 1987.

[275] M. Rueher. From specification to design: An approach based on rapid prototyping. In *Proc. 4th Intl. Wksp. on Software Specification and Design*, pp. 126–133, Los Alamitos, 1987.

[276] T. Sato and H. Tamaki. Enumeration of success patterns in logic programs. *Theoretical Comp. Sci.*, 34:227–240, 1984.

[277] T. Sato and H. Tamaki. Transformational logic program synthesis. In *Proc. of the Intl. Conf. on Fifth Generation Computer Systems*, pp. 195–201, Tokyo, 1984.

[278] L. Scharer. The prototyping alternative. *ITT Programming*, 1(1):34–43, 1983.

[279] J. Scheid and S. Anderson. The ina jo specification language reference manual. Tech.Rep. TM-(L)-6021/001/01, System Development Corp., Santa Monica, 1985.

[280] E. Schonberg, J. Schwartz, and M. Sharir. On automatic technique for selection of data representation in SETL programs. *ACM Trans. Prog. Lang. Syst.*, 3(2), 1981.

[281] R. Schultz and J. Geissman. Bridging the gap between static and dynamic verification. In *Proc. AAAI-88 Wksp. on Validation and Verification of Expert Systems*, pp. 1–9, 1988.

[282] J. Schwartz. Automatic data structure choice in a language of very high level. *Commun. ACM*, 18:722–728, 1975.

[283] R. Schwartz, P. Melliar-Smith, and F. Vogt. An interval based temporal logic. In *Proc. ACM Wksp. on the Logics of Programming*, pp. 443–457, 1983.

[284] R. Schwartz, P. Melliar-Smith, and F. Vogt. An interval logic for higher-level temporal reasoning. In *Proc. 2nd Ann. ACM Symp. Principles of Distributed Computing*, pp. 173–186, 1983.

[285] R. Sedlmeyer et al. Knowledge-based fault localization in debugging. In *Proc. ACM SIGSOFT SIGPlan Software Eng. Symp. High-Level Debugging*, pp. 25–31, New York, 1983. ACM.

[286] R. Seviora. Knowledge-based program debugging systems. *IEEE Software*, pp. 20–32, 1987.

[287] E. Shapiro. *Algorithmic Program Debugging.* MIT Pr., Cambridge, 1983.

[288] E. Shapiro. *Concurrent Prolog.* MIT Pr., Cambridge, 1987.

[289] A. Shaw. Reasoning about time in higher-level language software. *IEEE Trans. Softw. Eng.*, pp. 875–889, 1989.

[290] M. Shaw. Problems of validation in a knowledge acquisition system using multiple experts. In *Proc. European Knowledge Acquisition Wksp.*, nr. 143 in GMD Studien, pp. 5.1–5.15. 1988.

[291] R. Shostak. A practical decision procedure for proving Presburger arithmetic with function symbols. *J. ACM*, 26(2):351–360.

[292] R. Shyamasundar and J. Hooman. Reasoning of real-time distributed programming languages. *J. ACM*, pp. 91–99, 1989.

[293] D. Skillcorn and J. Glasgow. Real time specification using Lucid. *IEEE Trans. Softw. Eng.*, pp. 221–229, 1989.

[294] D. Smith. Top-down synthesis of divide-and-conquer algorithms. *Artificial Intelligence*, 27:43–96, 1985.

[295] D. Smith. KIDS: A semiautomatic program development system. *IEEE Trans. Softw. Eng.*, 16(9):1024–1043, 1990.

[296] D. Smith, G. Kotik, and S. Westfold. Research on knowledge-based software environments at Kestrel Institute. *IEEE Trans. Softw. Eng.*, 11(11), 1985.

[297] P. Smith, S. Ng, and A. Steward. Criteria for the validation of expert systems. In *Proc. World Congress on Expert Systems*, pp. 980–988, 1991.

[298] S. Smoliar. Operational requirements accommodation in distributed system design. *IEEE Trans. Softw. Eng.*, 7(6):531–537, 1981.

[299] G. Smolka. Making control and data flow in logic programs explicit. In *Proc. of the Symposium on LISP and Functional Programming '84*, Austin, 1984.

[300] G. Smolka and H. Aït-Kaci. Inheritance hierarchies: Semantics and unification. *J. Symbolic. Comp.*, (7):343–370, 1989.

[301] Special issue on artificial intelligence and software engineering. *IEEE Trans. Softw. Eng.*, 11(11), 1985.

[302] S. Squires, M. Branstad, and M. Zelkowitz, eds. *Working Papers from the ACM SIGSOFT Rapid Prototyping Wksp.*, Columbia, 1982.

[303] R. Stachowitz and C.-L. Chang. Completeness checking of expert systems. Tech.rep., Lockheed Missiles & Space Company, Austin, 1988.

[304] R. Stachowitz, C.-L. Chang, and J. Combs. Performance evaluation of knowledge-based systems. Tech.rep., Lockheed Missiles & Space Company, Austin, 1987.

[305] R. Stachowitz, C.-L. Chang, T. Stock, and J. Combs. Building validation tools for knowledge-based systems. Tech.rep., Lockheed Missiles & Space Company, Austin, 1987.

[306] R. Stachowitz and J. Combs. Validation of expert systems. Tech.rep., Lockheed Missiles & Space Company, Austin, 1988.

[307] R. Stachowitz, J. Combs, and C.-L. Chang. Validation of knowledge-based systems. Tech.rep., Lockheed Missiles & Space Company, Austin, 1987.

[308] L. Sterling and E. Shapiro. *The Art of Prolog.* MIT Pr., Cambridge, 1986.

[309] K. Stohl, W. Snopek, T. Weigert, and T. Moritz. Development of a scheduling expert system for a steelplant. In *Proc. IFAC Wksp. in Expert Systems in Mineral and Metal Processing*, Helsinki, 1991.

[310] B. Stroustrup. *The C++ Programming Language.* Addison-Wesley, Reading, 1986.

[311] W. Suwa, A. Scott, and E. Shortliffe. Completeness and consistency in a rule-based system. In B. Buchanan and E. Shortliffe, eds., *Rule-Based Expert Systems*, pp. 159–170. 1982.

[312] W. Suwa, A. Scott, and E. Shortliffe. An approach to verifying completeness and consistency in a rule-based expert system. *AI Magazine*, 3(4):16–21, 1988.

[313] I. Suzuki, Y. Motohashi, K. Taniguchi, T. Kasami, and T. Okamoto. Specification and verification of decentralized daisy chain arbiters with ω-extended regular expressions. *Theoretical Comput. Sci.*, 43:277–291, 1986.

[314] A. Symonds. Creating a software-engineering knowledge base. *IEEE Software*, pp. 50–56, 1988.

[315] D. Syners and A. Thayse. *From Logic Design to Logic Programming.* Springer Verlag, Berlin, 1987.

[316] A. Szalas. Concerning the semantic consequence relation in first-order temporal logic. *Theoretical Comput. Sci.*, (47):329–334, 1986.

[317] A. Szalas and L. Holenderski. Incompleteness of first-order temporal logic with until. *Theoretical Comput. Sci.*, (57):317–325, 1988.

[318] K. Takahashi and A. Takeuchi. A debugger for AND/OR parallel logic programming language ANDOR-II. Tech.Rep. ICOT TR-608, Institute for New Generation Computer Technology, Tokyo, 1990.

[319] A. Takeuchi. How to solve it in Concurrent Prolog. Unpublished note, 1983.

[320] H. Tamaki and T. Sato. Unfold/fold transformation of logic programs. In *Proc. 2nd Intl. Logic Programming Conference*, pp. 127–138, Upssala, 1984.

[321] T. Tanaka and K. Ishikawa. An ATMS-based knowledge verification system for diagnostic applications. In *Proc. World Congress on Expert Systems*, pp. 997–1004, 1991.

[322] A. Tarski. A lattice-theoretical fixpoint theorem and its applications. *Pacific J. Math.*, (5):285–309, 1955.

[323] J. Tatemura and H. Tanaka. Debugger for a parallel logic programming language Fleng. In *Proc. 8th Intl. Conf. Logic Programming*, pp. 86–96, Tokyo, 1991.

[324] R. Tavendale. A description and assessment of FDL. Tech.Rep. 84/67, Marconi Research Centre, 1984.

[325] R. Tavendale. A technique for prototyping directly from a specification. In *Proc. 8th Intl. Conf. on Software Eng.*, pp. 224–229, 1985.

[326] P. Tavolatto and K. Vincenna. A prototyping methodology and its tool. In R. Budde, K. Kuhlenkamp, L. Mathiassen, and H. Zullighoven, eds., *Approaches to Prototyping*, pp. 434–447. Springer Verlag, Berlin, 1984.

[327] A. Taylor. LIPS on a MIPS: Result from a Prolog compiler for a RISC. In *Proc. 7th Intl. Conf. Logic Programming*, 1990.

[328] T. Taylor and T. Standish. Initial thoughts on rapid prototyping. *ACM SIGSOFT*, pp. 160–166, 1982.

[329] P. Terpstra and M. van Someren. INDE: A system for knowledge refinement and machine learning. In *Proc. European Knowledge Acquisition Wksp.*, nr. 143 in GMD Studien, pp. 30.1–30.8. 1988.

[330] R. Terwilliger and R. Campbell. Please: Executable specifications for incremental software development. *The J. of Systems and Software*, (10):97–112, 1989.

[331] A. Thayse, ed. *From Modal Logic to Deductive Databases.* Wiley, Chicester, 1989.

[332] J. Tiernan. An efficient search algorithm to find the elementary circuits of a graph. *Commun. ACM*, 13(12):722–726, 1970.

[333] D. Touretzky. *The Mathematics of Inheritance Systems.* Morgan-Kaufmann, Los Altos, 1986.

[334] D. Troy, C. Yu, and W. Zhang. Linearization of nonlinear recursive databases. *IEEE Trans. Softw. Eng.*, 15(9):1109–1119, 1989.

[335] J.-P. Tsai. A knowledge-based approach to software design. *IEEE J. on Selected Areas in Communications*, 6(5):828–841, 1988.

[336] J.-P. Tsai, M. Aoyama, and Y. Chang. Rapid prototyping using frorl language. In *Proc. 12th IEEE Intl. Computer Software and Applications Conf.*, pp. 410–417, Chicago, 1988.

[337] J.-P. Tsai, K. Fang, and H. Chen. A knowledge-based debugger for real-time software systems based on a non-interference testing architecture. In *Proc. 13th IEEE Intl. Computer Software and Applications Conf.*, pp. 642–649, Orlando, 1989.

[338] J.-P. Tsai, K. Fang, and H. Chen. A noninvasive architecture to monitor real-time distributed systems. *IEEE Computer*, 23(4):11–23, 1990.

[339] J.-P. Tsai, K. Fang, H. Chen, and Y. Bi. A noninterference monitoring and replay mechanism for real-time software testing and debugging. *IEEE Trans. Softw. Eng.*, 16(8):897–916, 1990.

[340] J.-P. Tsai and H. Jang. A knowledge-based approach for the specification and analysis of real-time software systems. *Intl. J. of Artificial Intelligence Tools*, 1(1):1–37, 1992.

[341] J.-P. Tsai, H. Jang, and K. Schellinger. RT-FRORL: A formal requirements specification language for specifying and analyzing real-time systems. In *Proc. 14th IEEE Intl. Computer Software and Applications Conf.*, Tokyo, 1991.

[342] J.-P. Tsai and A. Liu. A knowledge-based system for rapid prototyping. *J. of Knowledge-Based Systems*, 2(4):239–248, 1989.

[343] J.-P. Tsai and J. Ridge. Intelligent support for specifications transformations. *IEEE Software*, 5(6):28–35, 1988.

[344] J.-P. Tsai and R. Sheu. A distributed cooperative agents architecture for software development. In *Proc. Intl. Joint Conf. on Artificial Intelligence Wksp. on Intelligent Cooperative Information Systems*, pp. 51–76, Sydney, 1991.

[345] J.-P. Tsai, R. Sheu, and S. Tsai. A knowledge-based system for ADA software development. In *Proc. 5th Ann. Conf. on Artificial Intelligence and Ada*, pp. 137–148, Fairfax, 1989.

[346] J.-P. Tsai and T. Weigert. Exploratory prototyping through the use of frame and production systems. In *Proc. 13th IEEE Intl. Computer Software and Applications Conf.*, pp. 445–462, Orlando, 1989.

[347] J.-P. Tsai and T. Weigert. A knowledge-based approach for checking software information using a nonmonotonic reasoning system. *J. of Knowledge-Based Systems*, 3(3):131–138, 1990.

[348] J.-P. Tsai and T. Weigert. HCLIE: A logic-based requirements language for new software engineering paradigms. *IEE Software Engineering J.*, 6(4):137–151, 1991.

[349] J.-P. Tsai and T. Weigert. An explication of reasoning in multiple inheritance system through non- monotonic horn clause logic. *J. of Information Sciences*, 63(3):261–283, 1992.

[350] J.-P. Tsai, T. Weigert, and M. Aoyama. A declarative approach to software requirements specification language. In *Proc. IEEE Computer Languages Conf. '88*, pp. 414–421, Miami Beach, 1988.

[351] J.-P. Tsai, T. Weigert, and H. Jang. Non-monotonic logic as a basis for requirements specification and analysis. In *Proc. Intl. Symp. on Artificial Intelligence*, pp. 13–15, 1991.

[352] J.-P. Tsai, T. Weigert, and H. Jang. A hybrid knowledge representation as a basis of requirement specification and specification analysis. *IEEE Trans. Softw. Eng.*, 18(12):1076–1100, 1992.

[353] M. Ueno and T. Kanamori. GHC program diagnosis using atom behavior. Tech.Rep. ICOT TR-550, Institute for New Generation Computer Technology, Tokyo, 1990.

[354] J. Ullman. Implementation of logical query languages for databases. *ACM Trans. Database Syst.*, 10(3), 1985.

[355] J. Ullman. *Principles of Database and Knowledge-Base Systems.* Computer Sciences Pr., 1989.

[356] U.S. Department of Defense. *Reference Manual for the Ada Programming Language*, ANSI/MIL-STD-11815A ed., 1983.

[357] M. van Emden and R. Kowalski. The semantics of predicate logic as a programming language. *J. ACM*, 23(4):733–742, 1976.

[358] M. Vardi and P. Wolper. An automata-theoretic approach to automatic program verification. In *Proc. Symp. Logic in Comp. Sci.*, pp. 332–344, 1986.

[359] K. Verschaetse and D. DeSchreye. Deriving termination proofs for logic programs, using abstract procedures. In *Proc. 7th Intl. Conf. Logic Programming.* MIT Pr., 1990.

[360] M. Volper. A temporal fixpoint calculus. In *Proc. 15th Ann. ACM Symp. Principles of Programming Languages*, pp. 250–259, San Diego, 1988.

[361] R. Waldinger and R. Lee. PROW: A step towards automatic program writing. In *Proc. 1st Intl. Joint Conf. on Artificial Intelligence*, pp. 241–252, Washington, 1969.

[362] D. Warren. An improved Prolog implementation which optimizes tail recursion. In *Proc. Logic Prog. Wksp*, Debrecen, 1980.

[363] D. Warren. An abstract Prolog instruction set. Tech.Rep. 309, SRI Intl., Menlo Park, 1983.

[364] R. Waters. The programmer's apprentice: A session with KBEmacs. *IEEE Trans. Softw. Eng.*, 11(11):1296–1320, 1985.

[365] D. Webster. Mapping the design information representation terrain. *IEEE Computer*, pp. 8–23, 1988.

[366] T. Weigert. *Logical Calculi for Reasoning in the Presence of Uncertainty.* PhD thesis, Dept. of Philosophy, Univ. of Illinois, Chicago, 1989.

[367] T. Weigert. Nonmonotonic logic as the basis for a requirement specification language. In *Proc. AAAI '89 - Wksp. Automating Software Design*, pp. 191–206, St. Paul, 1989.

[368] T. Weigert and T. Moritz. Development and verification of knowledge-based systems. Tech.rep., RISC Linz, 1992.

[369] D. Wile. Program development: Formal explanation of implementations. *Commun. ACM*, 1983.

[370] M. Wilson. A requirements and design aid for relational database. In *Proc. 5th Intl. Conf. on Software Eng.*, 1981.

[371] J. Wing. A study of 12 specifications for the library problem. *IEEE Software*, pp. 66–76, 1988.

[372] J. Wing. A specifier's introduction to formal methods. *IEEE Computer*, 23(9):8–24, 1990.

[373] J. Wing and M. Nixon. Extending Ina Jo with temporal logic. *IEEE Trans. Softw. Eng.*, pp. 181–197, 1989.

[374] P. Wolper. Temporal logic can be more expressive. In *Proc. 22nd Ann. IEEE Symp. Foundations of Comp. Sci.*, pp. 340–348, 1981.

[375] P. Wolper. Expressing interesting properties of programs in propositional temporal logic. In *Proc. 13th Ann. ACM Symp. Principles of Programming Languages*, pp. 184–193, 1986.

[376] P. Wolper. On the relation of programs and computation to models of temporal logic. In B. Banieqbal, H. Barringer, and A. Pnueli, eds., *Temporal Logic in Specification*, nr. 398 in Lect. Notes in Comp. Sci., pp. 75–123. Springer Verlag, Berlin, 1987.

[377] R. Yeh and R. Mittermeir. Conceptual modelling as a basis for deriving software requirements. In *Proc. Intl. Computer Symp.*, Taipei, 1980.

[378] K. Yue. What does it mean to say that a specification is complete? In *Proc. 4th Intl. Wksp. on Software Specification and Design*, pp. 42–49, Los Alamitos, 1987.

[379] P. Zave. The operational approach to requirements specification for embedded systems. *IEEE Trans. Softw. Eng.*, 8(3):250–269, 1982.

[380] P. Zave. The operational versus the conventional approach to software development. *Commun. ACM*, 27(2):104–118, 1984.

[381] P. Zave. An insider's evaluation of PAISLey. *IEEE Trans. Softw. Eng.*, 17(3):212–225, 1991.

[382] P. Zave and R. Yeh. Executable requirements for embedded systems. In N. Gehani and N. Mcgettrick, eds., *Software Specification Techniques*, pp. 341–360. Addison-Wesley, Reading, 1986.

[383] M. Zelkowitz, A. Shaw, and J. Gannon. *Principles of Software Engineering and Design*. Prentice-Hall, Englewood Cliffs, 1979.

[384] W. Zhang and C. Yu. Necessary and sufficient conditions to linearize doubly recursive programs in logic databases. *ACM Trans. Database Syst.*, 15(3):459–482, 1990.

[385] N. Zlatareva. Distributed verification: A new formal approach for verifying knowledge-based systems. In *Proc. World Congress on Expert Systems*, pp. 1021–1029, 1991.

[386] W. Zuberek. Timed Petri nets and preliminary performance evaluation. In *Proc. 7th Symposium Computer Architecture*, pp. 88–96, La Bank, 1980.

Appendix E

Index